# SCHOOLWIDE PREVENTION MODELS

*Lessons Learned in Elementary Schools*

Edited by

CHARLES R. GREENWOOD
THOMAS R. KRATOCHWILL
MELISSA CLEMENTS

THE GUILFORD PRESS
New York    London

KH

© 2008 The Guilford Press
A Division of Guilford Publications, Inc.
72 Spring Street, New York, NY 10012
www.guilford.com

Printed in the United States of America

This book is printed on acid-free paper.

Last digit is print number:   9   8   7   6   5   4   3   2   1

Library of Congress Cataloging-in-Publication Data available from the publisher.
ISBN 978-1-59385-839-1

11/2/09

# About the Editors

**Charles R. Greenwood, PhD,** is Director of the Juniper Gardens Children's Project (JGCP), Senior Scientist in the Schiefelbusch Institute for Life Span Studies, and Professor of Applied Behavioral Science and Special Education at the University of Kansas. A former teacher of students with behavior disorders and a school psychologist, he holds a PhD in educational psychology from the University of Utah. Dr. Greenwood is internationally recognized for his expertise in developing evidence-based instructional and behavioral interventions as well as methods of progress-monitoring measurement and classroom behavior observation. He is the author of over 100 articles, chapters, and books, and has served on the editorial boards of 12 different journals. Dr. Greenwood's work has been funded by the Office of Special Education Programs, the National Center for Special Education Research, and the National Institute of Child Health and Human Development. In 1996, under his leadership, the JGCP received the Council for Exceptional Children's Research Award in recognition of its substantial contribution to the education and treatment of children with disabilities. In 2001, he received the Fred S. Keller Award from Division 25 of the American Psychological Association (APA) for his distinguished contributions to the field of education.

**Thomas R. Kratochwill, PhD,** is Sears–Bascom Professor at the University of Wisconsin–Madison; Director of the Educational and Psychological Training Center, an interdisciplinary unit for clinical and applied training for counseling psychology, rehabilitation psychology and special education, and school psychology; and Co-Director of the Child and Adolescent Mental Health and Education Resource Center. He is the author of over 200 journal articles, book chapters, and monographs, and the recipient of numerous awards, including the 2007 APA Award for Distinguished Career Contributions to Education and Training in Psychology. Dr. Kratochwill has been Associate Editor of *Behavior Therapy*, the *Journal of Applied Behavior Analysis*, and *School Psychology Review*; Founding Editor of the APA Division 16 journal, *School Psychology Quarterly*, from 1984 to 1992; and Co-Editor of the special section of *School Psychology Quarterly* devoted to Evidence-Based Intervention Research. He is a Past President of the Society for the Study of School Psychology and Co-Chair (with Kimberly Hoagwood) of the Task Force on Evidence-Based Interventions in School Psychology. He is currently on the APA Board of Educational Affairs Task Force on Translating Psychological Science into Classroom Practice and the APA Task Force on Evidence-Based Practice for Children and Adolescents.

**Melissa Clements, PhD,** is a Senior Associate with MGT of America, Inc., a research firm based in Tallahassee, Florida. Prior to joining MGT, she served as Co-Director of the Coordination, Consultation, and Evaluation Center at the University of Wisconsin–Madison, the coordination center for the Office of Special Education Programs K–3 Reading and Behavior Intervention Models Project. Dr. Clements holds a PhD in developmental psychology from Wayne State University. Her research interests include early child development, education, special education, contextual influences, and evaluation of prevention and intervention programs for high-risk populations. Her research was recognized in 2000 with the Steven A. Lewis Memorial Research Award and in 2001 with the Wayne State Dissertation Fellowship Award.

# Contributors

**Mary Abbott, PhD,** Kansas Center for Early Intervention in Reading and Behavior, Juniper Gardens Children's Project, University of Kansas, Kansas City, Kansas

**Bob Algozzine, PhD,** Behavior and Reading Improvement Center, University of North Carolina at Charlotte, Charlotte, North Carolina

**Kate Algozzine, MS,** Behavior and Reading Improvement Center, University of North Carolina at Charlotte, Charlotte, North Carolina

**David J. Chard, PhD,** School of Education and Human Performance, Southern Methodist University, Dallas, Texas

**Melissa Clements, PhD,** Senior Associate, MGT of America, Inc., Tallahassee, Florida

**Nancy Cooke, PhD,** Behavior and Reading Improvement Center, University of North Carolina at Charlotte, Charlotte, North Carolina

**Harriet Dawson-Bannister, MA,** Kansas Center for Early Intervention in Reading and Behavior, Juniper Gardens Children's Project, University of Kansas, Kansas City, Kansas

**Celeste Rossetto Dickey, MEd,** Bethel School District and College of Education, University of Oregon, Eugene, Oregon

**Batya Elbaum, PhD,** Department of Teaching and Learning, School of Education, University of Miami, Coral Gables, Florida

**Michael H. Epstein, EdD,** Department of Special Education and Communication Disorders, University of Nebraska–Lincoln, Lincoln, Nebraska

**Debra Fillingin, BME,** Overland Park Elementary School, Shawnee Mission School District, Shawnee, Kansas

**Charles R. Greenwood, PhD,** Kansas Center for Early Intervention in Reading and Behavior, Juniper Gardens Children's Project, University of Kansas, Kansas City, Kansas

**Beth A. Harn, PhD,** Department of Special Education and Clinical Sciences, College of Education, University of Oregon, Eugene, Oregon

**Shawnna Helf, PhD,** Behavior and Reading Improvement Center, University of North Carolina at Charlotte, Charlotte, North Carolina

**Robert H. Horner, PhD,** College of Education, University of Oregon, Eugene, Oregon

**Kristin Duppong Hurley, PhD,** Center for At-Risk Children's Services, University of Nebraska–Lincoln, Lincoln, Nebraska

**Edward J. Kame'enui, PhD,** College of Education, University of Oregon, Eugene, Oregon

**Debra Kamps, PhD,** Kansas Center for Early Intervention in Reading and Behavior, Juniper Gardens Children's Project, University of Kansas, Kansas City, Kansas

**Jorun Kaufman, BA,** Kansas Center for Early Intervention in Reading and Behavior, Juniper Gardens Children's Project, University of Kansas, Kansas City, Kansas

**Thomas R. Kratochwill, PhD,** Department of Educational Psychology, University of Wisconsin–Madison, Madison, Wisconsin

**Sylvia Linan-Thompson, PhD,** Department of Special Education, University of Texas at Austin, Austin, Texas

**Tina McClanahan, BS,** Pre-Kindergarten Services Program, Charlotte–Mecklenburg Schools, Charlotte, North Carolina

**Christy S. Murray, MA,** Vaughn Gross Center for Reading and Language Arts, College of Education, University of Texas at Austin, Austin, Texas

**Ron Nelson, PhD,** Department of Special Education and Communication Disorders, University of Nebraska–Lincoln, Lincoln, Nebraska

**Greg Roberts, PhD,** Vaughn Gross Center for Reading and Language Arts, College of Education, University of Texas at Austin, Austin, Texas

**Nancy Scammacca, PhD,** Vaughn Gross Center for Reading and Language Arts, College of Education, University of Texas at Austin, Austin, Texas

**Deborah C. Simmons, PhD,** Department of Special Education and Clinical Sciences, College of Education, University of Oregon, Eugene, Oregon

**George Sugai, PhD,** Educational Psychology Department, Neag School of Education, University of Connecticut, Storrs, Connecticut

**Lori Synhorst, PhD,** Department of Special Education and Communication Disorders, University of Nebraska–Lincoln, Lincoln, Nebraska

**Tary J. Tobin, PhD,** Department of Special Education and Clinical Sciences, College of Education, University of Oregon, Eugene, Oregon

**Sharon Vaughn, PhD,** Vaughn Gross Center for Reading and Language Arts, College of Education, University of Texas at Austin, Austin, Texas

**Mary Baldwin Veerkamp, PhD,** Kansas Center for Early Intervention in Reading and Behavior, Juniper Gardens Children's Project, University of Kansas, Kansas City, Kansas

**Jeanne Wanzek, PhD,** The Florida Center for Reading Research, Florida State University, Tallahassee, Florida

**Richard White, EdD,** Department of Special Education and Child Development, University of North Carolina at Charlotte, Charlotte, North Carolina

**Howard Wills, PhD,** Kansas Center for Early Intervention in Reading and Behavior, Juniper Gardens Children's Project, University of Kansas, Kansas City, Kansas

**Althea L. Woodruff, PhD,** Vaughn Gross Center for Reading and Language Arts, College of Education, University of Texas at Austin, Austin, Texas

# Contents

**PART III. IMPLICATIONS AND CONCLUSIONS**

# PART I

# BACKGROUND
# AND RATIONALE

# CHAPTER 1

# Introduction

CHARLES R. GREENWOOD, ROBERT H. HORNER,
*and* THOMAS R. KRATOCHWILL

Two major themes in educational research guided the development of this volume. The first is the growing research evidence that the two most critical foundations for long-term educational success are development of early literacy and social-behavior skills (Committee on Integrating the Science of Early Childhood Development, 2000) and for both, growth in the number of evidence-based instructional interventions available for use in the schools. The second theme is recognition that an effective approach to education may well involve a multi-tiered model of prevention and early intervention similar to that used in community and public health (Costello & Angold, 2000; Gordon, 1983; H. M. Walker & Shinn, 2002). This approach was adopted because waiting to provide special education services as in the past is now recognized as a lost opportunity to prevent initial problems from becoming more serious problems later (President's Commission on Excellence in Special Education, 2002). Two key messages underpinning multi-tiered prevention models in education are (1) investment in efficient, evidence-based practices of instruction and behavior support that will be effective with most students, and (2) early identification and intervention for children who do not respond to universal practices. Implementation of this approach requires systematic concepts, tools, and procedures needed for the conduct of universal early screening that can guide decisions about early intervening with individual students. This approach is linked to individual differences in students' response to intervention (RTI). RTI asserts that children who are not responsive to instructional interventions that are effective with most students are in need of timely, frequent, and intensive intervention to accelerate their progress and thereby avoid delays in attaining short-term benchmark and annual, grade-level proficiencies (see Table 1.1). In the work reported in this book, formative measurement tools were used in schools to frequently monitor progress in support of decision making regarding individual response to instructional intervention; and whether each student needed more than the universal (Tier 1 level) instructional intervention services.

In response to these two themes, the U.S. Department of Education's Office of Special Education Programs (OSEP) beginning in 2001 made a major investment in six research centers. Each center was given the mandate to formally test the extent that these themes could be feasibly applied in elementary schools and produce measurably superior benefits for students. Each center proposed a variation on the three-tiered prevention model and, in collaboration with local area schools, conducted a 4-year program of field-based research designed to examine the efficacy of their approach.

In this book, we present illustrative findings from each center in one

**TABLE 1.1. Core Concepts of RTI**

The core concepts of RTI include the following:

- Students receive high-quality instruction in their general education setting.
- General education instruction is research based.
- General education instructors and staff assume an active role in students' assessment in that curriculum.
- School staff conduct universal screening of academics and behavior.
- Continuous progress monitoring of student performance occurs.
- Continuous progress monitoring pinpoints students' specific difficulties.
- School staff implement specific, research-based interventions to address students' difficulties.
- School staff use progress-monitoring data to determine interventions' effectiveness and to make any modifications as needed.
- Systematic assessment is completed of the fidelity or integrity with which instruction and interventions are implemented.
- The RTI model is well-described in written documents (so that the procedures and criteria used in schools can be compared to the documents).
- Sites can be designated as using a "standardized" treatment protocol or an individualized, problem-solving model.

*Note.* From the National Research Center on Learning Disabilities website: *www.nrcld.org/research/rti/concepts.html.*

or more elementary schools, as well as the integrated messages gleaned across the six centers. We focus in this volume on the feasibility and efficacy of the six tested approaches in anticipation of future reports on broader effectiveness on student outcomes. Now complete, the experiences and lessons learned from intensively working with 42 elementary schools in six states are the content of this volume. Because schoolwide prevention models reflect a rapidly emerging alternative to traditional practice they have implications for the design of contemporary systems of schooling. These implications reach multiple levels as we report below, including the student, school, district, state, and national levels.

Collectively, this work reflects a pioneering effort to reform schooling based on research evidence. The available resources for this work, however, did not allow addressing the sustainability of these models beyond the involvement of researchers over time. Long-term questions of sustainability and distal student outcomes thereafter (e.g., future need for services, grade retention, graduation, etc.) await future research.

This book is organized into three parts. In the first chapter of Part I, we provide a rationale for an emphasis on promotion of social behavior and early literacy as the core foundation for an effective education, followed by the conceptual and empirical rationale for the integration of evidence-based interventions within a three-tiered model of prevention. Chapter 2 describes the common-core implementation issues and procedures undergirding schoolwide, three-tiered prevention models in elementary schools. Chapters 3 through 8 in Part II each provide a detailed school-based example of each center's model approach including school characteristics, procedures, and outcomes. Finally, Chapter 9 in Part III examines the implications coming from this braided program of research. Our goal in this volume is to provide the readers with an accessible description of schoolwide prevention models including their foundations and evidence-based strategies for improving the effectiveness of elementary schooling. We also discuss the need for future research and translation to practice.

## FOUNDATIONAL ISSUES IN SCHOOLING: BEHAVIOR PROBLEMS AND LITERACY

The overly high prevalence of (1) student discipline problems and (2) academic underachievement in American elementary schools have been at the forefront of the public's perception of the challenges to schooling for years (e.g., National Commission on Excellence in Education, 1983). In the sections that follow, key literature relating to these fundamental educational issues is covered. Topics related to behavior and reading problems and factors that play a role in ameliorating these challenges are reviewed, followed by a discussion of the interconnectedness of these important educational outcomes.

## Prevalence of Behavior Problems

For the first 19 years of the Gallup Poll, school discipline was rated one of the top three problems confronting schools (Rose & Gallup, 2006). For example, school principals reported that 54% of public schools "took at least one serious disciplinary action against a student." Altogether, 1,163,000 serious disciplinary actions were taken in 2000–2001 (National Center for Education Statistics, 2005). Of these, 83% were suspensions for 5 days or more, 11% were removals with no services, and 7% were transfers to specialized schools. In the year prior to the Columbine High School massacre there were 17 homicides and 5 suicides. Teachers were the victims of 183,000 nonfatal crimes at school, including 119 thefts and 65,000 violent crimes (Bureau of Justice, 2005). Eighty percent of students in the eighth grade reported that their teacher stopped teaching to deal with student misbehavior in the classroom (Kaufman et al., 2000). School discipline and behavior problems are typically more frequent in central city, public, urban schools compared to suburban or rural schools where the vast majority of low-socioeconomic-status (SES) and minority/ethnic students are educated.

According to the Surgeon General's report, mental illness ranks second to cardiovascular disease in cost burden to the national economy per year (Child and Adolescent Health Measurement Initiative, 2003). One in five children will express at least one of the symptoms described in the *Diagnostic and Statistical Manual of Mental Disorders* (DSM-IV; American Psychiatric Association, 1994), and 5% of all children will experience "extreme functional impairment" due to mental illness (Child and Adolescent Health Measurement Initiative, 2003). Estimates are that 3–6% of children have serious emotional disability (Kauffman, 2001). The 24th Annual Report of OSEP to Congress reported in 2001 that 2,887,217 students with learning disabilities (LD), 473,663 with emotional and behavioral disorders (EBD), and 78,749 with autism received special education services in 2001 (ages 6 to 21). These figures were up from 2,247,000 (LD), 400,211 (EBD), and 5,415 (autism) reported 10 years early (Office of Special Education Programs, 2003). Results of the 2003 National Survey of Children's Health indicated that 11.5% of children had learning disabilities, 8.8% had attention-deficit/hyperactivity disorder (ADHD), and 6.3% had behavior problems. Six or seven children in 1,000 were reported with autism spectrum disorders (Centers for Disease Control and Prevention, 2007). As a group, these children with LD, ADHD, behavior problems, and autism had more learning problems, missed more school days, and were more depressed and anxious than children without these conditions (Blanchard, Gurka, & Blackman, 2006). The cost of long-term mental health care in the United States exceeds $67 billion (Hu, 2004).

Taken together, these data indicate a substantial problem at high cost under business as usual in elementary schooling. Prevention of behavioral and literacy failure and early intervening schoolwide potentially offers a solution for reducing the outcomes and costs associated with these problems. Thus, we now examine the specific social-behavioral and early literacy skills recommended by current research that underlie schoolwide prevention efforts.

## What Evidence-Based Behavioral Skills Are Necessary for Success in School?

"Readiness" for school implies that a specific set of knowledge and skills exist that students must have before they enter school. Defined by the National Education Goals Panel (Kagan, Moore, & Bredekamp, 1995), the critical dimensions are health and physical development, emotional well-being and social competence, approaches to learning, communicative skills, and cognitive and general knowledge. Children need to bring to school a range of established and growing personal conduct–social skills to benefit from schooling.

Personal conduct competencies include the ability to regulate attention, engagement, and emotion to focus on the teacher and engage instructional situations, participate in groups, make transitions to new activities, and work independently to complete tasks. Social competencies include the ability to initiate and receive social bids, work cooperatively toward common goals, navigate conflicting situations, and comply with conventions of behavior. And children in school are expected to be free of challenging, aggressive, and disruptive behaviors (Sainato & Carta, 1992). Children's social competencies and relationships with peers have an effect on whether their school grade transitions will be successful (Huffman, Mehlinger, & Kerivan, 2000). Children's classroom friendships relate to adjustment to school, need for mental health support, and overall school performance (Ladd, Kochenderfer, & Coleman, 1996). Children with language and reading disabilities are at high risk for impaired social interaction skill, social withdrawal, and peer rejection (Gertner, Rice, & Hadley, 1994; Lonigan, Bloomfield, et al., 1999). Children with developmental disabilities in particular are at risk for having fewer opportunities for interactions with their peers, being less successful in their social bids to peers, and for developing fewer friendships (Guralnick, Connor, Hammond, Gottman, & Kinnish, 1996).

For many kindergarteners, it is their first formal experience with schooling and of learning these many appropriate avenues of conduct. The students most at risk and least prepared for school are those without preschool and other schooling experiences prior to kindergarten (Barnett, 2001; Barnett, Young, & Schweinhart, 1998). It also is increasingly clear that even as early as preschool, children exhibit behavior problems severe enough to lead to their removal. Based on data from 40 states, the Yale University Child Study Center reported that preschool children were expelled 3 times more often than elementary and high school children (Gilliam, 2006). Expulsion rates varied considerably across states ranging from 4 to 10 per 1,000 students. Five-year-olds were expelled almost *twice* as often as 4-year-olds and 3 times as often as 3-year-olds. Boys in preschool were more than 4 times as likely to be expelled as girls, and African American children were about twice as likely to be expelled as European American children (Skiba, Rausch, & Ritter, 2004).

Research indicates that language and social communication skills are the early basis for learning to regulate behavior and how to comply with the behavioral expectations of the classroom and school. For students with language challenges and disabilities that adversely affect their communication, severe behavior problems are often more frequent and predicable. Behavior problems in this subpopulation, those who lack spoken and written communication skills, are known to function as primitive forms of communication (e.g., Repp & Deitz, 1990). Children with speech and language delays, for example, may be more likely to use physical actions such as aggression to communicate their wants and needs (Webster-Stratton, 1997). Interventions that teach alternative forms of communication to non-speaking children for purposes of choice and controlling their environment are effective means of reducing severe problem behavior (Reichle, York, & Eynon, 1989).

Students are expected to quickly learn how to function independently in the classroom (Carta, Sainato, & Greenwood, 1988). Kindergarten teachers reported that the skills most needed by children entering kindergarten were (1) the ability to complete work independently, (2) participate in groups, and (3) make timely, independent transitions between activities (Carta, Atwater, Schwartz, & Miller, 1990). The absence of explicit, systematic, and proactive teaching of these skills in a school population leads to increased behavior problems at school and potentially later behavior disorders (Kazdin, Mazurick, & Bass, 1993). Research clearly indicates that behavioral problems such as anxiety, disruption, noncompliance, and attention deficits are counterproductive to learning (DiPerna & Elliott, 2002). Serious behaviors such as aggression, arguing, and defiance are even greater threats to learning, and high rates of these problems schoolwide add to the cost burden of education and adversely affects the learning atmosphere in school and teacher retention/burnout.

Typical (average) K–5 grade trends in students' response to instruction sampled in observational research in three midwestern, urban, magnet elementary schools can be seen in Figure 1.1 in terms of engagement in classroom behaviors that either enable or detract from academic learning (i.e., active academic responding, task management behaviors, and inappropriate behavior) reported by Greenwood, Horton, and Utley (2002).

As can be seen across grades, acceleration in composite academic responding occurs after kindergarten and covaries with deceleration in task management. As students increase their time engaged in oral and silent reading, writing, and academic talk (academic responding) time spent simply attending to the teacher, following directions, raising their hand (task management behaviors), declines (refer to Greenwood et al., 2002). Both level off during third and fourth grades with academic responding becoming more frequent than task management as the curriculum advances and students engage in more independent work. Greater separation between the two occurs in fifth grade as academic responding

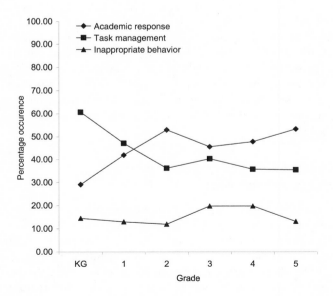

**FIGURE 1.1.** Grade trends in students' engagement in active academic responding. *Note.* From Greenwood, Horton, and Utley (2002). Copyright by the National Association of School Psychologists. Reprinted by permission.

increases even more. Along with these trends in classroom conduct over time, grade trends in inappropriate behaviors reflect a relatively constant background occurrence (e.g., of inappropriate locale, disruption, and other moderate intensity classroom behavior problems) ranging from 12 to 20% of time observed. A slightly declining trend is seen between kindergarten through second grade, thereafter increasing in third and fourth grades, and declining again in fifth grade.

The occurrence of behavior problems in schools serious enough to result in removal from the classroom for an office disciplinary referral for major problems like fighting, theft, inappropriate language, property destruction, and so on varies by age–grade level and school. For example, data reported on the School-Wide Information System (SWIS) website indicate that the mean number of major office referrals ($N_{schools}$ = 1,210; $N_{students}$ = 595,742) for the 2004–2005 school year was 0.39 per 100 students (grades K–6) compared to 1.28 in grades 6–9 (Seth et al., 2007). Thus for every 100 students, 39 versus 128 events occurred in that year in elementary versus junior/middle school. These numbers also vary by school, and by school SES conditions. For example, 884 office disciplinary referrals for major and minor infractions were reported by one low-SES elementary school in one year compared to only 22 in a mid to high-SES school. Grade trends in the low-SES school that year indicated high rates in second through fifth grades, lower in sixth grade (see Figure 1.2).

Behavioral skills are necessary for success in school, and some are required for school readiness. These skills cut across academic responding and task management skills. Others, like classroom behavior problems, actually compete with school success and risk removal of the student from the school, suspension from school negatively impacting academic learning and social adjustment. And both are learned at home and in school.

## Prevalence of Struggling Readers and Gaps in Academic Achievement

Closing the achievement gap between whites and minorities and students from low-income families is overwhelmingly rated as very important, and the public expects the schools to do this job (Rose & Gallup, 2006). Closing the achievement gap starts with reading (Burns, Griffin, & Snow, 1999; Snow, Burns, & Griffin, 1998). The larger the reading gap, the larger the gap in other subjects over time because reading comprehension is the key that unlocks the door to subject-matter knowledge (Torgesen, 2002).

The failure to learn to read is an impairment of ability that severely

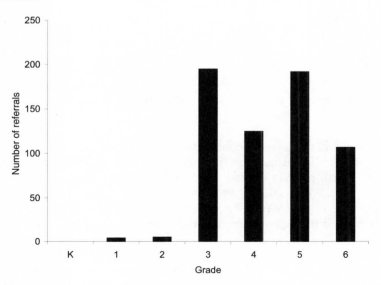

**FIGURE 1.2.** Grade trends in office disciplinary referrals for one school in the 2004–2005 school year (total number in 1 year = 844).

restricts competence because reading is a keystone necessary for future success. The prevalence of significant reading disability is 17–20% of children (1 in 5), and more than 33% (1 in 3) of children are struggling readers. Statistics indicate that 25% of 12th graders score below the basic level in reading (National Assessment of Educational Progress, 2002) with no significant change in fourth grade reading progress since 1992 (National Assessment of Educational Progress, 2003). Estimates are that 74% of poor readers in the third grade remain poor readers in ninth grade (Fletcher & Lyon, 1998). Struggling readers are more likely to drop out of school and to engage in criminal behavior and substance abuse (Whitehurst & Lonigan, 2001). Children and adults who cannot read are unable to address their health needs. Thus, reading failure is a personal, educational, economic, and public health problem.

Nationally,

> Between 1992 and 2005, there was no significant change in the percentage of fourth-graders performing at or above *Basic*, but the percentage performing at or above *Proficient* increased during this time. The percentage of eighth graders performing at or above Basic was higher in 2005 (73 percent) than in 1992 (69 percent), but there was no significant change in the percentage scoring at or above *Proficient* between these same years. (National Assessment of Educational Progress, 2005)

However, in 2007,

> 4th graders scored higher on average in 2007 than all previous years, while 8th graders were 1 point higher than 2005 and 3 points higher than 1992. There was no significant change in the percentage of students at the Proficient level. (National Assessment of Educational Progress, 2007).

Viewed in the international context, Baer, Baldi, Ayotte, and Green (2007) reported that in 2006 the average reading comprehension score of U.S. fourth graders ranked 22nd out of 44 countries. Fourth-grade students in 10 countries in the study had average scores higher than those in the United States. And, the performance of U.S. students was not improved in reading comprehension on this measure compared to 2001 in the Progress in International Reading Literacy Study (Baer et al., 2007).

Reading failure in the United States is greatest in central city, urban schools (National Assessment of Educational Progress, 2003). Students educated in central city schools perform lower in 4th-grade reading than do students attending urban-fringe or rural schools. Students who are free-lunch eligible (low-SES) perform lower than those who are not (average- and above-SES). Blacks and Hispanics perform lower in reading achievement than do white or Asian students (Lutkus, Grigg, & Donahue, 2007). Blacks and Hispanics are overrepresented in special education primarily due to reading difficulties and behavior problems (Ferguson, Kozleski, & Smith, 2003) and underrepresented in programs for the gifted. Teachers in urban schools are often the least qualified, lacking the needed credentials and/or are assigned to teach subjects out of their area of expertise (Cohen, 2003).

## What Evidence-Based Emerging Literacy and Reading Skills Are Needed for Success in School?

Students who have not experienced language and had the opportunity to learn from key early literacy experiences prior to kindergarten face significant challenges learning to read (Torgesen, 2002; Whitehurst & Lonigan, 1998, 2001). Adequate early literacy experience before kindergarten enables children to acquire knowledge of two interdependent domains of information needed to learn to read. First, children need sources of information that will directly support their understanding of the meaning of print in school. These include vocabulary knowledge, conceptual knowledge, story schemas, and story comprehension. Children from low-SES and minority group backgrounds are at high risk for not bringing these skills to kindergarten (Hart & Risley, 1995; Walker, Greenwood, Hart, & Carta, 1994). Children also need to be able to translate print into sounds and sounds into print. These skills include phonemic awareness, and letter–sound correspondence. Children from low-SES and minority group backgrounds are also at risk for not bringing these skills to kindergarten (Whitehurst & Lonigan, 2001). Chard and Kame'enui (2000) reported that students who displayed poor reading skills in first grade had a 90% chance of continuing poor reading skills 3 years later and began to actively dislike reading, reading less often in and out of school (Juel, 1988). Students showing reading problems at the end of third grade are not likely to improve significantly by the end of eighth grade (Felton & Wood, 1992).

To acquire literacy knowledge, it is increasingly clear that children must be taught through early experiences with parents and teachers (Whitehurst & Lonigan, 2001). Without such early learning experiences, students continue to struggle to read throughout the school years. Thus, the core elements of a science-based reading program prior to third grade include phonemic awareness, letter–sound relationships (phonics), an increasing lexicon of words (vocabulary) identifiable at a "single" glance (fluency), and comprehension. Students arriving in third grade with these skills will be able to read third-grade text accurately and fluently with adequate levels of understanding (Moats, 1999; National Reading Panel, 2000). Reading skill components that differentiate reading achievement after third grade include continued growth in the lexicon of words, acquisition of the complex vocabulary that appears primarily in written text, acquiring strategies for processing different types of text (e.g., narrative, expository), growth in conceptual and background knowledge, and growth in reasoning/inferential skills. The most important outcome of elementary reading instruction is comprehension of written material (Block, Gambrell, & Pressley, 2002; Torgesen, 1998, 2002).

## Are Behavior Problems and Literacy Problems Linked?

Learning to read in school depends on direction following, attention, processing abilities, and motivation to stay actively engaged with the teacher and instruction. Learning to read (or any school subject) is interrupted by problem behaviors in the classroom and school (H. M. Walker, Ramsey, & Gresham, 2005). In the context of these skills in the classroom, children's literacy skills are advanced through their conversational interactions with teachers, engagement with the curricula, and their social interactions with peers. These are the naturally supportive processes through which the majority of students learn to read in school.

When problems with these naturally supportive processes emerge, they instead become processes that impede and/or constrain one another—leading to behavior problems and delayed reading. They become social mechanisms by which falling behind in reading leads to behavior problems, and behavior problems lead to delays in learning to read (Reid & Eddy, 1997; Reid, Patterson, & Snyder, 2002). Students' lack of social competency often may lead to behavior problems that interrupt attention and engagement in classroom learning activities, leading to delays in learning to read. Just one example, the inability to communicate may interrupt the learning of phonological skills.

Evidence indicates that regulation of attention and engagement play key roles in children's classroom learning and that there is an overlap between attention, behavior problems, and reading disabilities (Greenwood et al., 2002; Lonigan, Anthony, Bloomfield, Dyer, & Samwel, 1999). Young children with poor attention skills have less developed emergent literacy skills (i.e., print knowledge, oral language). In addition to improving phonological awareness skills, interventions in phonological skills have been found to increase engagement and decrease behavior problems (Torgesen et al., 1999). Similar findings have been reported in randomized trials at the elementary school level targeting engagement in academic responding (e.g., Greenwood, Delquadri, & Hall, 1989). Child engagement in classroom activities is one of the best single behavioral correlates of children's developmental status (Ridley, McWilliam, & Oates, 2000). To maintain active engagement in learning to read, for example, direction following and sustained attention are necessary (Kamps, Greenwood, Arreaga-Mayer, Abbott, & Utley, 2002).

One particularly compelling conceptualization of this linkage between behavior problems and learning to read is that of Reid and Eddy (1997). The inability to perform reading tasks becomes aversive leading to increasingly severe behavior problems that function to avoid or escape classroom reading instruction (Wehby, Lane, & Falk, 2003). If not prevented early, the lack of reading skills at school entry can lead to these types of behavior problems because students readily learn that behavior problems reduce their time spent learning to read and therefore, increase the intensity and severity of their social conduct in the future (Patterson, Reid, & Dishion, 1992). Over weeks and months in school, behavior problems lead to reading failure and vice versa.

Other evidence indicates that 50% of students with EBD also meet one or more of the criteria for LD (Glassberg, Hooper, & Mattison, 1989). Students qualifying to receive special education services for EBD also are struggling readers (Mastropieri, Jenkins, & Scruggs, 1985). The estimated comorbidity between reading disorders and ADHD, a condition manifested by high levels of behaviors that interfere with learning including inattention, impulsivity, distractibility, and moodiness, is as high as 50% (Shaywitz & Shaywitz, 1993; Torgesen et al., 2001), and over 70% for children with language and behavior disorders (Benner, Nelson, & Epstein, 2002).

The social and behavioral difficulties related to reading disabilities not only impede later school outcomes, but also negatively affect children's interactions with teachers and peers, leading to social withdrawal, peer rejection and increased likelihood of referral for special education and psychiatric services (Gertner et al., 1994). Emergent patterns of social deficits, behavioral problems, and language delay have been reported even for children younger than kindergarten (Kaiser, Hancock, Cai, Foster, & Hester, 2000).

Reading and behavior problems after third grade, increasingly affect students' ability to learn and comprehend the subject matter taught in school. This cycle continues to compound over weeks and months in school eventually leading to drop out in adolescence and other adverse outcomes ranging from running away, delinquency, early parenthood, sexually transmitted diseases, drugs, and other high-risk behaviors (Reid & Eddy, 1997). Seventy-five percent of the prison populations are poor readers (Chard & Kame'enui, 2000).

Unfortunately, too many students take this path in school, and too little effort is made to anticipate these problems as early as kindergarten, and to prevent small early problems from becoming large problems later. As a result, students on this path reach a point in their schooling where reading instruction effective for the majority of students is not effective for them.

The consequences of this path to undereducation in America are staggering because education pays. Having less than a high school education leads to poverty, lower lifetime earnings, and unemployment (Baum & Ma, 2007). Even having a high school diploma in today's economy means lower pay. "Persons with a doctoral or professional degree are expected to earn about $3 million over a life time compared to only $1 million for a person without a high school degree" (Employment Policy Foundation, 2004). The costs of social services to children and young adults in poverty who are unemployed and perhaps early parents are also staggering (Center on Budget and Policy Priorities, 2006; Children's Defense Fund, 2005). Because this path prevents many students from learning from instruction that is effective with most students and because of the increasing numbers of children experiencing reading and behavior problems who are served by special education and mental health services, the overall K–12 costs to educate are greater than necessary. Loss to the national economy due to the lowered intellectual capacity of the workforce is huge (Brooks-Gunn, Currie, & Besharov, 2000;

Karoly et al., 1998). Continued school success from grade level to grade level is the greatest known protective factor.

In summary, the prevalence of school discipline and underachievement continues to be at the forefront of the public's concerns, and the public expects the schools to address these problems. Increasingly data exist documenting the high prevalence of reading and behavior problems in schools, and recent evidence suggests the two are linked, one affecting and supporting the other. Data exist showing which personal social conduct and literacy skills are needed by students at each grade level to be on target learning to read in elementary school. Research reveals an active, early pathway leading to reading failure, early school failure, and undereducation. The prevalence of these problems originating in early childhood and kindergarten when unaddressed powerfully affects each school's learning climate in positive and negative ways. Similarly affected are a host of other adverse outcomes including increased costs to educate, high rates of teacher burnout, failing schools, and crime and violence.

## Recent Accountability Policies Have Raised Expectations for Schooling Results

The No Child Left Behind Act (NCLB; 2001), the Individuals with Disabilities Act (IDEA; 2004), and related initiatives (Reading First, Safe Schools) as well as complementary state and local policies have raised public expectations for schooling results and how it can be achieved. Policymakers and parents expect that the path to improving results is through use of evidence-based, educational experiences in school proven to result in better learning outcomes. Consequently, a growing market for evidence-based practices in education has been created (see Table 1.2). For example, NCLB provisions for schools that receive federal funds require that (1) only evidence-based reading curricula may be purchased and supported by schools using federal funds, (2) reporting of students' annual yearly progress in the curriculum including minority subpopulations (e.g., race, language, and disability), and (3) inclusion of special education students in all areas including accountability testing.

Compared to earlier authorizations, IDEA 2004 policies included the provision that students' RTI could be used as a basis for special education eligibility for learning disabilities and intervention decision making. Because RTI relies on the concept of progress monitoring in the curriculum to qualify students for special education services, it also supports schools' use of evidence-based curricula and practices capable of supporting and accelerating students' growth and development.

**TABLE 1.2. Recent Policies Impacting the Prevalence of Evidence-Based Practice**

- 2001: No Child Left Behind Act (NCLB)
  - Mandates evidence-based reading practices.
  - Mandates annual yearly progress reporting.
  - Embraces special education.

- 2002–2003: Evidence-based practices scale up in local schools
  - Scientifically based reading curricula.
  - Schoolwide prevention models (positive behavior support; reading).
  - Progress monitoring and data-based decision making.

- 2004–present: Individuals with Disabilities Education Act (IDEA)
  - RTI and prereferral interventions.
  - Progress monitoring and data-based decision making.

Leading to NCLB 2001 and IDEA 2004, blue ribbon panels reported weaknesses and needed improvements in educational research (Coalition for Evidence-Based Policy, 2003; National Reading Panel, 2000; Shavelson & Towne, 2002). The report by the President's Commission on Excellence in Special Education (2002) recommended that the special education field should (1) strengthen its focus on results, rather than process; (2) embrace a model of prevention rather than failure; and that it (3) consider students with disabilities to be part of general education. Prevention models are also increasingly embraced by professional organizations in education including, for example, the National Association of School Psychology and National Association of State Directors of Special Education. Schoolwide prevention models are the topic of this volume.

Because policies have also supported research on effective practices, the good news is that we are faced with the prospects of new and emerging knowledge about effective practices—some that offer the potential of vastly reducing the number of struggling readers and students with behavior problems in local schools. This knowledge in several broad areas includes prevention science and schoolwide prevention models.

Prevention science is the application of problem-solving strategies linking severity of problems, risk and protective factors, and interventions with evidence indicating that interventions are capable of reducing the prevalence of poor outcomes. Schoolwide prevention models are strategies designed to apply prevention science knowledge to reduction of risk and poor education outcomes. Rather than waiting for children to "grow out of" early learning problems before providing special education services as in the past, schoolwide prevention models support intervening earlier to prevent small problems from becoming larger problems in the future. Intervening early is now possible using formative measurement tools to identify students who are not responsive to the universal reading instruction effective with most students. These students are provided earlier, intensive services to prevent emerging problems from becoming more serious and costly conditions. As we see, schoolwide prevention models are comprehensive strategies that guide action designed to reduce the prevalence of all negative outcomes. Prevention models do assume that many students at risk may be helped earlier. However, it is a fallacy to think that prevention models assume that all disabilities and problem conditions can be prevented entirely (e.g., Gordon, 1983; Merrell & Buchanan, 2006). Prevention models do embrace instructional interventions for all students including those with identified disabilities and high-risk conditions. Prevention models assume that those with disabilities can be helped to improve and maintain functioning and independence given comprehensive prevention–intervention services.

## FOUNDATIONAL ISSUES IN SCHOOLWIDE PREVENTION

The time to apply prevention science in elementary education has come. Providing impetus is the growth in science-based intervention practices for promoting positive social behavior, and literacy now and in the future. Many of these are discussed below and in other chapters in this volume. Several however qualify as foundational to schoolwide prevention.

First, there is considerable progress in the field of prevention science especially with regard to evidence-based practices (see Weissberg, Kumpfer, & Seligman, 2003). Specifically, a number of principles of effective prevention programs have been identified (Nation et. al., 2003), and are featured in the prevention models in this text. An important impetus to the prevention science movement within education has been the advances made in children's mental health through prevention initiatives (see Tolan & Dodge, 2005; Weisz, Sandler, Durlak, & Anton, 2005). Second, widespread use of continuous progress monitoring measures in education is based on more than 15 years of evidence showing that students of teachers who use progress monitoring receive a better instructional program and achieve more than students whose teachers don't (see, e.g. National Center for Progress Monitoring, 2006). Other evidence-based instructional interventions and strategies (What Works Clearing House, 2003), include evidence-based reading curricula (Kamps et al., 2003; Vaughn, Klingner, & Haager, 2007); positive behavior support (PBS; Marquis et al., 2000); and peer-assisted learning strategies

(PALS; Rohrbeck, Ginsberg-Block, Fantuzzo, & Miller, 2003), among others discussed in the following chapters.

Another impetus is the RTI policy in IDEA 2004 that allows states to use students' response to intervention as qualification for special education services and a means of intervention selection. These policies embrace the progress monitoring component of prevention science in that schools implementing a prevention approach will necessarily need rich sources of progress data available for all their students for decision making related to the need for differentiated interventions, including special education needed by individual students within a school (D. Fuchs & Fuchs, 2005; L. S. Fuchs & Fuchs, 2006). In the remainder of this chapter, we tie together themes previously discussed that inform schoolwide prevention and how these themes were linked to the six centers' work designing and implementing their individual models.

## How Might We Meet Expectations Using Schoolwide Prevention Models?

What distinguishes a prevention approach from traditional approaches to schooling, and the provision of special education in particular, is its strong emphasis on the whole school beginning in kindergarten. The goal is to prevent delays in educational outcomes by intensifying instructional supports, thereby allowing students' functional skills to emerge. This is achieved by universal progress monitoring to identify students at risk combined with early, differentiated tiers of intervention (universal, targeted, and indicated). In comparison, the traditional special education model for years has been one of waiting to provided intervention until the second or third grade for children to have sufficiently failed to qualify for individual special education services (President's Commission on Excellence in Special Education, 2002).

### Prevention in Schools

Prevention models are designed to manage risk in an elementary school across a series of steps linking an identified problem to exposure–disorder–outcomes knowledge. "The effort is to tie problem solving to the causes of problems, to onset and protection against onset, and to cure, impairment, or relapse of the problem" (Merrell & Buchanan, 2006, p. 171). Prevention models are designed to link quick, targeted actions of the system (e.g., a city health department or Whittier Elementary School faculty) to reductions in the range of negative outcomes associated with a disease or other undesirable outcomes such as a learning disability in reading or a serious behavior disorder.

The goal of a prevention model is to maximize all positive outcomes including those experienced by the individual, the system, and society. Prevention outcomes for some at-risk children may be to prevent the problem and its costs altogether. Where disease or disability is present, evidence-based treatments are used to ameliorate the condition and, to the extent possible, reduce its negative impact compared to the natural course of the disease (e.g., early onset, loss of function or life, etc.). Interventions in this case are designed to improve function and independence, thereby reducing costs compared to traditional practices. Frequently collected progress data reflecting all children's individual response to intervention is needed to assess if the universal intervention is sufficient, and to identify those students who need more intense support. Key decision making within a prevention framework seeks to move a child either into or out of secondary or tertiary intervention based on a student's response. The progress monitoring and problem solving (decision making) approaches of Deno (Deno, 2002; L. S. Fuchs & Deno, 1991) and Good (Good, Gruba, & Kaminski, 2002) in education provide two concrete methods widely used in schools that are consistent with prevention science and schoolwide three-tiered models.

### Three Tiers Differentiate Intervention

Many prevention approaches monitor outcomes relative to tiers or levels of risk: primary (universal), secondary (targeted), and tertiary (indicated) (H. M. Walker & Shinn, 2002). At the primary level, outcomes are monitored and "universal" practices implemented with all students in the school are intended to promote healthily development, and prevent the onset of a delay, and a delay from becoming a disability, thereby avoiding the problem. An example of universal prevention in public health would be a systematic advertising campaign explaining the importance of obtaining a flu shot in reducing chances of catching the flu. At the secondary level, children most at risk are "targeted" for treatment prior to the condition becoming a disability. In the case of education, kindergarteners targeted as at risk because of falling below benchmark on basic early literacy skills as compared to other children this age are provided additional small-group instruction. In the case of public health, a targeted intervention would be an immunization program exclusively for seniors and young children—subpopulation groups most at risk for the flu. Primary and secondary prevention working together reduce the full consequences of disability to individuals and the system (individual, school, and society stakeholders). At the tertiary level, children with an identified disability are treated to reduce the negative outcomes associated with the full disease. In the case of edu-

cation, children with a behavior disorder are provided highly individualized behavioral supports including interventions based on functional
assessments of the promoters of the student's problem behavior. In the
case of public health, individuals with the flu are treated with a complement of care and medicine to shorten their illness, and to reduce
transmission to others in the community. Often a reality of the tertiary
level is the fact that primary and secondary intervention efforts may
have failed for any one individual student. However, early detection
and intervention at the universal and targeted levels may very well
have minimized the overall negative impact of the disease or disability.
Typically in schoolwide prevention models, all students in a school
maintain receipt of universal intervention such as use of an evidence-
based reading curricula with either targeted or indicated interventions
added to intensify the overall strength of treatment, and the likelihood
of a positive response to intervention.

Schoolwide prevention models like Project CIRCUITS (Kame'enui,
Simmons, Good, & Chard, 2002) use a three-tiered model to reduce the
prevalence of reading problems. The authors defined "prevention" as an
action to prevent or stop something from happening, and also to reduce
the impact of a problem that is already identified. They described primary prevention (first circuit) as a systems-level effort to effectively reform an entire school's efforts to prevent reading difficulties, expected to
meet the needs of about 80% of the school population. Secondary prevention (second circuit) exposes high-risk students to strategies and procedures to supplement and enhance the effects of the primary prevention. Secondary prevention typically accommodates 15% of the K–3
students shown not to be benefiting from primary prevention alone and
is often based around small-group reading instruction and peer tutoring.
Tertiary prevention (third circuit) "represents reading instruction that is
specifically designed and customized for individual students with marked
difficulties in reading or reading disabilities, and who have not responded to primary and secondary prevention efforts" (p. 4). Tertiary
intervention is reserved for approximately 5% of students within a
school. Schoolwide positive behavior support (SWPBS; Horner, Sugai,
Todd, & Lewis-Palmer, 2003; Marquis et al., 2000; Sugai & Lewis,
1999) is another example of a tiered, schoolwide prevention model focused on positive approaches to school discipline and reduction in the
prevalence of behavior problems schoolwide.

## The K–3 OSEP Behavior and Reading Prevention Initiative

Based on these foundations, OSEP had become increasingly interested in
strategies for intervening earlier in student's development as a means of

improving reading and behavior outcomes. Such capacity appeared particularly important for two of the largest subpopulations of students served by IDEA, those eligible for special education services under the categories of emotional disturbance and specific learning disability (Federal Register, 2001b). The concern in the disability field was that these children were typically not identified and served prior to their disabilities becoming severe.

> Effective strategies that intervene early in a child's development are well recognized in improving results from children with disabilities. Unfortunately, approximately sixty percent of the children currently being served under IDEA are typically identified too late to receive full benefit from those interventions.
>
> There currently exists a substantial and compelling body of research describing how to assess, identify, and help these children. . . . For instance a substantial body of research indicates that both populations of children: Can be assessed and identified early with relative easy and accuracy; Are at high risk for dropping out of school, becoming discipline problems, and failing in school; Often fall behind because they do not receive appropriate interventions earlier; Can make tremendous gains when provided with effective services during early childhood; and May need individually tailored interventions because one approach may not fit all children (Federal Register, 2001a, p. 32878).

Thus OSEP decided to compete funding to sponsor six National Research Centers plus a separate coordinating center to conduct field-based research testing the efficacy of schoolwide prevention models. These centers were funded in 2003 with a common focus on early intervening for children in kindergarten through grade 3. Among the common specific goals of each center were development, implementation, and evaluation of a three-tiered Prevention Model in at least seven representative elementary schools. The primary aim of each funded center's prevention model was focused on (1) behavior, (2) reading, or (3) reading and behavior as follows:

- *Behavior prevention centers* were located at the University of Oregon (*www.wcer.wisc.edu/cce/behavior.html*) and the University of Nebraska (*www.wcer.wisc.edu/cce/nebraska.html*).
- *Reading prevention centers* were located at the University of Oregon (*www.wcer.wisc.edu/cce/reading.html*) and University of Texas-Austin (*www.wcer.wisc.edu/cce/texas.html*).
- *Reading and behavior prevention centers* were located at the University of Kansas (*www.wcer.wisc.edu/cce/kansas.html*) and

University of North Carolina–Charlotte (*www.wcer.wisc.edu/ cce/carolina.html*).

- The *coordinating center*, located at the University of Wisconsin–Madison (*www.wcer.wisc.edu/cce/index.htm*), was responsible for designing and coordinating implementation of a shared measurement model from which it would be possible to pool results across the centers.

## SUMMARY AND CONCLUSION

In this chapter, we introduced foundations and themes in contemporary education that point to schoolwide prevention models as a potential solution to the unacceptably high prevalence of students with (1) behavior problems, (2) reading problems, or (3) behavior and reading problems in local elementary schools. These models are solutions because they are responsive to schooling priorities as reported by the general public and parents. They are responsive to recent federal and state policies on educational practice and accountability. They are supported by principles grounded in prevention science and evidence-based practice. And they are informed by a growing number of behavioral and reading intervention practices that can be successfully implemented with good results in real schools and classrooms.

In Chapter 2, we present additional information on the core procedures and implementation approaches needed to successfully implement three-tiered schoolwide prevention models. Following Chapter 2, we present the individual school case studies contained in Part II. Informed by foundations and common themes as is seen, each center's model was uniquely developed. Major outcomes of this work include the practices employed and the variations in tiered models where the procedure common to all centers was the universal (Tier 1) application. In each center, the universal intervention was the initial intervention step in a sequence of implementing two or three tiers. Another outcome was each center's use of assessment tools and approaches for documenting that the universal literacy and behavior support practices that were actually implemented. Yet another outcome was use of implementation data in combination with the students' progress data to making "improving" decisions at multiple levels of the school system (i.e., student, teacher, class, grade, and school) and to inform continuing professional development efforts. In Chapter 9, we conclude the book with a discussion of outcomes and implications.

As we look across this entire effort, we encourage readers seriously considering implementing a schoolwide prevention model to evaluate six critically important issues (foundational components) across the remaining material in this volume and its relevance to their own circumstances. How these issues are addressed in any single effort, based on our experiences, will powerfully affect initial feasibility, and over time, the eventual success or failure.

1. Coordination of the schoolwide system that includes monitoring of progress combined with decision making, evidence-based practices, high-quality implementation, and professional development is a foundation. To maximize student outcome effectiveness, a feedback loop must be established between student progress and the practices implemented to fidelity so that needed improvements in practice and implementation thereof can be optimized relative to attained growth in desired student outcomes.

2. Universal screening, progress monitoring, and decision making based on locally collected data is a foundational component. Attend to the what, how, when, where, and why this was conducted in each model and how it was possible for faculty teams to access, review, and make informed decisions about the intervention needs of individual students.

3. The selection, adoption, and use of evidence-based instructional/intervention practices including progress monitoring (Number 1 above) is a foundation because it has been shown to reduce the prevalence of students in a school with behavior problems and/or who are struggling to learn to read. Of each center's model, ask the question, "What criteria were used and how were these decisions made—and can they be similarly made in my school?"

4. Leadership commitment and administrative buy-in and support for schoolwide implementation is critically important in concept and resources. The strategies and means of attaining this support reported below and how one's own access to such support are a necessary foundation.

5. Professional development that targets evidence-based practice and that is sufficiently intensive to lead to implementation is a foundation. Professional development in schoolwide prevention models must lead to implementation of the model schoolwide—nothing less is acceptable. Ongoing coaching and systematic training of new staff and retraining of old staff are also critical.

6. Monitoring effects and evaluating progress relative to goals and improving the action plan one year to the next is a foundation. This includes measuring the fidelity of intervention and a feedback loop between student progress and practices implemented used to optimize growth in desired outcomes (implementation and student outcome).

# REFERENCES

American Psychiatric Association. (1994). *Diagnostic and statistical manual of mental disorders* (4th ed.). Washington, DC: Author.

Baer, J., Baldi, S., Ayotte, K., & Green, J. G. (2007). *The reading literacy of U.S. fourth-grade students in an international context: Results from the 2001 and 2006 Progress in International Reading Literacy Study (PIRLS)*. Retrieved November 29, 2007, from *www.nces.ed. gov/pubsearch/pubsinfo.asp?pubid= 2008017*.

Barnett, W. S. (2001). Preschool education for economically disadvantaged children: Effects on reading achievement and related outcomes. In S. B. Neuman & D. K. Dickinson (Eds.), *Handbook of early literacy research* (pp. 421–443). New York: Guilford Press.

Barnett, W. S., Young, J., & Schweinhart, L. J. (1998). How preschool education contributes to cognitive development and school success: An empirical model. In W. S. Barnett & S. S. Boocock (Eds.), *Early care and education for children in poverty: Promises, programs, and long-term outcomes* (pp. 167–184). Buffalo: State University of New York Press.

Baum, S., & Ma, J. (2007). Education pays: The benefits of higher education for individuals and society. Retrieved March 2, 2007, from *www.collegeboard.com/ prod_downloads/ about/news_info/trends/ed_pays_2007.pdf*.

Benner, G. J., Nelson, J. R., & Epstein, M. H. (2002). Language skills of children with EBD: A literature review. *Journal of Emotional and Behavioral Disorders, 10*, 43–59.

Blanchard, L. T., Gurka, M. J., & Blackman, J. A. (2006). Emotional, developmental and behavioral health of American children and their families: A report of from the 2003 national survey of children's health. *Pediatrics, 117*(6), 1202.

Block, C. C., Gambrell, L. B., & Pressley, M. (2002). *Improving comprehension instruction: Rethinking research, theory, and classroom practice*. New York: Jossey-Bass.

Brooks-Gunn, J., Currie, J., & Besharov, D. J. (2000, May 10). *Early childhood intervention programs: What are the costs and benefits?* (Congressional Research Briefing Summary). Washington, DC: U. S. Department of Health and Human Services.

Bureau of Justice. (2005). *Indicators of school crime and safety 2005*. Retrieved November 5, 2007, from *www.ojp.gov/bjs/pub/press/iscs05pr.htm*. Washington, DC: Bureau of Justice, Bureau of Justice Statistics.

Burns, M. S., Griffin, P., & Snow, C. E. (1999). *Starting out right: A guide to promoting children's reading success*. Washington, DC: Commission on the Prevention of Reading Difficulties in Young Children, National Research Council.

Carta, J. J., Atwater, J. B., Schwartz, I. S., & Miller, P.A. (1990). Applications of ecobehavioral analysis to the study of transitions across early education settings. *Education and Treatment of Children, 13*, 298–315.

Carta, J. J., Sainato, D. M., & Greenwood, C. R. (1988). Advances in the ecological assessment of classroom instruction for young children with handicaps. In S. L. Odom & M. B. Karnes (Eds.), *Research perspectives in early childhood special education* (pp. 217–239). MD: Paul H. Brookes.

Center on Budget and Policy Priorities. (2006). *What does the safety net accomplish*. Washington, DC: Author.

Centers for Disease Control and Prevention. (2007). Prevalence of autism spectrum disorders. *Morbidity and Mortality Weekly Report, 56*(SS-1), 12–28.

Chard, D. J., & Kame'enui, E. J. (2000). Struggling first-grade readers: The frequency and progress of their reading. *Journal of Special Education, 34*(1), 28–38.

Child and Adolescent Health Measurement Initiative: National Survey of Children's Health (2003). Data Resource Center on Child and Adolescent Health website. Retrieved May 5, 2008, from *www.childhealthdata.org*.

Children's Defense Fund. (2005). *Defining poverty and why it matters for children.* Washington, DC: Author.

Coalition for Evidence-Based Policy. (2003). *Identifying and implementing educational practices supported by rigorous evidence.* Washington, DC: U.S. Department of Education, Insititute of Education Science.

Cohen, J. S. (2003, December 20). Poor kids get least qualified teachers: Illinois' standards too lax, critics say. *Chicago Tribune,* pp. 1, 22.

Committee on Integrating the Science of Early Childhood Development. (2000). *From neurons to neighborhoods: The science of early childhood development.* Washington, DC: National Academies Press.

Costello, E. J., & Angold, A. (2000). Developmental epideminology: A framework for developmental psychopathology. In A. J. Sameroff, M. Lewis, & S. M. Miller (Eds.), *Handbook of developmental psychopathology* (2nd ed., pp. 57–73). New York: Kluwer/ Plenum.

Deno, S. L. (2002). Problem solving as "best practice." In A. Thomas & J. Grimes (Eds.), *Best practices in school psychology IV* (Vol. 1, pp. 37–56). Washington, DC: National Association of School Psychologists.

DiPerna, J., & Elliott, S. (2002). Promoting enablers to improve student achievement: An introduction to the miniseries. *School Psychology Review, 31*(3), 1–12.

Employment Policy Foundation. (2004, February). Education pays: Stay in school. *IssueBackgrounder, Contemporary Issues in Employment and the Workplace.*

Federal Register. (2001a, Monday, June 18). Department of Education, Office of Special Education and Rehabilitation Services; Special Education—Research and Innovation to Improve Services and Results for Children with Disabilities Program Notice. *Federal Register, 66,* 32878–32882.

Federal Register. (2001b, June 18). Priority—Centers for implementing K–3 behavior and reading Intervention Models (CFDA 84.324 X). *Federal Register, 66*(117).

Felton, R. H., & Wood, F. B. (1992). A reading level match study of nonword reading skills in poor readers with varying IQ. *Journal of Learning Disabilities, 25,* 318–326.

Ferguson, D., Kozleski, E., & Smith, A. (2003). Transforming general and special education in urban schools. In F. E. Obiakor, C. A. Utley, & A. F. Rotatori (Eds.), *Effective education for learners with exceptionalities* (Vol. 15, pp. 43–74). New York: JAI Press.

Fletcher, J. M., & Lyon, G. R. (1998). Reading: A research-based approach. In W. M. Evers (Ed.), *What's gone wrong in America's classrooms* (pp. 49–90). Palo Alto, CA: Board of Trustees of the Leland Stanford Junior University, Hoover Institution Press.

Fuchs, D., & Fuchs, L. S. (2005). Responsiveness-to-intervention: A blueprint for practitioners, policymakers, and parents. *Teaching Exceptional Children, 38*(1), 57–61.

Fuchs, L. S., & Deno, S. L. (1991). Paradigmatic distinctions between instructionally relevant measurement models. *Exceptional Children, 57,* 488–500.

Fuchs, L. S., & Fuchs, D. (2006). Implementing responsiveness-to-intervention to identify learning disabilities. *Perspectives, 32*(1), 39–43.

Gertner, B. L., Rice, M. L., & Hadley, P. A. (1994). Influence of communicative competence of peer preferences a preschool classroom. *Journal of Speech and Hearing Research, 37,* 913–923.

Gilliam, W. S. (2006). *Prekindergartners left behind: Expulsion rates in state prekindergarten systems.* New Haven, CT: Yale University Child Study Center. Retrieved November 8, 2007, from *www.fcd-us.org/PDFs/NationalPre KExpulsionPaper03.02_new.pdf.*

Glassberg, L. A., Hooper, S. R., & Mattison, R. E. (1989). Prevalence of learning disabilities at enrollment in special education students with behavior disorders. *Behavioral Journal of Dyslexia, 44,* 81–102.

Good, R. H., Gruba, J., & Kaminski, R. A. (2002). Best practices in using dynamic indicators of basic early literacy skills (DIBELS) in an outcomes-driven model. In A. Thomas & J. Grimes (Eds.), *Best practices in school psychology* ( 4th ed., pp. 699–720). Washington, DC: National Association of School Psychologists.

Gordon, R. S. (1983). An operational classification of disease prevention. *Public Health Reports, 98*, 107–109.

Greenwood, C. R., Delquadri, J., & Hall, R. V. (1989). Longitudinal effects of classwide peer tutoring. *Journal of Educational Psychology, 81*, 371–383.

Greenwood, C. R., Horton, B. T., & Utley, C. A. (2002). Academic engagement: Current perspectives on research and practice. *School Psychology Review, 31*(3), 328–349.

Guralnick, M. J., Connor, R. T., Hammond, M. A., Gottman, J. M., & Kinnish, K. (1996). The peer relations of preschool children with communication disorders. *Child Development, 67*, 471–489.

Hart, B., & Risley, T. R. (1995). *Meaningful differences in the everyday experience of young American children.* Baltimore: Brookes.

Horner, R. H., Sugai, G., Todd, A. W., & Lewis-Palmer, T. (2003). School-wide positive behavior support. In L. Bambara & L. Kern (Eds.), *Individualized supports for students problem behaviors: Designing positive behavior support plans* (pp. 359–390). New York: Guilford Press.

Hu, T. (2004). *An international review of the economic costs of mental illness* (Working Paper 31). Washington DC: A joint project of the World Bank, the Fogerty International Center of the National Institutes of Health, the Bill and Melinda Gates Foundation, and the World Health Organization.

Huffman, L. C., Mehlinger, S. L., & Kerivan, A. S. (2000). *Risk factors for academic and behavioral problems at the beginning of school.* Palo Alto, CA: Stanford University School of Medicine, Department of Pediatrics, and The Children's Health Council.

Juel, C. (1988). Learning to read and write: A longitudinal study of 54 children from first through fourth grades. *Journal of Educational Psychology, 80*, 437–447.

Kagan, S. L., Moore, E., & Bredekamp, S. (1995). *Reconsidering children's early development and learning: Toward common views and vocabulary.* Washington, DC: National Education Goals Panel.

Kaiser, A. P., Hancock, T. B., Cai, X., Foster, E. M., & Hester, P. P. (2000). Parent reported behavioral problems and language delays in boys and girls enrolled in head start classrooms. *Behavioral Disorders, 26*(1), 26–41.

Kame'enui, E. J., Simmons, D.C., Good, R, H., & Chard, D. J. (2002). *Focus and nature of primary, secondary, and tertiary prevention: CIRCUITS model.* Unpublished manuscript, Center for Teaching and Learning, Eugene, OR.

Kamps, D., Greenwood, C. R., Arreaga-Mayer, C., Abbott, M., & Utley, C. (2002). *Center for early intervention in reading and behavior to improve the performance of young children.* Kansas City: University of Kansas, Juniper Gardens Children's Project.

Kamps, D., Wills, H. P., Greenwood, C. R., Thorne, S., Lazo, J. F., Crockett, J. L., et al. (2003). A descriptive study of curriculum influences on the early reading fluency of students with academic and behavioral risks. *Journal of Emotional and Behavioral Disorders, 11*(4), 211–224.

Karoly, L. A., Greenwood, P. W., Everingham, S. S., Hoube, J., Kilburn, M. R., Peters, S., et al. (1998). *Investing in our children: What we know and don't know about costs and benefits of early childhood interventions.* Santa Monica, CA: RAND.

Kauffman, J. M. (2001). *Characteristics of emotional and behavioral disorders of children and youth* (7th ed.). Columbus, OH: Merrill Publishers.

Kaufman, P., Chen, X., Choy, S. , Ruddy, S. A., Miller, A. K., Fleury, J. K., et al. (2000). *Indicators of school crime and safety, 2000.* Washington, DC: U.S. Department of Education, Office of Educational Research and Improvement, National Center for Education

Statistics, and U.S. Department of Justice, Office of Justice Programs, Bureau of Justice Statistics.

Kazdin, A. E., Mazurick, J. L., & Bass, D. (1993). Risk for attrition in treatment of antisocial children and families. *Journal of Clinical Child Psychology, 22*, 2–16.

Kratochwill, T. R., & Shernoff, E. S. (2004). Evidence-based practice: Promoting evidence based practice interventions in school psychology. *School Psychology Review, 33*(1), 34–48.

Ladd, G. W., Kochenderfer, B. J., & Coleman, C. C. (1996). Friendship quality as a predictor of young children's early school adjustment. *Child Development, 67*, 1103–1118.

Lonigan, C. J., Anthony, J. L., Bloomfield, B. G., Dyer, S. M., & Samwel, C. S. (1999). Effects of two preschool shared reading interventions on the emergent literacy skills of children from low income families. *Journal of Early Intervention, 22*, 306–322.

Lonigan, C. J., Bloomfield, B. G., Anthony, J. L., Bacon, K. D., Phillips, B. M., & Samwel, C. S. (1999). Relations among emergent literacy skills, behavior problems, and social competence in preschool children from low- and middle-income backgrounds. *Topics in Early Childhood Special Education, 19*, 40–53.

Lutkus, A. D., Grigg, W. S., & Donahue, P. L. (2007). *The nation's record card: 2007 trial urban district assessment in reading.* Retrieved November 29 2007, from *www.nces.ed.gov/pubsearch/pubsinfo.asp?pubid=2008455.*

Marquis, J. G., Horner, R. H., Carr, E. G., Turnbull, A. P., Thompson, M., Beherns, G. A., et al. (2000). A meta-analysis of positive behavior support. In R. Gersten, E. Schiller, & S. Vaughn (Eds.), *Contemporary special education research: Syntheses of the knowledge base on critical instructional issues* (pp. 137–178). Mahwah, NJ: Erlbaum.

Mastropieri, M., Jenkins, V., & Scruggs, T. (1985). Academic and intellectual characteristics of behavior disordered children and youth. In R. B. Rutherford, Jr. (Ed.), *Severe behavior disorders of children and youth* (pp. 86–140). Reston, VA: Council for Children with Behavior Disorders.

Merrell, K. W., & Buchanan, R. (2006). Intervention selection in school-based practice: Using public health models to enhance systems capacity of schools. *School Psychology Review, 35*(2), 167–180.

Moats, L. (1999). *Teaching reading is rocket science: What expert teachers of reading should know and be able to do.* Washington, DC: American Federation of Teachers.

Nation, M., Crusto, C., Wandersman, A., Kumpfer, K. L., Seybolt, D., et al. (2003). What works in prevention principles of effective prevention programs. *American Psychologists, 58*(6/7), 449–456.

National Assessment of Educational Progress. (2002). *12th grade report card: Math and reading.* Retrieved November 20, 2007, from *www.nces.ed.gov/nationsreportcard/reading/results.*

National Assessment of Education Progress. (2003). *12th grade report card: Math and reading.* Retrieved March 2, 2008, from *http://www.nagb.org/release/musick_6_03.html.*

National Assessment of Education Progress. (2005). *Reading results: Executive summary for grades 4 and 8.* Retrieved March 2, 2008, from *http://nationsreportcard.gov/reading_math_2005/s0002.asp.*

National Center for Education Statistics. (2005). *Indicators of school crime and safety: 2005.* Washington, DC: U.S. Department of Education, Institute for Education Science. Retrieved March 2, 2008, from *www.nces.ed.gov/programs/crimeindicators/Indicators.asp?PubPageNumber=19.*

National Center for Progress Monitoring. (2006). *Review of progress monitoring tools: Standards* (Website). Retrieved October 16, 2006, from *www.student progress.org/chart/chart.asp.*

National Commission on Excellence in Education. (1983). *A nation at risk: The imperative for educational reform.* Washington, DC: U.S. Government Printing Office.

National Reading Panel. (2000). *Teaching children to read: An evidence-based assessment of the scientific research literature on reading and its implications for reading instruction.* Washington DC: National Institute of Child Health and Human Development.

Office of Special Education Programs. (2003). *Twenty-fourth Annual Report to Congress on the Implementation of the Individuals with Disabilities Act.* Washington, DC: U. S. Department of Education, Office of Special Education Programs.

Patterson, G. R., Reid, J. B., & Dishion, T. J. (1992). *Antisocial boys.* Eugene, OR: Castalia Press.

President's Commission on Excellence in Special Education, (2002). *A new era: Revitalizing special education for children and families.* Washington, DC: U.S. Department of Education.

Reichle, J., York, J., & Eynon, D. (1989). Influence of indicating preferences for initiating, maintaining, and terminating interactions. In In F. Brown & D. Lehr (Eds.), *Persons with profound disabilities: Issues and practices* (pp. 191–211). Baltimore, MD: Brookes.

Reid, J. B., & Eddy, J. M. (1997). The prevention of antisocial behavior: Some considerations in the search for effective interventions. In D. M. Stoff, J. Breiling, & J. D. Master (Eds.), *Handbook of antisocial behavior* (pp. 343–356). New York: Wiley.

Reid, J. B., Patterson, G. R., & Snyder, J. J. (2002). *Antisocial behavior in children and adolescents: A developmental analysis and the Oregon model for intervention.* Washington, DC: APA Books.

Repp, A. C., & Deitz, D. E. D. (1990). Using an ecobehavioral analysis to determine a taxonomy for stereotyped responding. In S. Schroeder (Ed.), *Ecobehavioral analysis and developmental disabilities: The twenty-first century* (pp. 122–140). New York: Springer-Verlag.

Ridley, S. M., McWilliam, R. A., & Oates, C. S. (2000). Observing children at play: Using engagement to evaluate activities and the classroom environment. *Children and Families, 14*(3), 36–38.

Rohrbeck, C. A., Ginsberg-Block, M. D., Fantuzzo, J. W., & Miller, T. R. (2003). Peer-assisted learning interventions with elementary school students: A meta-analytic review. *Journal of Educational Psychology, 95*(2), 240–257.

Rose, L. C., & Gallup, A. M. (2006). *The 38th annual Phi Delta Kappa/ Gallup Poll of the public's attitudes toward the public schools.* Washington, DC: Phi Delta Kappa. Retrieved November 25, 2007, from *www.pdkmembers.org/e-GALLUP/kpoll_pdfs/pdk poll38_2006.pdf.*

Sainato, D. M., & Carta, J. J. (1992). Classroom influences on the development of social competence in young children with disabilities: In S. L. Odom, S. R. McConnell, & M. A. McEvoy (Eds.), *Social competence of young children with disabilities Issues and strategies for intervention* (pp. 93–109). Baltimore: Brookes.

Seth, M., William, A. I., Todd, A. W., Horner, R. H., Sugai, G., Glasgow, A., et al. (2007). *School-Wide Information System (SWIS) data.* Eugene: University of Oregon. Retrieved November 28, 2007, from *www.swis.org/users.php?p=resources.*

Shavelson, R. J., & Towne, L. (2002). *Scientific research in education.* Washington, DC: National Academy Press.

Shaywitz, S. E., & Shaywitz, B. A. (1993). Learning disabilities and attention deficits in the school setting. In L. J. Meltzer (Ed.), *Strategy assessment and instruction for students with learning disabilities: From theory to practice* (pp. 221–245). Austin Tx: Pro-Ed.

Skiba, R., Rausch, M. K., & Ritter, S. (2004). Children left behind: Series summary and recommendations. *Education Policy Briefs, 2*(4), 1–4.

Snow, C. E., Burns, M. S., & Griffin, P. (1998). *Preventing reading difficulties in young children.* Washington, DC: National Research Council, National Academy Press.

Sugai, G., & Lewis, T. J. (1999). *Developing positive behavior support for students with challenging behaviors.* Reston, VA: Council for Children with Behavior Disorders.

Tolan, P. H., & Dodge, K. A. (2005). Children's mental health as a primary care and concern: A system for comprehensive support and service. *American Psychologists, 60*(6), 601–614.

Torgesen, J. K. (1998). Catch them before they fall: Identification and assessment to prevent reading failure in young children. *American Educator, 22,* 32–39.

Torgesen, J. K. (2002). The prevention of reading difficulties. *Journal of School Psychology, 40,* 7–26.

Torgesen, J. K., Alexander, A. W., Wagner, R., K., Rashotte, C. A., Voeller, K. S., & Conway, T. (2001). Intensive remedial instruction for children with severe reading disabilities: Immediate and long-term outcomes from two instructional approaches. *Journal of Learning Disabilities, 34,* 33–58.

Torgesen, J. K., Wagner, R. K., Rashotte, C. A., Rose, E., Lindamood, P., Conway, T., et al. (1999). Preventing reading failure in young children with phonological processing disabilities: Group and individual responses to instruction. *Journal of Educational Psychology, 91,* 579–593.

Vaughn, S., Klingner, J., & Haager, D. (Eds.). *Validated reading practices for three tiers of intervention.* Baltimore: Brookes.

Walker, D., Greenwood, C. R., Hart, B., & Carta, J. J. (1994). Improving the prediction of early school academic outcomes using socioeconomic status and early language production. *Child Development, 65,* 606–621.

Walker, H. M., Ramsey, E., & Gresham, R. M. (2005). *Antisocial behavior in school: Evidence-based practices* (2nd ed.). Belmont, CA: Wadsworth/Thomson Learning.

Walker, H. M., & Shinn, M. R. (2002). Structuring school-based interventions to achieve intregrated primary, secondary, and tertiary prevention goals for safe and effective schools. In S. R. Shinn, H. M. Walker, & G. Stoner (Eds.), *Academic and behavioral interventions II: Preventive and remedial approaches* (pp. 1–27). Washington, DC: National Association of School Psychologists.

Webster-Stratton, C. (1997). Early intervention for families of preschool children with conduct problems. In M. Guralnick (Ed.), *The effectiveness of early intervention* (pp. 429–453). Baltimore: Brookes.

Wehby, J. H., Lane, K. L., & Falk, K. B. (2003). Academic instruction of students with emotional and behavior disorders. *Journal of Emotional and Behavioral Disorders, 11,* 194–197.

Weissberg, R. P., Kumpfer, K. L., & Seligman, M. E. P. (2003). Prevention that works for children and youths—An introduction. *American Psychologist, 58*(6–7), 425–432.

Weisz, J. R., Sandler, I. N., Durlak, J. A., & Anton, B. S. (2005). Promoting and protecting youth mental health through evidence-based prevention and treatment. *American Psychologist, 60*(6), 628–648.

What Works Clearing House. (2003). *Study design and implementation assessment device (Study DIAD): Version 6.* Washington, DC: U. S. Department of Education, Institute for Education Science.

Whitehurst, G. J., & Lonigan, C. J. (1998). Child development and emergent literacy. *Child Development, 69,* 848–872.

Whitehurst, G. J., & Lonigan, C. J. (2001). Emergent literacy: Development from prereaders to readers. In S. B. Neuman & D. K. Dickinson (Eds.), *Handbook of early literacy research* (pp. 11–29). New York: Guilford Press.

CHAPTER 2

# Core Features of Multi-tiered Systems of Reading and Behavioral Support

DAVID J. CHARD, BETH A. HARN, GEORGE SUGAI, ROBERT H. HORNER,
DEBORAH C. SIMMONS, *and* EDWARD J. KAME'ENUI

Chapter 1 described the need for schools to consider the implementation of schoolwide, multi-tiered systems of prevention for reading instruction and behavioral intervention and the research that supports these approaches. Difficulties with learning to read and with school-related behavior problems have been documented in the public media and in the research literature for decades (e.g.; Committee on the Prevention of Readng Difficulties, 1998; Bennett, Brown, Boyle, Racine, & Offord, 2003). Fortunately, the research literature supports the use of sustained and systemic approaches to preventing behavior and reading difficulties (National Research Council, 1998; Dwyer, Osher, & Hoffman, 2000; Horner, Sugai, Todd, & Lewis-Palmer, 2005; Lipsey, 1992; Nelson, 1996; Simmons, Kame'enui, Stoolmiller, Coyne, & Harn, 2003). Thus, as Kame'enui, Good, and Harn (2005) observed, prevention is possible if the problem you are attempting to prevent actually exists, is understood, and evidence exists that prevention is possible.

We believe that these conditions have been achieved in the areas of reading failure and problem behavior. However, the emerging research on the efficacy of multi-tiered approaches does not yet lend itself to creating prescriptions of exactly how to create and implement the perfect system for a particular school or school district. For example, researchers have yet to identify one specific means of determining an individual student's response to intervention and level of risk. Benchmarks, benchmarks plus growth, growth alone, and even educator judgment have been used and recommended in the literature (e.g., D. Fuchs, Fuchs, & Compton, 2004). Another example is the increasingly important pre-K movement in the United States that is including preschool programs in existing K–5/6 elementary schools. As a result, downward extensions of progress monitoring measures are needed for use with preschool children (McConnell & Missall, 2008) as are evidence-based early literacy preschool curricula, thus making it possible for individual schools to integrate preschool within their planned or existing multi-tiered systems.

There are more than 85,000 public schools in the United States of all sizes and student diversity (i.e. cultures, languages, and developmental status). Some elementary schools now include preschool (Barnett, Hustedt, Hawkinson, & Robin, 2006). Some have argued that the precise nature of a schoolwide, multi-tiered system as described in Chapter 1 must be shaped by the school and community contexts in which it is implemented (Zins & Ponti, 1990), and we agree. However, we also contend that the organizing principles and strategies for conceptualizing, designing, implementing, and sustaining instructional and behavioral change are fundamentally the same for individual schools. In this chapter, we describe the key components in a common, shared framework we believe to be essential for successful implementation of multi-tiered systems of support for reading and behavior.

The six experiences detailed in this book offer one overarching lesson: the common features implemented and tested in each project were only effective when the challenges of creating and implementing these models were identified, anticipated, and addressed proactively. Implementation of features like those described below is a complex, organizational process that is unlikely to be successful if a "one-size-fits-all" approach is employed (Gersten, Chard, & Baker, 2000; Elmore, 1996). Thus, meeting the challenges of establishing and maintaining schoolwide, multi-tiered systems of reading and behavior support requires (1) understanding and accommodating the contextual factors at work in schools and communities and also (2) making and sustaining a commitment to system implementation quality.

The purpose of this chapter is to describe and illustrate common features of multi-tiered models of reading instruction and behavior support as they have been conceptualized by the centers and schools highlighted in this book. The details of these features should be considered by schools in their efforts to establish effective, efficient, and relevant schoolwide multi-tiered models of support and how these essential features would be addressed and implemented within their context. Each of these features is discussed as a practice in which schools will need to engage to successfully implement a similar schoolwide approach. The discussions also provide evidence that supports the stated practice and examples of how the practices were implemented in the reading and behavior centers.

## WHAT CORE SCHOOLWIDE PREVENTION PRACTICES WERE USED BY THE CENTERS?

The collective experiences of the researchers, psychologists, administrators, teachers, and interventionists who worked on these projects have identified several keys to meeting the implementation challenges successfully. The common implementation features include

1. Coordinated universal, targeted, and indicated systems of support.
2. Universal screening, progress monitoring, and decision making.
3. Selection, adoption, and use of evidence-based instructional/intervention practices.
4. Leadership commitment from administrators and school-based leadership teams.
5. Professional development that targets evidence-based practice.
6. Monitoring effects and evaluating progress relative to goals and improve the action plan (also see Kame'enui et al., 2005; Sugai & Horner, 2006).

The *coordination feature* guided design of the school's program in terms of universal, targeted, and indicated intervention tiers and rules for moving students between different levels in intensity (i.e., the patterns of individuals' participation in three tiers) of support based on individuals' response to intervention. The *universal screening feature* established and maintained a schoolwide assessment plan wherein all students were assessed at least in the fall (if not winter and spring as well) and benchmarks used to identify students not responsive to Tier 1 intervention. The *use of evidence-based instructional interventions* ensured that effective practices were capable of differentiating and intensifying the effectiveness of support provided. The *leadership feature* ensured the coordinated participation of all administrators, faculty, students, and parents. The *professional development feature* ensured that administrators, faculty, students, and parents learned and implemented their roles in the system with fidelity. The *monitoring effects and evaluating progress feature* ensured that the short- and long-term outcomes of the multi-tiered system were known and continuous program improvement plans were in place.

## COORDINATED UNIVERSAL, TARGETED, AND INDICATED SYSTEMS OF SUPPORT

Historically, general education and special education systems were operated independently in schools, and students were moved from one system to the other as a consequence of their achievement or behavior. Prevailing data from the remediation approach indicated that once in special education students rarely left the program (e.g., Ferguson, Kozleski, & Smith, 2003). Historically, schools have often taken a "one-size-fits-all" approach to teaching reading and providing discipline. When students experienced difficulties, their problems were attributed to their inability to succeed rather than to the school's inability to effectively accommodate their learning needs. Likewise, if students engaged in antisocial or disruptive behavior, the response was to treat the behavior as idiosyncratic to the student and not a function of the school environment or a lack of behavioral support (President's Commission on Excellence in Special Education, 2002).

In contrast, schoolwide, multitiered support systems are designed to expect and accommodate the full range of student needs by increasing the instructional and behavioral supports in relation to the magnitude of need of each student (Tilley, 2003). Differentiating support is a significant challenge in schools without a systemic, coordinated approach to meeting student needs (Denton, Vaughn, & Fletcher, 2003). Successful differentiation within schools and across the contexts described in the subsequent chapters in this book is achieved by essential allocating support resources in relation to student need schoolwide. The resources involved are not only personnel, but also time, scheduling, materials, progress monitoring, and evaluating student response to intervention. In many cases, resource allocations are changed regularly to provide timely response to individual student learning as well as adjusted in relation to changes in support needs in the building (i.e., personnel, programs, etc.).

At the heart of each schoolwide model described in subsequent chapters was systematic implementation of a multitiered prevention approach (e.g., universal, targeted, and indicated) to provide differential levels of behavioral support, reading instruction, or both as discussed in Chapter 1. The conceptual coordination of the majority of models was guided by three tiers of prevention/intervention (see Table 2.1). Each model articulated in subsequent chapters took a purposeful, overt approach to integrating all resources within the school building to design a tiered, early intervening system. The model was then applied schoolwide in a responsive and timely manner based on knowledge of individual students' response to intervention. Thus, these models represent a major theoretical shift from the remediation of the past to a future of prevention.

Movement of students in and out of tiers was guided by the following principles with some individual program variations (see Kratochwill, Clements, & Kalymon, 2007, for a detailed discussion):

- All students receive the *universal* level of support.
- Those who were *not responsive* to intervention were moved to more intensive levels of support; to targeted, or to indicated, while continuing to receive the universal level of support.
- Those who *were responsive* to intervention became candidates for moving toward less intensive levels of support (e.g., tertiary to targeted).
- Thus, within and over years, it was possible for individual students to move forward or backward in receipt of tier supports based on their individual rate of progress.

As discussed below, onset of support decisions were made by classroom teachers and/or building leadership teams charged with this responsibility.

## Universal and Targeted Systems of Support

### Behavioral Supports

The majority of models reported using universal and targeted systems of support for reading, behavior, or both at school- and classwide levels of implementation. For example, the behavior models at the University of Nebraska and University of Oregon uniquely adapted these core features. The Tier 1 (universal) intervention was designed to prevent behavior problems by actively teaching a common set of school rules and expectations for behavior supported by evidence-based research. Based on typical experiences with universal intervention, it was expected that approximately 80% of students would respond to the universal intervention (Horner, Sugai, Todd, & Lewis-Palmer, 2005). The rules were displayed throughout the school in classrooms and common areas. The rules were also actively taught schoolwide and reviewed on numerous occasions. Fidelity of implementation of this universal intervention by teachers and school staff was monitored to ensure that individuals had

the knowledge and were providing the desired instruction and consequences included in the schoolwide behavior plan. The emphasis on fidelity of implementation was based on knowledge that superior outcomes are obtained when evidence-based programs are implemented as
designed (Shadish, Cook, & Campbell, 2002).

The Tier 2 (targeted) interventions were purposely integrated with
the Tier 1 system (e.g., using the same set of expectations) and intensified through small-group delivery methods or by meeting individual student needs. These included use of classroom rules instruction, group re
inforcement contingencies, and teacher praise to reinforce desired student
response. Other examples included two additional strategies: compliance
training and variations of daily behavior check-in/check-out systems
(e.g., Crone, Horner, & Hawken, 2004; Kamps, Kravits, Stolze, &
Swaggart, 1999; Walker, Colvin, & Ramsey, 1995).

## Reading Supports

The reading models relied on the school's adoption and use of evidence-
based reading curricula with all students (Haager, Klingner, & Vaughn,
2007). The implications of schools not choosing to employ evidence-
based reading curricula are that from year to year they will be more
likely to be faced with increasing numbers of children struggling to learn
to read and qualifying for special education services to learn to read
compared to schools using evidence-based curricula. For example,
Kamps et al. (2003) reported that students' growth in lettering naming
fluency, nonsense word fluency, and oral reading fluency was differentially influenced by the school's choice of reading curriculum. Students
in the same grades in Reading Mastery and Success for All, two evidence-based reading curricula, made significantly greater progress learning to read (i.e., rate of growth over time and endpoint scores) as indicated by all three measures (i.e., letters, nonsense word, and oral reading
fluencies) than did the literature-based reading curricula. And Reading
Mastery outperformed Success for All (Kamps et al., 2003). Without appropriate change in reading instruction, struggling readers do not make
progress on their own (Chard & Kame'enui, 2000; Juel, 1988; Kamps et
al., 1989).

Like universal, schoolwide expectations and rules for behavior,
evidence-based reading curricula was a proactive step in the effort to
provide effective instruction to all students early–thus, prevent reading
problems from arising in the first place (Torgesen et al., 2001). Because
these curricula teach evidence-based reading skills, the probability that
students will be proficient with the precursors needed to be successful
readers is increased. Universal, evidence-based reading instruction also

accelerates student results because it is explicit, that is, all steps are taught directly (Foorman, Francis, Fletcher, & Schatschneider, 1998; Mathes, Torgesen, Allen, & Allor, 2002). This is compared to implicit reading instruction, wherein too many students are unable to learn the skills that teachers do not directly teach.

From a prevention perspective, use of a evidence-based reading curriculum as "universal intervention" was the first step in improving the instructional environment of children in poverty schools, improving student outcomes, and reducing the subpopulation of struggling readers and students with reading disabilities (Kamps & Greenwood, 2005). In most cases, this included explicit teaching of phonemic awareness skills and the alphabetic principle with sufficient intensity (Simmons, Kuykendall, King, Cornachione, & Kame'enui, 2000). As with behavior, it was expected that 80% of students would respond to universal intervention.

The formulation of targeted reading supports was guided by evidence supporting the effectiveness of (1) small groups of three to six participating students and low student teacher ratio, (2) explicit, phonics-based instruction, and peer tutoring. Exemplars of curricula used for this purpose were Reading Mastery (Engelmann & Bruner, 1995) and Open Court (McGraw Hill, 2005).

## Indicated Systems of Support for Individual Students

### Behavioral Supports

The majority of models reported providing Tier 3 (indicated) behavioral supports to individual students needing them. For example, the Tier 3 behavioral supports were based on contemporary knowledge of comprehensive, function-based support for nonresponders. These included interventions based on individualized functional assessment and analysis (Hanley, Iwata, & McCord, 2003), individual contingencies of reinforcement, and individual behavioral contracts involving home and school coordination (Kamps & Kay, 2001; Kamps, Kravits, & Ross, 2002).

### Reading Supports

The formulation of indicated reading supports was guided by evidence supporting the efficacy of (1) one-to-one instruction delivered by an adult, (2) highly individualized, explicit instruction, and (3) special education services. One exemplar was the Language Arts Multisensory Program (LAMP; Abbott, 2002) used by the Kansas Reading Center. LAMP is specifically designed for use with students with severe reading chal-

lenges and differed substantially from literacy instruction effective with
the majority of learners.

The first difference was that it promoted the use of kinesthetic and
tactile experiences in addition to the standard visual and auditory ones.
The second difference was the direct instruction of a specific sequence of
phonological skills with the use of restricted text—an Alphabetic Pho-
nics/Orton–Gillingham approach (Foorman, Francis, Fletcher et al.,
2001). The third difference was that early in the LAMP sequence of
skills to be taught literature is used combined with tutor–student choral
readings. Uses of literature increased as word recognition skills improved. Fourth, the LAMP has an extended emphasis on phonemic
awareness skills. And fifth, an adult teacher works with the student one-
to-one. The big idea was to increase intensity and strength of treatment
for students who had not learned to read using other procedures.

In summary, it is necessary to identify the level of supports students
need to be successful in a multi-tiered approach to be sufficiently agile in
responding to changes in student needs and patterns of growth. This
agility is predicated on the coordination of instructional and behavioral
supports that can be allocated based on formative assessment information. The role and nature of formative assessment systems and practices
are the focus of the next section.

## UNIVERSAL SCREENING, PROGRESS MONITORING, AND DECISION MAKING

The efficacy of a schoolwide system of instructional or behavioral support hinges on the school personnel's ability to ensure students are on a
trajectory toward long-term educational success through the use of measures designed for early identification (Irvin, Tobin, Sprague, Sugai, &
Vincent, 2004; Kame'enui et al., 2005; Merrell & Buchanan, 2006).
Collecting data and acting upon those data in a formative, dynamic, and
responsive way has not been typical in traditional schools. Although
norm-referenced, commercially published measures of reading achievement do an adequate job of documenting groups of learners' performance at a given point in time (e.g., every spring), their purpose is not to
inform the instruction of individual learners nor to monitor performance
formatively over time. In the schoolwide, multi-tiered models described
in this book, each school used assessment systems for early screening
and regular progress monitoring to make timely decisions about changes
needed in the amount or level of support students needed and allocated
resources accordingly. Screening and regular progress monitoring not
only enable the evaluation of the Tier 1 (universal) intervention efforts,

but also allows early identification and intervention for those students in need of more intense support (Grimes, Kurns, & Tilly, 2006). Using progress monitoring data to assist in determining the allocation of resources necessary to improve student performance is a key part of successful differentiation.

Data-based decision making is not new to education. In fact, formative evaluation has been used to improve educational decision making and student achievement for over 30 years (Deno, 1985; L. S. Fuchs, Fuchs, & Hamlett, 1989; Shinn, 1989, 1998). Formative evaluation is measurement conducted frequently enough that short-term growth in students' proficiency can be measured. It is an evidence-based practice (Stecker & Fuchs, 2005). The advantage of indicators of short-term growth is that teachers can act on this information within the school in ways that will accelerate progress. This approach is quite different from using only end-of-year achievement data to attempt to make large-scale instructional adjustments for the following school year. Such adjustments have failed to address the needs of students who were experiencing difficulties in the short term during the year, and this kind of disconnect between when change in instruction is needed and when change in instruction is actually made does not advance student growth in the same way (Salvia & Ysseldyke, 2006). Today, with technically adequate formative measures that can be used for screening and progress monitoring, data-based decisions can be made to change instructional support in much shorter timeframes (e.g., daily, weekly, monthly) to increase the sensitivity of instructional decision making the benefit to students (Ervin, Schaughency, Matthews, Goodman, & McGlinchey, 2007; L. S. Fuchs et al., 1989). Multilevel systems described in this book all employed data-based decision making to answer questions such as:

*System-level questions*

1. How well are we implementing our program?
2. How well are our reading/behavioral program practices meeting the needs of our second-grade students relative to benchmarks and earlier measurements?
3. Which evidence-based practices may help students be more successful?
4. Which students have similar instructional needs and what is the most appropriate tier for instruction?
5. Are we meeting the needs of more students in third grade than we did last year?
6. How effective are our instructional supports for students needing Tier 2 or 3?

7. Do we need to reallocate our resources (intensify supports) to accelerate learning?
8. Do we need better practices?

*Student-level questions*

1. Which students are at risk for experiencing academic or behavioral difficulties and need additional support to reach their end-of-year goals?
2. Are students on track to meet their end-of-year goals?
3. Which skills have students mastered, what do they need to learn?
4. How might we adjust our support for this student to help her be more successful?

## Formative Measurement Tools

Dynamic Indicators of Basic Early Literacy Skills (DIBELS) was the common assessment system implemented across all projects to monitor the development of early literacy skills (Good, Gruba, & Kaminski, 2002; Kaminski & Good, 1998). These measures are particularly appropriate within multi-tiered models because of their sensitivity to prereading skills and the opportunity they provide to link these results with monitoring earlier skill development in oral reading fluency. DIBELS assists in completing two functions, (1) identifying children who are at risk for reading difficulties because they are not acquiring prereading skills (i.e., letter naming, initial sounds fluency, blending sounds in nonsense words) and oral reading fluency, and (2) monitoring how students are responding to the increased support and interventions. DIBELS is widely used, and "benchmarks" for student performance across each of the measures and skills have been empirically determined to assist in determining satisfactory levels of progress (Good, Simmons, Kame'enui, Kaminski, & Wallin, 2002). Once students are screened, teachers can then identify students needing differential instruction to accelerate learning— to put a student back on track as quickly as possible. In the next section we describe the research on evidence-based reading and behavior intervention practices and illustrate how these practices can be implemented as part of the model.

The School-Wide Information System (SWIS) was used as a common source of progress monitoring data and decision making in most of the behavior models (May et al., 2000). Developed by the Oregon Behavior Center, SWIS is a computerized system for monitoring all office referrals and reporting trends in office disciplinary referrals for behavior problems over time (Irvin et al., 2006). These data are used by school leadership teams to evaluate and plan individual student and schoolwide progress reducing behavior problems serious enough to prompt office referral and well as school suspensions. Other data collection systems used for this purpose included Systematic Screening for Behavior Disorders (Walker & Severson, 1992) and the Early Screening Project (Walker, Severson, & Feil, 1995).

Too often early screening and progress monitoring have been unavailable in schools. However, formative measurement systems are increasingly adopted and institutionalized for making decisions about the type and intensity of student support needed for effective implementation of a multi-tiered support model, attention also must be given to identifying and implementing evidence-based instructional practices and interventions that will increase the likelihood of student success.

## SELECTION, ADOPTION, AND SUSTAINED USE OF EVIDENCE-BASED INSTRUCTIONAL/INTERVENTION PRACTICES

Key to the effectiveness of multi-tiered support models is the systemic and sustained use of instructional/intervention practices that are associated with successful school outcomes for all children (Grimes & Tilly, 1996). In behavioral supports and reading instruction, extensive literatures have converged to guide the development and implementation of specific instructional/intervention practices (e.g., see What Works Clearinghouse, 2007). The advantage of using evidence-based reading curricula or behavioral interventions is that what, when, and how skills should be taught is informed by evidence derived from studies that were designed to be capable of generating causal results, designs known to produce rigorous, unbiased, and believable findings.

### Reading

Over the past decade and a half, research syntheses have reported the importance of teaching several key skills that include phonological awareness, phonics, fluency, vocabulary, and reading comprehension (e.g., Committee on the Prevention of Reading Difficulties, 1998; Gersten, Fuchs, Williams, & Baker, 2001; National Reading Panel, 2000; Swanson & Hoskyn, 1998). Moreover, these key skills need to be taught systematically, explicitly, and with attention to the instructional environment to ensure that the widest range of learners have sufficient opportunities to learn (Chard & Kame'enui, 2000; Elbaum, Vaughn, Hughes, & Moody, 2000; Foorman & Torgesen, 2001; Kame'enui & Simmons, 1998; Shaywitz, 2003).

Despite this converging evidence, it is important to keep in mind that different students will always have different instructional needs that may require increasing instructional intensity through modifying or increasing the use of explicit modeling, more frequent practice opportunities, and detailed instructional feedback, and a more systematic instructional pace (Greenwood, Kamps, Terry, & Linebarger, 2007; Harn, Kame'ennui, & Simmons, 2007; Kame'enui, Simmons, Good, & Chard, 2002; Vaughn, Gersten, & Chard, 2000).

## Behavior

Converging research findings have also pointed to key skills and effective practices for supporting students at risk for behavioral difficulties. These practices promote explicitly teaching expected behaviors to all students, rewarding students for exhibiting these expected behaviors, providing additional instruction and practice for students who are experiencing difficulties demonstrating appropriate behaviors (Lewis & Sugai, 1999; Metzler, Biglan, Rusby, & Sprague, 2001; Nelson, Martella, & Galand, 1998; Scott, 2001; Sugai & Horner, 2002; Sugai, Horner, & Gresham, 2002). As in reading, some students will continue to need additional and intensive behavioral supports despite the implementation of effective preventive practices. Effective interventions for students experiencing behavioral problems focus on teaching desired alternative behaviors. Doing so requires consistent monitoring with use of contingent reinforcement and specific teaching of individual self-monitoring strategies. In reading and behavior support systems, decisions about adjusting these variables of instruction are guided and evaluated by data (e.g., SWIS).

## Reading and Behavior

Evidence discussed in Chapter 1 described the mutual relationship between academic outcomes and behavioral outcomes. Specifically, persistent academic failure may lead to aggression, disruption, and other antisocial behavior (Hinshaw, 1992; Maguin & Loeber, 1995; Morrison, Furlong, & Morrison, 1997), or negative self-attributions, learned helplessness, or depression (Dweck & Leggett, 1988; Dweck & Wortman, 1982; Sheridan, Hungelmann, & Maughan, 1999). Likewise, problem behaviors may prevent students from accessing and benefiting from academic instruction (McIntosh, Chard, Boland, & Horner, 2006). Evidence-based behavior support practices and systems include increasing academic engagement and improving academic achievement. Similarly, efforts to improve academic outcomes through evidence-based instructional approaches to promote appropriate student behavior and safe classroom settings have also been demonstrated (McIntosh et al., 2006).

Identifying evidence-based practices and curricular programs that support their effective use in schools is challenging and requires continued investigation by school staff. The key study designs to look for in research reports of the effects of instructional practices are those associated with high standards of evidence (What Works Clearinghouse, 2007; Gersten et al., 2005). In the models described below, supporting evidence was based on randomized trial, regression-discontinuity designs, and single-case experimental designs (Horner et al., 2005). Knowledge of the research basis for program practices adopted and used within buildings enables all personnel to "understand" *why* as well as *what* is being used across levels of support. Once identified and adopted, systemic and sustained use of evidence-based practices within and across schools is the next critical challenge to overcome (Adelman & Taylor, 1998; Greenwood, Delquadri, & Bulgren, 1993). Sustained implementation of three-tiered models requires substantial administrative commitment and ongoing support. In the next section, we discuss the important role that administrators and school leaders play in ensuring the success of multi-tiered models.

## LEADERSHIP COMMITMENT FROM ADMINISTRATORS AND SCHOOL-BASED TEAMS SUPPORTING SCHOOLWIDE IMPLEMENTATION

Administrators and boards of education control the resources and set the policies, standards, and practices of the school. They also are considered to be leaders of effective instructional and curricular practices, behavior and classroom management, and schoolwide behavioral support practices and policies. Their leadership serves as the critical link between teachers, parents, school boards, and the communities. To this end, administrative leadership must not be viewed as gratuitous or token. Instead, the administrator must embrace the details of the three-tiered system and be considered more knowledgeable of the system than anyone in the school building. Administrators need to be willing to commit resources and empower others in schools to design, implement, and sustain implementation of these programs. Finally, he or she must lead by example, if indeed staff members are to implement the system reliably and relentlessly.

Decisions that focus on school building resource management and allocation, personnel issues, budget allocations, and policy interpretations require a strong and skilled principal. Decisions on the operation and management of the three-tiered system also require a team-based leadership approach to implementing the core features previously discussed, but also those features considered unique to the individual school. In the models described below, the principal and faculty leadership teams provided the organizational infrastructure needed to implement. Leadership teams also supported participation by a large proportion of school staff, increasing the collective expertise of the group, providing opportunity for greater staff input, leveraging a broad-based staff commitment, and enhancing the impact of implementation and sustainability efforts.

Lessons learned suggest that reading instructional and/or behavioral leadership teams should consist of (1) an administrator, (2) teachers who are representative of grade levels (or departments in high schools), (3) parents, and (4) support staff (e.g., counselor, school psychologist). The team members should bring together the best instructional and behavioral expertise in the school to manage, improve, and sustain the system. Some of important skills of team members included the ability to conduct instructional or environmental analysis, collect and analyze formative data, develop academic or social skills lessons, and develop and make accommodations to specialized academic or behavioral support plans. Reading and/or behavioral leadership teams should meet on a regularly scheduled basis, as often as once every 2 weeks, and the primary focus of the meetings should be on reviewing student performance data (e.g., reading progress and/or office disciplinary referral data, etc.) to determine if students are making adequate and timely progress.

Finally, the building leadership teams should be given high status in the coordination or governing structure of the school by the administration, the team members should be respected by other school faculty. Because concerns about discipline and student achievement have been consistently among the top concerns for parents, school personnel, and community members for years, schools should establish and maintain structures that allow for regular monitoring of the status of discipline and student performance, development of policies and practices that prevent the initiation and growth of discipline and learning problems, and systems of curricular and instructional support for staff, students, and parents. *High status* in this case means that the leadership team provides schoolwide leadership, establishes school improvement and professional development priorities and policies, and takes priority in resource allocations.

For example, administrative and school leadership played a particularly important role in centers that combined behavior and reading support models. The unique challenge of these two centers (University of

Kansas and University of North Carolina) was to blend and integrate these evidence-based strategies for use in individual schools. With considerable overlap in practices used, unique work was necessary to develop each school's capacity to implement and coordinate two prevention initiatives simultaneously. In the case of Kansas (Chapter 8), this was accomplished by establishing two parallel schoolwide systems, one for reading and one for behavior. Each operated relatively independently from the other, supervised and implemented by staff with different skills and roles. In the case of North Carolina (Chapter 7), key faculty members (literacy coordinator and principal) served as common members of reading and behavior teams. Other members included specialists in either reading or behavior serving on one team or the other. An additional role of these teams is to identify and assist in prioritizing the professional development needs within the building.

To this point we have considered three tiers of support: universal screening, progress monitoring, and decision making; selection and use of evidence-based practice; and administrative commitment and school-based leadership teams. Moving to a schoolwide multi-tiered model of reading and behavioral supports will require a significant change in practices and policies that will necessitate professional development. Putting all of this in place depends additionally on professional development.

## PROFESSIONAL DEVELOPMENT THAT TARGETS EVIDENCE-BASED PRACTICE

We know that expectations that professionals will adopt and implement evidence-based practices without significant support are naïve and counterproductive (Elmore, 2002). Although the initiation of evidence-based practices may either be policy mandates such as NCLB, or "grass-root" efforts with the school, the research evidence on changing educational practices seems to suggest that sustained change occurs as a result of teachers and other educational professionals mastering the newly adopted practice, being provided a clear rationale for the change, as well as demonstrating improved student outcomes (Gersten et al., 2000; Huberman & Miles, 1984).

Most of the centers and schools had multiple foci for their professional development efforts, but with a common goal on improved instructional and behavioral practices. For example, the Texas center spent considerable time and effort on enhancing the universal reading curricula (Tier 1) in terms of teachers' deep understanding and improved skills in delivering high-quality and comprehensive reading instruction. These efforts were systematic and coordinated to ensure each teacher had the skills necessary to meet the needs of a full range of learners and demonstrated a purposeful focus on prevention by providing all students high-quality instruction.

Oregon's Reading Center focused most of its professional development efforts on Tiers 2 and 3 as well as targeted support for individuals. To enhance the effectiveness of Tier 2 and Tier 3 supports, center researchers and staff provided support in the use of additional evidence-based programs. Within these professional development efforts, personnel were not only shown how to use the program and provided a rationale for its use, but also sessions overtly focused on effective instructional practices that would generalize staff's skills in meeting learners' needs beyond that specific program practice (e.g., small-group behavior management, pacing, corrective feedback, explicit instruction, etc.). Additionally, support was ongoing and iterative.

Regular follow-up sessions were scheduled a few weeks after beginning new practices to address concerns and questions to increase high-quality implementation. Implementation was also monitored regularly at both reading centers with fidelity observations. If concerns were noted during the observation, additional "coaching" support was provided based upon the needs of the interventionist (i.e., behavior or program management, pacing, etc.). This individualized and supportive approach was welcomed as interventionists noted the improvement in student skills and behavior. Additional areas targeted for professional development included methods to improve leadership and coordination.

In both reading centers, district administrators and principals were provided professional development on the system-level rationale for program selection and interpreting systems-level student performance data. School-level leadership team members (i.e., literacy or Title I coordinators) were also targeted for more systematic professional development that focused not only on data-based decision making and program usage, but also methods for increasing coordination of instructional supports and overcoming the logistical challenges of scheduling and grouping that often interfere with the schools' ability to best meet students' instructional needs. More informal support and discussions were provided to support these school-based leaders on how to provide ongoing and supportive individualized "coaching" to their school staff to sustain long-term implementation of effective practices. All of the professional development practices were implemented in relation to the district's or school's established implementation plans or established long-term instructional goals, the importance of which is discussed next.

## MONITOR EFFECTS AND EVALUATE PROGRESS
## RELATIVE TO GOALS AND IMPROVE THE ACTION PLAN

Regular monitoring and evaluation of the schools that attempt to implement a schoolwide system of reading and/or behavioral support are needed to (1) prevent ineffective practices from wasting time and resources, (2) improve the efficiency and effectiveness of current procedures, (3) eliminate elements of the system that are ineffective or inefficient, and (4) make modifications before academic difficulties or problem behavior patterns become too severe and difficult to change. In fact, in the absence of obtaining frequent, reliable, and valid indicators of student performance in reading, for example, or discipline, it would be enormously difficult to ascertain whether a school-adopted intervention—that is, a reading curriculum program or a schoolwide discipline plan—represents a wise investment.

Here again we recommend a formative approach to evaluation at the program level. End-of-year evaluation, though necessary for accountability purposes, is not a sufficient approach to "take stock" and make the timely modification to supports students need to prevent long-term difficulties. Given the core features previously discussed, schools are in a position to employ a system of self-assessment and continuous improvement that includes monitoring (1) the status of schoolwide discipline and classroom management, (2) levels of staff implementation, (3) rates of student academic competence and fluency, and (4) levels of administrative and staff commitment. Having covered these core features, we now turn to the individual reports of the experiences of individual schools each working with a center and their efforts to implement multi-tier prevention models.

### Synthesis of Six Programs' Procedures

A synthesis of features and detailed procedures used in each center and school model is contained in Table 2.1 in a side-by-side comparison. As previously mentioned, two programs implemented behavioral models (Nebraska and Oregon), two implemented reading models (Texas and Oregon), and two implemented behavior and reading models (North Carolina and Kansas). In most cases, the aim of each program was to test the efficacy of implementing three tiers of prevention (see Table 2.1). In these programs, center and school staff worked to implement three tiers, usually beginning with Tier 1 in year 1 followed by Tiers 2 and 3 in year 2, in most cases requiring more than one school year to achieve full implementation. The Texas and Oregon reading programs differed in these aims however. The aim in Texas was to test the efficacy of an enhanced Tier 1 only, whereas in Oregon the aim was to investigate the effects of improvements made in an already existing three-tiered program.

Overall, school-based case study designs were used to describe the prospective implementations of three tiers. At Texas, a historical control group was used allowing a before-and-after comparison of the effects of enhancing Tier 1 with evidence-based reading practices on student learning. Similarly with Oregon Reading, a before-and-after improvement strategy was used. With regards to universal student screening to assess individuals' response to intervention, all programs conducted screening in the fall soon after the start of school. Four of the programs also screened at the middle and end of the year (Oregon Reading, Oregon Behavior, North Carolina, Kansas, and Texas). All screening assessments were direct measures of student performance, in the case of Oregon Behavior, screening for behavior problems also was teacher determined.

## Reading

Four of the programs implemented three-tiered reading models (Texas, Oregon, North Carolina, and Kansas). At Tier 1, the evidence-based Open Court curriculum was used schoolwide in all but Texas. In Oregon Reading and North Carolina, additional reading curriculum components were used in combination with Open Court. In Texas, teachers were provided intensive professional development in evidence-based reading practice (see Chapter 5 for details). At Tier 2, additional evidence-based curriculum components were used in small groups (see Table 2.1). Tier 2 and Tier 3 reading components were not implemented in Texas. Tier 3 reading used additional curriculum components including Reading Mastery in Oregon and North Carolina, and Early Reading Interventions (EIR) and the Language Arts Multi-sensory Program (LAMP) in Kansas with one-on-one or very small groups (see Table 2.1).

## Behavior

Four the programs implemented behavior prevention models (Nebraska, Oregon Behavior, North Carolina, and Kansas). All four used some form of schoolwide positive behavior support (Horner et al., 2005). Nebraska and North Carolina used their own evidence-based versions, The Behavior and Academic Support and Enhancement (BASE) program and schoolwide positive *unified* behavior support, respectively. At Tier 2, multiple behavior supports were selected and used, varying across individual programs (see Table 2.1). The check-in/check-out system (Crone et al., 2004) was used in Oregon and Kansas. It involved a morning check-in during which students receive a behavior monitoring sheet for

**TABLE 2.1. Comparison of K–3 Reading and Behavior Three-Tiered Schoolwide Case Studies**

| Feature | Chapter | | | | | |
|---|---|---|---|---|---|---|
| | 3 | 4 | 5 | 6 | 7 | 8 |
| Author | Nelson et al. | Tobin et al. | Vaughn et al. | Chard & Harn | Algozzine et al. | Abbott et al. |
| Center | Nebraska | Oregon | Texas | Oregon | North Carolina | Kansas |
| Focus | Behavior | Behavior | Reading | Reading | Reading and Behavior | Reading and Behavior |
| Age/Grade | K–3 | K–3 | K–1, over 3-year span | K–3; followed one cohort from Grades 1 to 3 | K–2 reading; K–5 behavior | K–6 inclusive; K–3 focused |
| Chapter aim | Test the efficacy of implementing three tiers of prevention | Test the efficacy of implementing three tiers of prevention | Test the efficacy of enhanced Tier 1 for at-risk students | Describe, evaluate, and improve an established ongoing multi-tiered approach | Test the efficacy of implementing three tiers of prevention | Test the efficacy of implementing three tiers of prevention |
| Study design | School-based case study of the implementation of three tiers over multiple years | School-based case study of the implementation of three tiers over multiple years | One historical control grade-cohort versus two sequential experimental cohorts; with a qualitative case study of one school principal | Description of an ongoing multi-tiered model followed by the effects of focused improvement in Tier 2 and Tier 3 | School-based case study of the implementation of three tiers over several years | School-based case study of the implementation of three tiers over several years |
| Screening | Annual screen | One-time screen; thereafter, teacher determined | January of kindergarten to identify students for study reported; beginning, middle, and end of year for all students in school | Beginning, middle, and end of year | Beginning, middle, and end of year | Beginning, middle, and end of year |

(continued)

**TABLE 2.1.** (continued)

| Feature | 3 | 4 | 5 | 6 | 7 | 8 |
|---|---|---|---|---|---|---|
| Reading: Tier 1 | | | Professional development in the use of progress monitoring and evidence-based reading practices; in-class research team support | Open Court; Success for All; and Reading Mastery, plus some small group | Open Court with added components | Open Court |
| Reading: Tier 2 | | | None for participants in study reported | Varied by grade level: first—intensified sections of core in small groups; second—Phonics for Reading and Read Naturally; third—Researcher developed core literature support vocabulary and comprehension focus, and Read Naturally | Early Reading Tutor (formerly Practice Court) | Small Group: Early Interventions in Reading, Read Naturally |
| Reading: Tier 3 | | | None for participants reported in study | Reading Mastery; with Read Naturally | Reading Mastery Classic | One-on-one: Early Interventions in Reading (double dose) or Language Arts Multisensory Program |

| | | | | | | |
|---|---|---|---|---|---|---|
| Behavior: Tier 1 | Behavior and Academic Support and Enhancement (BASE) program (i.e., common areas procedures; Think Time Strategy, continuum of responsibility) | Schoolwide positive behavior support, with classwide systems | | | Schoolwide positive unified behavior support, with classwide systems | Schoolwide positive behavior support, with classwide systems |
| Behavior: Tier 2 | First Step to Success; Home Base module | Check-in/check-out | | | Behavior contracting, self-monitoring and evaluation; Boys Town interventions | Classwide group contingency; small groups: social skills club, mentoring; check-in/check-out |
| Behavior: Tier 3 | Multisystemic therapy (MST) | Functional behavioral assessment and related function-based support; teacher assist team; behavior support team | | | Boys Town interventions; functional behavioral assessment | One-on-one, social skills club, check-in/check-out; functional behavioral assessment |
| Level of Adoption | Fidelity of implementation | Fidelity of implementation, action plan, monitoring, evaluating, and adjusting the program based on SWIS and other data | Fidelity of implementation; evidence-based practices were evident in the classrooms and school | Fidelity of implementation; leadership; schoolwide model; data systems for screening, diagnosis, progress monitoring; evidence-based practices; and professional development | Fidelity of implementation; DIBELS after year 2; SWIS; school-staff-implemented interventions; faculty-team-implemented decision making | Fidelity of implementation; school-staff-implemented interventions; faculty-team-implemented decision making; DIBELS and SWIS data |

the day. Sheets list behavioral expectations and provide a grid for evaluating student's behavior during each major setting and subject of the day by the teacher or adult responsible for that time/activity. Students checked out at the end of day with their check-out teacher and points counted for meeting expectations and awards earned. At Tier 3, more one-on-one procedures were used including functional behavioral assessments used to develop individual behavior plans (Sugai, Lewis-Palmer, & Hagan, 1998), and a range of other procedures (e.g., multisystemic therapy, teacher assistance teams, Boys Town interventions, check-in/check-out, and social skills club; see Table 2.1).

Last, the procedures used to advance school's adoption of the three-tiered models were noted and varied (see Table 2.1). Fidelity of implementation data as a common indicator of the extent to which implementation occurred in all schools. School staff leadership teams also were a common procedure, supported by action plans, and decision making based on efficacy as measured by reduction in office disciplinary referrals using SWIS progress monitoring and numbers of students meeting literacy skill benchmarks using DIBELS progress monitoring (Oregon Behavior, Oregon Reading, North Carolina, and Kansas).

## DISCUSSION AND CONCLUSION

The major challenge with implementing any new practices is not necessarily found in the practices themselves. Instead, the major challenge is that the *processes*, *structures*, and *routines* of the schools in which the implementation efforts are taking place often are not sufficient to support the adoption and sustained use of research-validated practices.

Although student performance is paramount, it doesn't take place in a vacuum or a single context but in a complex environment (Sugai & Horner, 1999) of classrooms and schools that involves professionals, policies, programs, and practices that interact in complex ways (Simmons, Kame'enui et al., 2003). At least three important reasons may explain why effective practices, programs, and accommodations have not been adopted, implemented, or sustained in most school settings.

First, interventions including curricular programs or specific strategies tailored to address a particular problem (academic or behavioral) are too often adopted and implemented before an assessment is conducted of the contextual fit between the intervention and the "host environment" (e.g., school, classroom). For example, before purchasing a new reading program, schools should consider how the new program aligns with current instructional supports or determine if it fills a critical gap identified for the building. Second, an intervention is frequently adopted before a formative, continuous feedback loop is established at the school-building level to provide information on its effectiveness in a timely manner. Third, a new intervention is adopted for the short term and not the long haul. This newly adopted intervention is not embraced and conceptualized as part of the primary program of prevention and intervention from the very outset. In short, there is no commitment to using the program that pervades the school or school district environment.

An effective behavioral and instructional approach begins with a serious commitment to providing an environment that supports effective and sustained implementation. Few schools have made this kind of commitment, however, those that have committed resist the temptation to abandon tried, true, and trustworthy practices for fads that lack empirical evidence of their effectiveness, are based on invalid theoretical tenets, or overemphasize social or emotional appeal (Carnine, 1997).

In this chapter, we describe core features of a systemic approach toward implementing effective reading and behavioral supports, with an emphasis on schoolwide approaches to discipline and early literacy. These features were derived from the combined work of the six centers that are further detailed in the remainder of this book. In particular, we emphasize the importance of taking a prevention approach focused on features that can be applied similarly to improving academic and behavioral outcomes. Although not necessarily integral to all of the models described in the following chapters, each feature plays an essential role in most of the models. The multi-tiered models described in the following chapters must be considered in the context of the challenges related to implementing innovative systems and practices. The keys to successful implementation lie in the commitment of school leadership and staff members to creating and maintaining an environment in which a systems approach to reading and behavioral support can be successful.

## REFERENCES

Abbott, M. (2002). *Language Arts Multisensory Program (LAMP)—Levels 1–3 teacher manual and student workbook*. Kansas City: University of Kansas, Juniper Gardens Children's Project, Kansas K–3 Reading and Behavior Center.

Adelman, H. S., & Taylor, L. (1998). Involving teachers in collaborative efforts to better address the barriers to student learning. *Preventing School Failure, 42*(2), 55–60.

Barnett, W. S., Hustedt, J. T., Hawkinson, L. E., & Robin, K. B. (2006). *The state of preschool 2006*. National Institute of Early Education Research. New Brunswick, NJ: Rutgers University. Retrieved October 14, 2007, from nieer.org/yearbook/pdf/yearbook.pdf

Bennett, K. J., Brown, K. S., Boyle, M., Racine, Y., & Offord, D. (2003). Does low reading achievement at school entry cause conduct problems? *Social Science Medicine, 56*(12), 2443–2448.

Carnine, D. (1997). Bridging the research-to-practice gap. *Exceptional Children, 63*(4), 513–521.

Chard, D. J., & Kame'enui, E. J. (2000). Struggling first-grade readers: The frequency and progress of their reading. *Journal of Special Education, 34*(1), 28–38.

Committee on the Prevention of Reading Difficulties in Children. (1998). *Preventing reading difficulties in young children.* Washington, DC: National Research Council, National Academy Press.

Crone, D. A., Horner, R. H., & Hawken, L. S. (2004). *Responding to problem behavior in schools: The behavior education program.* New York: Guilford Press.

Deno, S. L., (1985). Curriculum-based measurement: the emerging alternative. *Exceptional Children, 52*(3), 219–232.

Denton, C. A., Vaughn, S., & Fletcher, J. M. (2003). Bringing research-based practice in reading intervention to scale. *Learning Disabilities Research and Practice, 18*(3), 201–211.

Dweck, C. S., & Leggett, E. (1988). A social-cognitive approach to motivation and personality *Psychological Review, 95*, 256-273.

Dweck, C. S., & Wortman, C. B. (1982). Learned helplessness, anxiety, and achievement motivation: Neglected parallels in cognitive, affective, and coping responses. In H. Krohne & L. Laux (Eds.), *Achievement, stress and anxiety* (pp. 93–125). Washington, DC: Hemisphere.

Dwyer, K. P., Osher, D., & Hoffman, C. C. (2000). Creating responsive school communities: The context of early warning, timely response: A guide to safe schools. *Exceptional Children, 66*, 347–365.

Elbaum, B., Vaughn, S., Hughes, M., & Moody, S. (2000). How effective are one-to-one tutoring programs in reading for elementary students at risk for reading failure? A meta-analysis of the intervention research. *Journal of Educational Psychology, 92*(4), 605–619.

Elmore, R. F. (1996). Getting to scale with good educational practice. *Harvard Educational Review, 66*, 1–26.

Elmore, R. F. (2002). *Bridging the gap between standards and achievement: The imperative for professional development in education.* Washington, DC: Shanker Institute.

Engelmann, S., & Bruner, E. C. (1995). *Reading mastery.* New York: SRA McMillan/McGraw-Hill.

Ervin, R. A., Schaughency, E., Matthews, A. Goodman, S. D., & McGlinchey, M. T. (2007). Primary and secondary prevention of behavior difficulties: Developing a data-informed problem-solving model to guide decision making at a schoolwide level. *Psychology in the Schools, 44*(1), 7–18.

Feil, E. G., Severson, H. H., & Walker, H. M. (1998). Screening for emotional and behavioral delays: Early screening project. *Journal of Early Intervention, 21*(3), 252–266.

Ferguson, D., Kozleski, E., & Smith, A. (2003). Transforming general and special education in urban schools. In F. E. Obiakor, C. A. Utley, & A. F. Rotatori (Eds.), *Effective education for learners with exceptionalities* (Vol. 15, pp. 43–74). New York: JAI Press.

Foorman, B., & Torgesen, J. (2001). Critical elements of classroom and small-group instruction promote reading success in all children. *Learning Disabilities Research & Practice, 16*(4), 203–212.

Foorman, B. R., Francis, D. J., Fletcher, J. M., Schatschneider, C., & Mehta, P. (1998). The role of instruction in learning to read: Preventing reading failure in at-risk children. *Journal of Educational Psychology, 90*, 37–55.

Fuchs, D., Fuchs, L. S., & Compton, D. (2004). Identifying reading disabilities by responsiveness-to-instruction: Specifying measures and criteria. *Learning Disability Quarterly, 27*, 216–227.

Fuchs, L. S., Fuchs, D., & Hamlett, C. (1989). Effects of instructional use of curriculum-based measurment to enhance instructional programs. *Remedial and Special Education, 10*, 43–52.

Gersten, R., Chard, D. J., & Baker, S. (2000). Factors enhancing sustained use of research-based instructional practices. *Journal of Learning Disabilities, 33*, 445–457.

Gersten, R., Fuchs, L. S., Williams, J. P., & Baker, S. (2001). Teaching reading comprehension strategies to students with learning disabilities: A review of research. *Review of Educational Research, 71*(2), 279–320.

Gersten, R., Fuchs, L. S., Compton, D., Coyne, M., Greenwood, C., & Innocenti, M. (2005). Quality indicators for group experimental and quasi-experimental research in special education. *Exceptional Children, 71*, 149–164.

Good, R. H., Gruba, J., & Kaminski, R. A. (2002). Best practices in using dynamic indicators of basic early literacy skills (DIBELS) in an outcomes-driven model. In A. Thomas & J. Grimes (Eds.), *Best practices in school psychology* (4th ed., pp. 699–720). Washington, DC: National Association of School Psychologists.

Good, R. H., Simmons, D. C., Kame'enui, E. J., Kaminski, R., & Wallin, J. (2002). *Summary of decision rules for intensive, strategic, and benchmark instructional recommendations in kindergarten through third grade* (Technical Report 11). Eugene: University of Oregon.

Greenwood, C. R., Delquadri, J., & Bulgren, J. (1993). Current challenges to behavioral technology in the reform of schooling: Large-scale high-quality implementation and sustained use of effective educational practices. *Education and Treatment of Children, 16*, 401–440.

Greenwood, C. R., Kamps, D., Terry, B., & Linebarger, D. (2007). Primary intervention: A means of preventing special education? In D. Haager, J. Klingner, & S. Vaughn (Eds.), *Evidence-based reading practices for response to intervention* (pp. 73–103)Baltimore: Brookes.

Grimes, J., Kurns, S., & Tilly, D. (2006). Sustainability: An enduring commitment to success. *School Psychology Review, 35*, 224–244.

Grimes, J., & Tilly, W. D. (1996). Policy and process: Means to lasting educational change. *School Psychological Review, 25*, 465–476.

Haager, D., Klingner, J., & Vaughn, S. (Eds.). (2007). *Evidence-based reading practices for response to intervention.* Baltimore: Brookes.

Hanley, G. P., Iwata, B. A., & McCord, B. (2003). Functional analysis of problem behavior: A review. *Journal of Applied Behavior Analysis, 36*,147–186.

Harn, B. A., Kame'enui, E. J., & Simmons, D. C. (2007). The nature and role of the third tier in a prevention model for kindergarten students. In D. Haager, J. Klingner, & S. Vaughn (Eds.), *Evidence-based reading practices for response to intervention* (pp. 161–184). Baltimore: Brookes.

Hinshaw, S. P. (1992). Academic underachievement, attention deficits, and aggression: Comorbidity and implications for intervention. *Journal of Consulting and Clinical Psychology, 60*, 893–903.

Horner, R. H., Carr, E. G., Halle, J., McGee, G., Odom, S., & Wolery, M. (2005). The use of single-subject research to identify evidence-based practice in special education. *Exceptional Children, 71*(2), 165–180.

Horner, R. H., Sugai, G., Todd, A. W., & Lewis-Palmer, T. (2005). School-wide positive behavior support. In L. Bambara & L. Kern (Eds.), *Individualized supports for students with problem behaviors: Designing positive behavior plans* (pp. 359–390). New York: Guilford Press.

Huberman, A. M., & Miles, M. N. B. (1984). *Innovation up close: How school improvement works.* New York: Springer.

Irvin, L. K., Horner, R. H., Ingram, K., Todd, A. W., Sugai, G., Sampson, N. K., et al. (2006). Using office discipline referral data for decision making about student behavior in elementary and middle schools. *Journal of Positive Behavior Interventions, 8*, 10–23.

Irvin, L. K., Tobin, T. J., Sprague, J. R., Sugai, G., & Vincent, C. G. (2004). Validity of office discipline referral measures as indicies of schoolwide behavioral status and effects of schoolwide behavioral interventions. *Journal of Positive Behavior Interventions, 6,* 131–147.

Juel, C. (1988). Learning to read and write: A longitudinal study of 54 children from first through fourth grades. *Journal of Educational Psychology, 80,* 437–447.

Kame'enui, E. J., Good, R. H., & Harn, B. A. (2005). Beginning reading failure and the quantification of risk. In W. L. Heward et al. (Eds.), *Focus on behavior analysis in education: Achievements, challenges, and opportunities* (pp. 70–89). Upper Saddle River, NJ: Pearson.

Kame'enui, E. J., Good, R. H., & Harn, B. A. (2005). Quantifying risk for beginning reading failure: Reading behavior as the supreme index for assessment in a primary intervention model. In W. L. Heward, T. E. Heron, N. A. Neef, S. M. Peterson, D. M. Sainato, G. Cartledge, I. Gardner, R. L. D. Peterson, S. B. Hersh, & J. C. Dardig (Eds.), *Focus on behavior analysis in education: Achievements, challenges, and opportunities* (pp. 69–89). Upper Saddle River, NJ: Prentice Hall.

Kame'enui, E. J., & Simmons, D. C. (1998). Beyond effective practice to schools as host environments: Building and sustaining a schoolwide intervention model in reading. *OSSC Bulletin, 41*(3), 3–24.

Kame'enui, E. J., & Simmons, D. C. (1999). *Planning and evaluation tool for effective schoolwide reading programs.* Unpublished document.

Kame'enui, E. J., Simmons, D. C., Good, R. H., & Chard, D. J. (2002). *Focus and nature of primary, secondary, and tertiary prevention: CIRCUITS model.* Unpublished manuscript. Eugene, OR: Center for Teaching and Learning.

Kaminski, R., & Good, R. H. (1998). Assessing early literacy skills in a problem-solving model: Dynamic indicators of basic literacy skills. In M. Shinn (Ed.), *Advanced applications of curriculum-based measurement* (pp. 113–142). New York: Guilford Press.

Kamps, D., Carta, J., Delquadri, J., Arreaga-Mayer, C., Terry, B., & Greenwood, C. R. (1989). School-based research and intervention. *Education and Treatment of Children, 12,* 359–390.

Kamps, D., & Greenwood, C. R. (2005, September 29–30). *Session III: Database Presentation III and Q & A.* Paper presented at the Topical Forum I: Applying RTI to SLD Determination Decisions. National Research Center Learning Disablities, University of Kansas, Kansas City, MO.

Kamps, D., & Kay, P. (2001). Preventing problems through social skills instruction. In R. Algozzine & P. Kay (Eds.), *What works: How schools can prevent behavior problems*(pp.57–84). Thousand Oaks: Corwin Press.

Kamps, D., Kravits, T., & Ross, R. (2002). Social-communicative strategies for school-age children. In H. Goldstein, L. A. Kaczmarek, & K. M. English (Eds.), *Promoting social communication: Child with developmental disabilities from birth to adolescence* (Vol. 10, pp. 239–277). Baltimore: Brookes.

Kamps, D., Kravits, T., Stolze, J., & Swaggart, B. (1999). Prevention strategies for students at risk and identified as serious emotionally disturbed in urban, elementary school settings. *Journal of Emotional and Behavioral Disorders, 7,* 178–188.

Kamps, D., Wills, H. P., Greenwood, C. R., Thorne, S., Lazo, J. F., Crockett, J. L., et al. (2003). A descriptive study of curriculum influences on the early reading fluency of students with academic and behavioral risks. *Journal of Emotional and Behavioral Disorders, 11*(4), 211–224.

Kratchowill, T., Clements, M., & Kalymon, K. M. (2007). Response to intervention: Conceptual and methodological issues in implementation. In S. R. Jimerson, M. K. Burns, & A. VanDerHeyden (Eds.), *The handbook of response to intervention: The science and practice of assessment and intervention*(pp.25–52). New York: Springer.

Lewis, T. J., & Sugai, G. (1999). Effective behavior support: A systems approach to proactive schoolwide management. *Focus on Exceptional Children, 31,* 1–24.

Lipsey, M. W. (1992). The effect of treatment on juvenile delinquents: Results from meta-analysis. In F. Losel, D. Bender, & T. Bliesener (Eds.), *Psychology and law*(pp.131–143). New York: Walter de Gruyter.

Maguin, E., & Loeber, R. (1995). Academic performance and delinquency. In M. Tonry (Ed.), *Crime and justice: An annual review of research: Vol. 20* (pp. 145–264). Chicago: University of Chicago Press.

Mathes, P. G., Torgesen, J. K., Allen, S. H., & Allor, J. H. (2002). *First grade PALS (Peer-Assisted Literacy Strategies)*. Longmont, CO: Sopris West.

May, S., Ard, W. III., Todd, A.W., Horner, R. H., Glasgow, A., Sugai, G., et al. (2000). *Schoolwide information system. Educational and Community Supports*, Eugene: University of Oregon.

McConnell, S. R., & Missall, K. N. (2008). Best practices in monitoring progress for preschool children. In A. Thomas & J. Grimes (Eds.), *Best practices in school psychology* (5th ed.). Washington, DC: National Association of School Psychologists.

McGraw Hill. (2005). *Open Court Reading Series*. DeSoto, Tx: Author.

McIntosh, K., Chard, D. J., Boland, J. B., & Horner, R. H. (2006). Demonstration of combined efforts in schoolwide academic and behavioral systems and incidence of reading and behavior challenges in early elementary grades. *Journal of Positive Behavior Interventions, 8*(3), 146–154.

Merrell, K. W., & Buchanan, R. (2006). Intervention selection in school-based practice: Using public health models to enhance systems capacity of schools. *School Psychology Review, 35*(2), 167–180.

Metzler, C. W., Biglan, A., Rusby, J. C., & Sprague, J. R. (2001). Evaluation of a comprehensive behavior management program to improve schoolwide positive behavior support. *Education and Treatment of Children, 24*(4), 448–479.

Morrison, G. M., Furlong, M. J., & Morrison, R. L. (1997). The safe school: Moving beyond crime prevention to school empowerment. In A. Goldstein & J. Cooley (Eds.), *The handbook of violence prevention* (pp. 236–264). New York: Guilford Press.

National Reading Panel. (2000). *Teaching students to read: An evidence-based assessment of the scientific research literature on reading and its implications for reading instruction.* Bethesda, MD: National Institute of Child Health and Human Development.

National Research Council. (1998). *Preventing reading difficulties in young children.* Washington, DC: National Academy Press.

Nelson, J. R. (1996). Designing schools to meet the needs of students who exhibit disruptive behavior. *Journal of Emotional and Behavioral Disorders, 4,* 147–161.

Nelson, J. R., Martella, R., & Galand, B. (1998). The effects of teaching school expectations and establishing a consistent consequence on formal office disciplinary actions. *Journal of Emotional and Behavioral Disorders, 6,* 153–161.

President's Commission on Excellence in Special Education. (2002). *A new era: Revitalizing special education for children and families.* Washington, DC: U.S. Department of Education.

Salvia, J., Ysseldyke, J. E., & Bolt, S. (2006). *Assessment: In special and inclusive eucation (10th edition).* Riverside, CA: Houghton Mifflin.

Scott, T. M. (2001). A schoolwide example of positive behavioral support *Journal of Positive Behavior Interventions, 3,* 88-94.

Shadish, W. R., Cook, T. D., & Campbell, D. T. (2002). *Experimental and quasi-experimental designs for generalized causal inference.* Boston: Houghton Mifflin.

Shaywitz, S. (2003). *Overcoming dyslexia: A new and complete science-based program for reading problems at any level.* New York: Knopf.

Sheridan, S. M., Hungelmann, A., & Maughan, D. P. (1999). A contextualized framework for social skills assessment, intervention, and generalization. *School Psychology Review, 28*(1), 84–103.

Shinn, M. R. (1989). *Curriculum-based measurement: Assessing special children.* New York: Guilford Press.

Shinn, M R. (1998). *Advanced applications of curriculum-based measurement*. New York: Guilford Press.

Simmons, D. C., Kame'enui, E. J., Stoolmiller, M., Coyne, M. D., & Harn, B. (2003). Accelerating growth and maintaining proficiency: A two-year intervention study of kindergarten and first-grade children at risk for reading difficulties. In B. Foorman (Ed.), *Preventing and remediating reading difficulties: Bringing science to scale* (pp. 197–228). Timonium, MD: York Press.

Simmons, D. C., Kuykendall, K., King, K., Cornachione, C., & Kame'enui, E. J. (2000). Implementation of a schoolwide reading improvement model: "No one ever told us it would be this hard!" *Learning Disabilities Research & Practice, 15*, 92–100.

Stecker, P. M., & Fuchs, L. S. (2000). Effecting superior achievement using curriculum-based measurement: The importance of individual progress monitoring. *Learning Disabilities Research & Practice, 15*, 128–134.

Stecker, P. M., & Fuchs, L. S. (2005). Using curriculum-based measurement to improve student achievement: Review of research. *Psychology in the Schools, 42*(8), 795–819.

Sugai, G., & Horner, R. H. (1999). Discipline and behavioral support: Practices, pitfalls, and promises. *Effective School Practices, 17*(4), 10–22.

Sugai, G., & Horner, R. H. (2002). The evolution of discipline practices: School-wide positive behavior supports. *Child and Family Behavior Therapy 24*, 23–50.

Sugai, G., & Horner, R. (2006). A promising approach for expanding and sustaining the implementation of schoolwide positive behavior support. *School Psychology Review, 35*, 245–259.

Sugai, G., Horner, R. H., & Gresham, F. M. (2002). Behaviorally effective school environments In M. R. Shinn, H. M. Walker, & G. Stoner (Eds.), *Interventions for academic and behavior problems II: Preventive and remedial approaches* (pp. 315–350). Bethesda, MD: National Association of School Psychologists.

Sugai, G., Lewis-Palmer, T., & Hagan, S. (1998). Using functional assessments to develop behavior support plans. *Preventing School Failure, 43*, 6–13.

Swanson, H. L., & Hoskyn, M. (1998). Experimental intervention research on students with learning disabilities: A meta-analysis of treatment outcomes. *Review of Educational Research, 68*(3), 277–321.

Tilly, W. D (2003, December). *How many tiers are needed for successful prevention and early intervention? Heartland Area Education Agency's evolution from four to three tiers.* Presented at the National Research Center on Learning Disabilities Response to Intervention Symposium, Kansas City, MO.

Torgesen, J. K., Alexander, A. W., Wagner, R. K., Rashotte, C. A., Voeller, K. S., & Conway, T. (2001). Intensive remedial instruction for children with severe reading disabilities: Immediate and long-term outcomes from two instructional approaches. *Journal of Learning Disabilities, 34*, 33–58.

Vaughn, S., Gersten, R., & Chard, D. J. (2000). The underlying message in LD intervention research: Findings from research syntheses. *Exceptional Children, 67*, 99–114.

Walker, H. M., Colvin, G., & Ramsey, E. (1995). *Antisocial behavior in school: Strategies and best practices*. Pacific Grove, CA: Brookes/Cole.

Walker, H. M., & Severson, H. H. (1992). *Systematic Screening for Behavior Disorders (SSBD)*. Longmont, CO: Sopris West.

Walker, H. M., Severson, H., & Feil, E. G. (1995). *E.S.P. Early screening project: A proven child find process*. Longmont, CO: Sopris West.

What Works Clearing House. (2007). Evidence standards. U. S. Department of Education, Institute for Education Science, Washington, DC. Retrieved July 12, 2007 from www.what works.ed.gov/reviewprocess/standards.html.

Zins, J. E., & Ponti, C. R. (1990). Best practices in school-based consultation. In A. Thomas & J. Grimes (Eds.), *Best practices in school psychology–II* (pp. 673–694). Washington, DC: National Association of School Psychologists.

# PART II

## CASE STUDIES

# CHAPTER 3

# The Nebraska Three-Tiered Behavioral Prevention Model Case Study

RON NELSON, KRISTIN DUPPONG HURLEY, LORI SYNHORST, *and* MICHAEL H. EPSTEIN

Estimates provided in the *Surgeon General's Report on Children and Mental Health* (Department of Health and Human Services, 2000) indicated that 21% of youth within the general population have a diagnosable mental health disorder. Approximately 11% of youth meet the diagnostic criteria for a significant impairment that adversely affects relationships at home, with peers, and in the community. Unfortunately, many teachers and parents report that they are unprepared to deal with problem behavior exhibited by students with such disorders (Furlong, Morrison, & Dear, 1994; Lowry, Sleet, Duncan, Powell, & Kolbe, 1995). Even special education teachers report feeling ill prepared to deal with students' problem behavior (Baum, Duffelmeyer, & Geelan, 1988). Parents are also concerned about problem behavior within schools, as 36% of general public school parents rated fighting/violence/gangs, lack of discipline, lack of funding, and use of drugs as the top four largest problems facing local schools; these four problems have been rated the top four for over 15 years (Rose & Gallup, 1998).

In response to this growing concern, three-tiered behavior prevention programs have been recommended to help schools create more effective teaching and learning environments (e.g., Nelson, Martella, & Marchand-Martella, 2002; Sugai, Sprague, Horner, & Walker, 2000; Walker et al., 1996). Such programs are designed to help schools link information about the physical school environment, administrative and management practices of the school, neighborhood and family characteristics, and characteristics of the student population to the development of a set of progressively more comprehensive, intense, and specific intervention programs designed to improve the teaching and learning environment as evidenced by reductions in school behavior problems and prevention of behavior disorders. The purpose of this chapter is to describe the implementation of the Nebraska three-tiered behavior prevention model in the context of a single elementary school. In this chapter, we first describe the elementary school setting in which the three-tiered behavior prevention model was implemented. We then describe the conceptual framework for the three-tiered prevention model and the criteria used to select the primary, secondary, and tertiary interventions. Next, we describe the implementation, professional development and key elements of the program. Then, we present a pre- and postintervention case study of the child outcomes for the primary, secondary, and tertiary interventions. Finally, we provide a discussion of lessons learned.

## SCHOOL SETTING

Roosevelt Elementary School (a pseudonym) is located in a low- to moderate-income neighborhood in a medium-sized city in the Midwest. Roosevelt serves approximately 370 students in grades K–5. The average student class size is 19, and the mobility rate is approximately 20%. A majority of the students are eligible for free or reduced lunch (53%) and 20% receive special education services. The overall race breakdown of the students includes 75% European Americans, 15% African Americans, 6% Hispanics/Latinos, 2% Native Americans, and 2% Asian Americans. In 2005, the average percentile scores on the Metropolitan Achievement Test (MAT;8th edition) (Harcourt Assessment) in reading and mathematics were 65 and 74, respectively.

Roosevelt is one of 36 elementary schools located in the local school district, serving over 32,000 students. The school district is typical of medium-sized districts across the country in that there is wide variance in the school populations served by each elementary school in terms of the number of students served (range = 200–800), free and reduced lunch rates (range = 4–95%), percent students of color (range = 6–65%), and mobility rates (range = 6–0%). The average percentile scores on the MAT in reading and mathematics in the 2005 academic year were 77 (range = 41–98) and 85 (range = 41–98), respectively. Further, the school district, like most public schools, initiated several programs in response to the sweeping reforms of No Child Left Behind (NCLB) throughout the project. In addition to instituting annual testing of all students in reading and math and annual report cards on school performance in 2005, the district sequentially adopted a new core reading (second project year) program (i.e., Houghton Mifflin, 2003). The school district initiated intensive and sustained professional development activities to facilitate teachers' adoption of the core reading program.

## CONCEPTUAL FRAMEWORK AND CORE PROCEDURES

The conceptual model for the Nebraska three-tiered behavior prevention model is based on the risk factor causal theory (Hawkins, VonCleve, & Catalano, 1991; Lynam, 1996). The risk factor causal theory is rooted in the notion that pervasive exposure to key risk factors is associated with negative, destructive long-term outcomes (Patterson, Reid, & Dishion, 1992). Empirical evidence suggests that this process likely operates in the following manner: (1) students and youth are exposed to a host of risk factors over time (e.g., family problems, child neglect/abuse); (2) risk factors are associated with the development of early maladaptive behavior (e.g., defiance of adults, aggression, lack of self-regulation); (3) short-term outcomes include truancy, peer and teacher rejection, low academic achievement, school discipline contacts and referrals, and a larger-than-normal number of schools attended; and (4) these short-term outcomes, in turn, are predictive of much more serious, longer term outcomes including emotional and behavioral disorders (EBD), school failure and dropout, delinquency, drug and alcohol use, gang membership, adult criminality, and, in some cases, serious violent acts (Cicchetti & Nurcombe, 1993). Thus, school programs need to implement a progressive set of primary, secondary, and tertiary interventions that represent greater comprehensiveness and intensity to prevent EBD in the face of individual's need for such intervention.

### Intervention Selection Criteria

The primary, secondary, and tertiary prevention interventions were selected based on the following criteria. First, the interventions had to represent greater comprehensiveness and intensity relative to those typically implemented by schools. Second, the interventions had to address one or more known causal risk factors. Third, the interventions had to be manualized or standardized to ensure that they could be replicated reliably by others. Fourth, the interventions had to fit within the context of a school and its educational mission. Finally, the interventions had to be fully developed and validated as evidenced by applied research studies. The studies associated with the primary, secondary, and tertiary interventions are cited below.

## Primary Prevention Program

The primary prevention program selected was Behavior and Academic Support and Enhancement (BASE) (Nelson, 1996; Nelson et al., 2002). BASE is a whole-school reform primary-level behavior program that has been developed and systematically refined over the past 15 years. The primary goals of the BASE are to develop, implement, and sustain a prevention-oriented schoolwide discipline program that can be implemented reliably by schools. Several experimental studies have documented the short- and long-term outcomes of BASE (Nelson, 1996; Nelson, Martella, & Galand, 1998; Nelson et al., 2002). Two U.S. Department of Education Grants from the Office of Special Education Programs (OSEP) and Office of Educational Research and Innovation (OERI) supported the development of BASE.

BASE included three primary elements: (1) common areas procedures and behavioral expectations, (2) the Think Time Strategy (a consistent classroom management strategy applied schoolwide), and (3) continuum of administrative disciplinary responses. The common areas procedures were designed to promote positive student behavior. For example, the lunch/recess schedule was designed to reduce wait time in the lunch line and maximize the level of supervision. Established patterns of supervision were also developed to enable staff to provide a more complete and balanced coverage of the common areas. In addition to procedures, behavioral expectations for each common area were developed and taught to students. The focus was on arrival, lunch/recess, and dismissal because a majority of the problems occur in these areas. Teachers actively taught students the routines and rewarded students (e.g., lunch with the principal, stickers). Periodic reviews of the routines were then conducted throughout the remainder of the year.

The Think Time Strategy (Nelson & Carr, 2000) was implemented schoolwide. The Think Time Strategy provided the basis for a more collaborative and less confrontational classroom management approach. Instead of reinforcing disruptive behavior by using punitive measures, the Think Time Strategy is designed to help staff facilitate corrective social interaction patterns and emotional experiences as well as enhance students' self-regulation skills (i.e., control impulses and emotions). Specifically, the Think Time Strategy is a collaborative process between two or more teachers (i.e., the homeroom teacher and a cooperating teacher[s] who provide the designated Think Time area). The Think Time Strategy includes three components: (1) precision request (i.e., teacher uses a short verbal statement to encourage the child to exhibit positive social behavior and does not use threats, ultimatums, warnings, or repeated request), (2) antiseptic bounding condition (i.e., reflective period to enable the child to gain self-control), and (3) behavioral debriefing process (i.e., teacher checks for self-control and initiates a positive interaction with the child).

The continuum of administrative disciplinary responses included those commonly used by schools (i.e., lunch time detention, performance-based in-school suspension, out-of-school suspension) as well as an administrative antiseptic bounding and debriefing intervention. The administrative antiseptic bounding and debriefing intervention was the primary administrative disciplinary response used by school staff. This disciplinary response was applied when students were noncompliant or highly disruptive during Think Time. The role of the administrator was to simply deescalate and help the student gain self-control. The role of the teacher was to ensure that the student completes Think Time successfully following the administrative antiseptic bounding and debriefing intervention. These coordinated administrator–teacher roles ensure that teacher authority was maintained.

## Secondary Prevention Program

The secondary prevention program selected was First Step to Success (Walker, Stiller, Golly, Kavanagh, Severson, & Feil, 1998). First Step to Success is an early-intervention program targeting kindergarten and first grade students at risk for EBD (Golly, Stiller, & Walker, 1998; Walker, Kavanagh, Stiller, Golly, Severson, & Feil, 1998; Walker, Stiller, Severson, Feil, & Golly, 1998). Teachers, peers, and parents or caregivers participate in the intervention as implementation agents, under the direction and supervision of a behavioral consultant who has primary responsibility for coordinating the intervention. Several studies have been conducted validating the use of First Step to Success as a secondary prevention program (Golly et al., 1998; Walker, Kavanagh, et al., 1998). First Step to Success has been included and/or featured in six compilations of effective interventions to address at-risk students and to identify approaches for making schools safer and violence free (e.g., Greenberg, 2000).

First Step to Success consists of three modules implementing a series of activities designed to be applied in concert with each other. The modules include (1) proactive, universal screening of all kindergarten and first-grade populations, (2) consultant-based school interventions involving the target child, peers, and teachers, and (3) parent training in caregiver skills for supporting and improving the child's school adjustment performance in the home.

### Screening Module

First Step includes a multigate screening process used to identify students at risk of behavior problems. The process relied on a series of teacher ratings of student behavior. The module is described in detail later in the chapter.

### School Module

The school module of First Step is an adapted version of the CLASS (Contingencies for Learning Academic and Social Skills) program for the acting-out child developed by Hops and Walker (1988). CLASS is divided into three successive phases: consultant, teacher, and maintenance. The consultant phase (program days 1–5) is the responsibility of an adult who coordinates the implementation process. In the target schools it is a paraprofessional or behavioral coach who serves as the consultant. The consultant performs the following key program tasks:

1. explains the CLASS program to the teacher, parents, target child, and peers;
2. secures the cooperation and consent of all parties to participate in the program's implementation;
3. operates the program in the classroom for the first five program days during a daily 20- to 30-minute sessions;
4. negotiates earned school and home privileges with the child, teacher, and parents;
5. demonstrates the program's operation and trains the teacher in how to apply it; and
6. turns over the program to the teacher and supervises his operation of it during the teacher phase of the CLASS program.

The consultant phase begins with a daily 20-minute session with the child, called the Green–Red Card Game. Initially, the consultant, in close proximity to the target child, monitors her classroom behavior using a red and green card. During this time, there are random moments when the coach will check if the card is displaying green or red. If the card is on green the child will earn a point. To meet criterion, the child must earn a minimum of 80% of the possible points for the session. For those that meet criterion, they earn a prearranged classroom reward, such as playing a game with the whole class. The child will also earn a special reward activity with her parents at home. The parents are given daily feedback regarding their child's progress and are encouraged to provide home activities, such as reading a book or playing a game as a reward for days the child earned a reward at school. As the game progresses the session length become longer and the interval in which points and praise can be earned is gradually extended from 30 seconds to 10 minutes. Additionally, in later stages of the program, the target child must work in blocks of multiple days to earn a reward. Thus, the program becomes more demanding as the student progresses through it, and the student must sustain acceptable performance for progressively longer periods of time to be successful.

The teacher phase (program days 6–20) is operated by the classroom teacher in whose room the program is initially implemented. The teacher assumes control of the program's operation on program day 6, but with close supervision and support provided by the First Step coach. The consultant provides monitoring and technical assistance on an as-needed basis for the teacher throughout the remainder of the teacher phase. Teacher phase implementation tasks include (1) operating the program daily, (2) awarding praise and points according to program guidelines and contingent on child performance, (3) supervising delivery of group activity and school rewards, and (4) communicating with parents on a regular basis regarding the target child's performance. The teacher works closely with the behavioral coach, child, parents, and peers throughout the total implementation period.

The maintenance phase lasts from program days 21–30 after which the school intervention is terminated. In this final phase, the target child is rewarded primarily with praise and expressions of approval/recognition from the teacher at school and the parents at home. An attempt is made during this phase to reduce the child's dependence on the program by substituting adult praise for points, reducing the amount of daily feedback given, and making occasional rewards available contingent on exemplary performance. In the majority of the cases, target students who successfully complete the teacher phase of the program are able to sustain their improved behavior in this phase despite these program changes.

## Home Module

The home module (homeBase) consists of a series of six lessons designed to enable parents and caregivers to build child competencies and skills in six areas that affect school adjustment and performance: (1) communication and sharing in school, (2) cooperation, (3) limit setting, (4) problem solving, (5) friendship making, and (6) development of confidence. HomeBase contains lessons, instructional guidelines, and parent–child games and activities for teaching these skills. HomeBase requires 6 weeks for implementation and begins after the target child has completed program day 10 of the First Step program.

The First Step behavioral coach visits the parents' home weekly and conducts the homeBase lessons in that setting. Following each session, materials are left with the parents that facilitate daily review and practice of each skill with the target child. The homeBase lessons require approximately 1 hour each. Parents are encouraged to work with their students 10 to 15 minutes daily and to focus on practicing the homeBase skills being taught.

## Tertiary Prevention Program

The tertiary prevention program selected was MultiSystemic Therapy (MST) (Henggeler et al., 1998). MST is an evidence-based family- and home-based treatment that views individuals as being surrounded by a network of interconnected systems that encompass individual, family, and extrafamilial (peer, school, neighborhood) factors and recognizes that intervention is often a necessary combination of these systems. A core feature of MST is its emphasis on altering the social ecology of youth and families in ways that promote positive adjustment and attenuate emotional and behavioral difficulties. For this reason, MST is a home-based model of service delivery. The effectiveness of MST with students who engage in serious antisocial behavior has been evaluated through several experimental and quasi-experimental studies (Bourdin, Henggeler, Blaske, & Stein, 1990; Bourdin et al., 1995; Brunk, Henggeler, & Whelan, 1987; Henggeler et al., 1991; Henggeler, Melton, & Smith, 1992, Henggeler, Pickrel, & Bourduin, 1999; Henggeler et al., 1986). MST has been included in the following compilations of effective interventions: U.S Department of Justice, National Institute on Drug Abuse, Center for Substance Abuse Treatment, Center for Substance Abuse Prevention, Blueprints for Violence Prevention, National Institute of Mental Health, and Center for Mental Health Services.

### Treatment Approach

This "multisystemic" approach views individuals as being surrounded by a network of interconnected systems that encompass individual, family, and extrafamilial (peer, school, neighborhood) factors and recognizes that intervention is often a necessary combination of these systems. As noted above, a core feature of MST is its emphasis on altering the social ecology of youth and families in ways that promote positive adjustment and attenuate emotional and behavioral difficulties. Based on the belief that the most effective and ethical route to helping students is through helping their families, MST views parent(s) or guardians(s) as valuable resources, even when they have serious and multiple needs of their own. The primary goals of MST are to 1) reduce the frequency and severity of mental health problems, 2) reduce other types of antisocial behavior, and 3) achieve these outcomes at a cost savings by decreasing rates of incarceration and out-of-home placements. MST achieves these goals through adherence to nine MST treatment principles:

1. The primary purpose of assessment is to understand the fit between the identified problems and their broader systemic context.
2. Therapeutic contacts emphasize the positive and use systemic strengths as levers for change.
3. Interventions are designed to promote responsible behavior and decrease irresponsible behavior among family members.
4. Interventions are present focused and action oriented, targeting specific and well-defined problems.
5. Interventions target sequences of behavior within and between multiple systems that maintain the identified problems.
6. Interventions are developmentally appropriate and fit the developmental needs of the students.
7. Interventions are designed to require daily or weekly effort by family members.
8. Intervention effectiveness is evaluated continuously from multiple perspectives with providers assuming accountability for overcoming barriers to successful outcomes.
9. Interventions are designed to promote treatment generalization and long-term maintenance of therapeutic change by empowering caregivers to address family members' needs across multiple systemic contexts.

Key characteristics of this model are as follows:

1. low caseloads, typically three to six families per full-time therapist;
2. Provision of services in the family's natural environment—home, school, and neighborhood settings;
3 time-limited duration of treatments, 3–5 months per family de-

pending on the seriousness of the problems and successes of interventions;
4. therapist functioning within a team of three to four practitioners,
   though each has an individual caseload;
5. 24-hours-per-day and 7-days-per-week availability of therapists,
   or at least one practitioner on the MST team;
6. Scheduling appointments at the family's convenience, such as
   evening hours and weekends; and
7. daily contact, face-to-face or by phone, with families.

MST therapists focus on empowering parents by using identified strengths
to develop natural support systems (e.g., extended family, neighbors)
and remove barriers (e.g., high stress, poor relations with spouse) to improve their capacity to function as effective parents. This process is
viewed as collaboration between the family and therapist, with the family taking the lead in setting treatment goals and the therapist suggesting
ways to accomplish these goals. Once engaged, the parents(s) or guard-
ian(s) consult with the MST therapist on the best strategies to, for example, set and enforce curfews and rules in the home, decrease the child's
friendships with deviant peers, or improve the child's academic performance.

MST therapists are asked to follow a consistent strategy:

1. develop and refine a multisystemic conceptualization of the
   causes of identified problems presented by each client family;
2. design and effectively implement intervention strategies that em-
   body the nine treatment principles;
3. identify barriers to the successful engagement of key participants
   (family members, school personnel, sources of parental social
   support) and implement strategies to overcome these barriers;
4. logically and clearly connect intermediary and ultimate goals;
   and
5. identify barriers to the successful implementation of interventions and implement strategies to overcome them.

## IMPLEMENTATION APPROACH

The three-tiered behavior prevention model was implemented at Roosevelt Elementary School during the 2002–2006 academic years. In 2002–
2003, the infrastructure for the primary prevention program was put in
place at the school. In 2003–2006, the interventions at each of the three

levels were implemented. During those school years the average enroll-ment at the school was 370 students who were served by the BASE pro-gram. Also, First Step served 34 students at risk of behavior problems, and MST enrolled 16 students identified with emotional or behavior dis-orders.

## Implementation of BASE

Implementation of BASE was achieved through a representative leader-ship team. The leadership team included the principal, school psycholo-gist, general education teacher and special education team leaders, and a community representative. The leadership team participated in a 6-hour workshop designed to enhance their knowledge and competencies in the BASE model. The training content included (1) primary-level school or-ganizational systems (i.e., leadership, schoolwide, nonclassroom, class-room) that would be evaluated (i.e., current status, identification of gaps; (2) specific elements of primary-level school organizational sys-tems; (3) how the School Evaluation Rubric (SER) is used to evaluate the school's current status (i.e., beginning, developing, exemplary) and ser-vice gaps (i.e., specific elements within each organizational system that need to be added or revised); and (4) implementation procedures and strategies.

The SER encompasses a three-step planning model develop and im-plement BASE. First, the leadership team conducted a consensus-based administration of the SER with all staff (approximately 1 hour) to iden-tify the current status of the schoolwide discipline program and identify service gaps in the four organizational systems. Second, based on the re-sults of the SER, the leadership team met 3 times (approximately 8 hours) to develop a strategic implementation plan. Finally, the leadership team guided the implementation of each of the components of the schoolwide discipline program across the remainder of the school year and continued to monitor its effectiveness and make adjustments as nec-essary over the project years. Project staff held collaborative problem-solving meetings with the school's leadership team when necessary. Additionally, a half-day training session and three problem-solving meetings were conducted on the Think Time Strategy (Nelson & Carr, 2000) and associated administrative disciplinary responses (described below) with staff. The content was as follows: (1) theoretical model (i.e., social learning theory); (2) preventative classroom management (e.g., teaching expectations); (3) key elements (i.e., precision request, antisep-tic bounding, debriefing); (4) implementation steps; (5) use with admin-istrative discipline procedures; and (6) common questions.

## Implementation of First Step

A First Step to Success behavior coach (i.e., paraprofessional levels) was hired by the project to implement the program. The coach was supervised by a project supervisor who was hired to oversee the implementation of First Step in all schools. A 2-hour training session prior to the beginning of the school year with kindergarten and first-grade teachers as well as the behavioral coach and supervisor was conducted as a scaling-up activity. The content included an overview of First Step, a description of antisocial behavior in young students, and a discussion of how First Step assists students and teachers to improve student behavior. The trainer provided examples of how First Step helps students and distributed copies of the First Step training guide to teachers.

Prior to implementation the behavioral coach attended a 6-day training session. (Note that length and intensiveness of the training session exceeded what is typically used to implement First Step.) This training session content included (1) understanding the underlying principles of First Step; (2) research regarding serious EBD; (3) screening procedures for identifying students eligible for First Step; (4) the role of the child, teacher, parent, and coach with regard to implementing First Step; (5) viewing and discussing training videos; and (6) role-playing behavioral coach duties (i.e., conducting initial child meetings, starting the program in the classroom, and using the Green–Red card appropriately).

After the initial training session, a 2-day training on the homeBase (described below) module was conducted. The homeBase training content was as follows: (1) review of the six lessons delivered to parents regarding improving home and school interactions; (2) review of the parent and child activities presented in the homeBase materials; and (3) discussion of common questions asked by parents during homeBase sessions. In addition to presentations and discussions, role-plays were used for the coaches to practice conducting the home sessions.

Finally, two single-day booster trainings were scheduled between the First Step to Success program developer and project staff. One booster session occurred in the fall as implementation was beginning, and the other in the winter after the first group of students had completed the program. This training consisted of a review of First Step, along with a troubleshooting session to discuss questions regarding implementation. Throughout early implementation of First Step, ongoing discussions via e-mail and phone between project staff and the First Step program developer regarding implementation issues were used to problem solve implementation issues. Likewise, weekly First Step team meetings occurred throughout the project. These meetings included the supervisor and behavioral coaches. The weekly meetings provided an opportunity to discuss implementation concerns, problem-solve difficult implementation issues, and overcome obstacles to consistently implement First Step.

### Screening Module

Each year, students attending kindergarten at Roosevelt were screened using a modified version of the Early Screening Project (ESP; Walker, Severson, & Feil, 1995). Likewise, first-grade students were screened using a modified version of the Systematic Screening for Behavior Disorders program (SSBD; Walker & Severson, 1990). The SSBD and ESP are similar screening measures that consist of "gates" that provide progressively more intensive levels of screening whereby only those students meeting or exceeding the predetermined cut-off criteria move on to the next step. At Gate I, teachers were asked to list the five students who best evince externalizing characteristics and five students who best evince internalizing ones. At Gate II, teachers completed the following rating scales on the five externalizers and five internalizers from Gate I: (1) Critical Events Index that asks respondents to check the occurrence or nonoccurrence of 30 items (e.g., steals, suddenly cries); (2) an Adaptive Behavior Scale (i.e., nine items representing prosocial behavior); and (3) a Maladaptive Behavior Scale (i.e., 10 items representing inappropriate social behaviors). Those students who exceed the normative criteria on one or more of the scales became eligible for First Step.

A total of 34 selected kindergarten and first-grade students identified as at risk for EBD received First Step to Success. A majority of the First Step students were male (53%), European American (83%), and eligible for free or reduced lunch (65%). First Step students met the respective specified ESP and SSBD criteria (see ESP and SSBD screening procedures above). The eligibility criteria for First Step identified students at the 20th percentile or less on the ESP and SSBD. Specifically, kindergarten students with $t$ scores of 60 or more on the ESP Adaptive Behavior and Maladaptive Behavior Scales or with $t$ scores of 70 or more on the ESP Critical Events Scale were eligible for participation. First-grade students whose characteristic behavior pattern most closely resembled the externalizing behavior description with $t$ scores of 43 or less and 56 or more on the Adaptive Behavior and Maladaptive Behavior Scales, respectively, or $t$ scores of 55 or more on the SSBD Critical Events Index were eligible for participation. First-grade students whose characteristic behavior pattern most closely resembled the internalizing behavior description with $t$ scores of 43 or less and 53 or more on the Adaptive Behavior and Maladaptive Behavior Scales, respectively, or $t$ scores of 60 or more on the SSBD Critical Events Index were eligible for participation.

A criterion sample ($n$ = 34) was identified in the school and provided a comparative framework with which to assess the outcomes of First Step to Success. A majority of the criterion students were male (83%) and European American (79%). Forty-six percent qualified for free or reduced lunch. The criterion students were those students who fell between the 21st and 30th percentile on the ESP and SSBD screening scales. Specifically, criterion kindergarten students were those with $t$ scores that ranged from 55 to 59 on the ESP Adaptive Behavior and Maladaptive Behavior Scales. First-grade criterion students whose characteristic behavior pattern most closely resembled the externalizing behavior description with a $t$ score of 43 or less on the Adaptive Behavior Scale or scores of 56 or more on the Maladaptive Behavior Scale, respectively. First-grade criterion students whose characteristic behavior pattern most closely resembled the internalizing behavior description with $t$ scores of 43 or less and 53 or more on the Adaptive Behavior and Maladaptive Behavior Scales, respectively, or $t$ scores of 60 or more on the SSBD Critical Events Index were eligible for participation.

## Implementation of MST

A MST therapist, one of three, was hired by the project to implement the program in the target school. The MST therapist had a master's degree and experience with students with mental health disorders. The therapist was supervised by an individual with a master's degree who was state certified as a clinical therapist. The MST therapists and supervisor underwent specific training and supervision as indicated by the developers of MST. A 1-day scaling-up training session was conducted by staff from MST Services Inc. The audience included the MST supervisor, key staff from the local mental health center, community leaders including local school district administrators and mental health agency administrators, and two or three representatives from Roosevelt Elementary School as well as the other participating schools. The training content was as follows: (1) an overview of MST including the scope, correlates, and causes of the serious behavior problems addressed with MST; (2) the theoretical and empirical underpinnings of the treatment model; and (3) a description of the family, peer, school, and individual intervention strategies used.

Prior to the beginning of the school year the MST therapist and supervisor attended a 5-day MST training session. The initial 5 days of training included didactic and experiential components. Didactic components included (1) systems theories, social learning theory, and major psychological and sociological models; (2) research regarding serious emotional disturbance in youth; (3) research relevant to problems experienced by target youth (e.g., learning disabilities); and (4) research on interventions used in MST (e.g., empirically validated family and marital therapy approaches). Additionally, the training utilized role-plays and exercises designed to stimulate critical thinking about the treatment process; client engagement; individual, family, and systems-level assessments; the evaluation of what evidence therapists use to draw conclusions about the correlates/causes of a problem; the development of intervention strategies and specific interventions; and how to determine whether an intervention is being effective.

Two-day quarterly booster trainings were provided throughout the project period by a consultant from MST Services Inc. As therapists gained field experience with MST, quarterly booster sessions were conducted on-site. The purpose of these boosters was to provide additional training in areas identified by therapists (e.g., marital interventions, treatment of parental depression in the context of MST) and to facilitate in-depth examination, enactment, and problem solving of particularly difficult cases. MST consultants were responsible for designing and delivering the booster training.

Weekly telephone consultation was also provided by MST Services Inc. The consultation was provided by the MST consultant assigned to the project and the codeveloper of MST. The consultation lasted 1 hour. Consultation sessions focused on promoting adherence to MST treatment principles, developing solutions to difficult clinical problems, and designing plans to overcome any barriers to obtaining strong treatment adherence and favorable outcomes for youths and families.

*Screening*

Students were identified for the MST program based on the following criteria: (1) is a K–3 grader; (2) is currently receiving special education services for emotional disturbance or has a *DSM-IV* (American Psychiatric Association [APA], 1994) diagnosis; (3) exhibits behaviors that are symptomatic of a serious mental health problem (as determined by performance on the Child Behavior Checklist or the Teacher Report Form; Achenbach, 1991); and (4) has special service needs that may include a history of multiple agency involvement and/or require the coordination of two or more service systems or agencies. A rolling referral process was used whereby students could be referred anytime throughout the school year.

A total of 16 selected K–3 grade students with EBD received MST. A majority of the MST students were male (75%), European American (93%), and eligible for free or reduced lunch (63%). As noted above, students met the MST eligibility criteria if they were a K–3 grader, currently receiving special education services for emotional disturbance or had a *DSM-IV* (APA, 1994) diagnosis, exhibiting behaviors that were symptomatic of a serious mental health problem (scores in the borderline to clinical range on the Child Behavior Checklist or the Teacher Report Form; Achenbach, 1991), and/or in need of special service coordination across two or more service systems or agencies. No criterion sample was identified for comparison purposes.

## OUTCOMES

The Nebraska Three-Tiered behavior prevention model was designed to enhance the behavioral and academic functioning of students at Roosevelt Elementary school. Yet we also recognized that there is evidence suggesting behavioral and academic performance, particularly in the area of reading, is related to one another (Nelson, Benner, Lane, & Smith, 2004). For this reason, the outcome evaluation that was conducted assessed behavioral adjustment and reading performance for the students who received the secondary or tertiary prevention programs. The dependent measures used and the outcomes achieved for each of the three tiers are reported below.

### Primary Prevention Outcomes

Third-grade mean Total Reading normal curve equivalent (NCE) scores on the Metropolitan Achievement Test (MAT) (Harcourt Assessment) were used to assess the outcomes of BASE. MAT scores 5 years prior (1996–2001 assessment periods) to the implementation of BASE and each of the five project years (2002–2006 assessment periods) are presented in Figure 3.1. Three major events occurred during the project implementation period. First, the school district adopted the MAT 8 (8th edition) in the 2003 assessment period. Prior to this the school district used the MAT 7 (7th edition). Second, as noted earlier, the school district implemented a new core reading program in the 2003 assessment period. Finally, the district responded to the NCLB requirement that all students in grades 3–12 (with few exceptions) participate in state and district assessment programs beginning in 2005 assessment period. Thus, the NCLB assessment requirement expanded the range of third-grade students taking the MAT in the 2005 and 2006 assessment periods.

Inspection of Figure 3.1 reveals that the MAT NCE Total Reading scores of third-grade students ranged from 48.4 to 58. 6 ($M = 53.9$, $SD = 3.5$) in the 5 years prior to the implementation of BASE. The MAT NCE

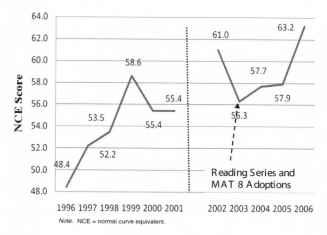

**FIGURE 3.1.** Metropolitan Achievement Test (MAT) Total Reading scores.

Total Reading scores of students increased, ranging from 56.3 to 63.2 ($M = 59.2$, $SD = 2.8$) in the years following. The mean pre- and postimplementation change score was 5.3.

## Secondary Prevention Outcomes

The First Step program was evaluated by assessing the behavioral adjustment and reading skills of the participants. The measures used in the evaluation and the outcomes are reported below.

### Behavioral Adjustment

Two measures were used to assess the behavioral adjustment of students. The Social Skills Rating System (SSRS), Social Skills, Problem Behaviors, and Academic Competence Scales (Elliott & Gresham, 1991) were used to assess teacher ratings of students' behavioral adjustment. Teachers rate student behaviors on a 3-point, Likert-type scale in two areas, how often behaviors occur and how important each behavior is to the respondent. The SSRS test–retest and internal consistency values for the Social Skills, Problem Behaviors, and Academic Competence Scales range from 0.84 to 0.93 and 0.82 to 0.85, respectively (Elliott & Gresham, 1991).

The Child Behavior Checklist (CBCL; Achenbach, 1991) Total Problems, Externalizing, and Internalizing broadband scales were used to assess parent ratings of students' behavioral adjustment. The parent/

guardian rates the child on each item indicating the severity of the problem on a scale of 0 (*no problem*) to 2 (*severe problem*). The CBCL test–retest and internal consistency values for the Total Problems, Externalizing, and Internalizing broadband scales ranged from 0.72 to 0.95 and 0.65 to 0.92, respectively (Achenbach, 1991). These data were collected on students who received First Step to Success but not on the criterion sample.

The pre- and posttest SSRS Social Skills, Problem Behavior, and Academic Competence Scale scores of First Step to Success and criterion students and the associated pre- and posttest effect size comparisons between these students are presented in Table 3.1. One-way analyses of covariance (ANCOVAs) were conducted on the posttest SSRS scale scores using the pre-test means as the covariate. The difference in the posttest SSRS Academic Competence, $F(1,67) = 4.62$, $p = 0.034$, Scale scores of criterion and First Step students scores of First Step and criterion students was statistically significant. There were no statistically significant differences in the posttest SSRS Social Skills, $F(1,67) = 0.15$, $p = 0.703$ and Problem Behavior, $F(1,67) = 0.81$, $p = 0.349$, Scale scores of First Step and criterion students.

Inspection of Table 3.1 reveals that all of the pretest SSRS mean scale scores of First Step students were substantially higher than the standardized mean score ($M = 100$, $SD = 15$). In contrast, the pretest SSRS mean scale scores of the criterion students all fell within the average range provided by the SSRS interpretation guidelines. Additionally, the pretest effect size comparisons between the First Step and criterion (i.e., nontreated students who scored between the 21st and 30th percentile on screening measures) students were moderate to large, ranging from −0.62 to −1.77. The formula used to compute the effect sizes was as follows:

$$\text{Effect size} = (M_{\text{First Step to Success students}} - M_{\text{criterion students}})/\text{Pooled } SD$$

Inspection of Table 3.1 shows that the posttest SSRS Social Skills and Problem Behavior mean scale scores of the criterion students deteriorated across the assessment period, whereas, their posttest SSRS Academic Competence Scale scores remained relatively stable. In contrast, the posttest SSRS Social Skills, Problem Behavior, and Academic Competence Scale scores of First Step students showed improvements across the assessment period. Additionally, the posttest SSRS mean scale scores of First Step and criterion students fell within the average range. Relative to the pretest, the posttest effect size comparisons indicated that differences between First Step and criterion students had decreased substantially following the intervention period (range = −0.16 to −0.55).

**TABLE 3.1. Students' Mean Pre, Post, and Follow-Up Scores on the Social SSRS and WRMT-R/NU**

| Measure and scale | Criterion | | | | First Step | | | | Effect size | |
|---|---|---|---|---|---|---|---|---|---|---|
| | Pre | | Post | | Pre | | Post | | Pre | Post |
| | $M$ | $SD$ | $M$ | $SD$ | $M$ | $SD$ | $M$ | $SD$ | | |
| SSRS | | | | | | | | | | |
| Social Skills | 98.56 | 13.07 | 95.53 | 14.34 | 83.23 | 11.95 | 93.32 | 12.43 | -1.22 | -0.16 |
| Problem Behavior | 99.71 | 10.33 | 103.09 | 12.16 | 118.34 | 10.73 | 109.44 | 11.54 | -1.77 | -0.55 |
| Academic Competence | 90.68 | 10.70 | 90.06 | 12.86 | 84.23 | 10.27 | 88.47 | 8.76 | -0.62 | -0.14 |
| WRMT-R/NU | | | | | | | | | | |
| Total Reading | 98.65 | 9.29 | 100.50 | 9.26 | 96.43 | 8.94 | 98.71 | 7.63 | -0.24 | -0.21 |

*Note.* SSRS, Social Skills Rating Scale. WRMT-R/NU, Woodcock Reading Mastery Test—Revised/Normative Update.

79

The mean pre- and posttest CBCL Total Problems, Externalizing, and Internalizing scores of First Step students are presented in Figure 3.2. Inspection of Figure 3.2 reveals that the pre- and posttest scores of students were below the established CBCL borderline criteria (60 to 63). However, the pretest CBCL Total Problems ($M = 59.1$, $SD = 9.14$) and Externalizing ($M = 59.8$, $SD = 9.32$) scores approached the borderline criteria. Students showed small to moderate concurrent decreases (mean CBCL pre–post change scores) in their levels of total problem ($M = -3.6$, $SD = 6.98$), externalizing ($M = -1.7$, $SD = 6.37$), and internalizing ($M = -3.6$, $SD = 8.38$) behavior following the intervention period. Positive changes in teacher ratings (SSRS) of the behavioral adjustment of students were consistent with those of parents (CBCL).

### Reading Skills

The Woodcock Reading Mastery Test–Revised/Normative Update (WRMT-R/NU; Woodcock, 1998) Total Reading (Word Identification, Word Attack, Word Comprehension, Passage Comprehension) Scale was used to assess students' reading skills. The internal consistency of the Total Reading Scale is .94 (Woodcock, 1998). The pre- and posttest WRMT-R/NU Total Reading scale scores of First Step to Success and criterion students and the associated pre- and posttest effect size comparisons between these students are presented in Table 3.1. A one-way ANCOVA was conducted on the WRMT-R/NU B Total Reading scale scores using the pretest mean as the covariate. The difference in the posttest mean

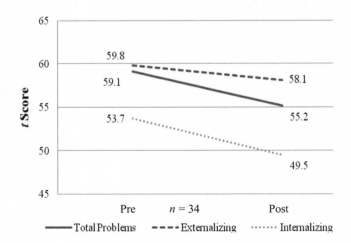

**FIGURE 3.2.** Mean pre- and posttest Child Behavior Checklist scores of students receiving First Step to Success.

scores of the First Step to Success and criterion students, $F(1,67) = 0.24$, $p = 0.625$, was not statistically significant. Inspection of Table 3.1 reveals that the pre- and posttest mean scores of both groups of students did not depart substantially from the standardized mean score (standardized mean score = 100; SD = 15). The effect sizes for the pre- and posttest comparisons between the First Step to Success and criterion students were –0.24 and –0.21, respectively.

## Tertiary Prevention Outcomes

As with the secondary prevention program, the SSRS and CBCL were used to assess the behavioral adjustment of students. The WRMT-R was used to assess students' reading skills. The outcomes are reported below.

### Behavioral Adjustment

The mean pre- and posttest CBCL Total Problems, Externalizing, and Internalizing scores of students are presented in Figure 3.3. These data reveal that all of the pretest and posttest scores of students departed substantially from the borderline criteria (60 to 63). Further, the pretest CBCL Total Problems ($x = 69.5$, SD = 8.94) and Externalizing ($x = 74.1$, SD = 6.74) scores exceeded the clinical criteria ($\geq 64$). Students showed large concurrent decreases (mean CBCL pre-post change scores) in their levels of total problem ($x = -11.0$, SD = 8.43) and externalizing ($x = -11.0$,

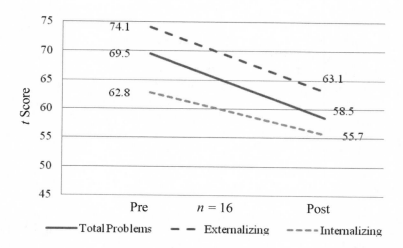

FIGURE 3.3. Mean pre- and posttest Child Behavior Checklist scores of students receiving multisystemic therapy.

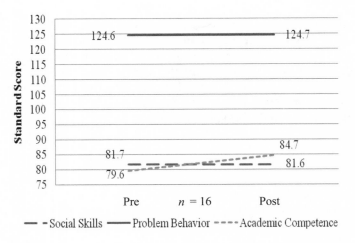

**FIGURE 3.4.** Mean pre- and posttest Social Skills Rating Scale scores of students receiving MultiSystemic Therapy.

$SD = 7.76$) following the intervention periods. Students evidenced moderate decreases in their levels of internalizing ($x = -7.1$, $SD = 9.64$) behavior following the intervention period. Inspection of Figure 3.3 reveals that the posttest CBCL Externalizing and Internalizing scores of students were below the established CBCL borderline criteria ($< 60$). Further, the posttest CBCL Externalizing scores of students fell within the borderline range (60 to 63).

The mean pre- and posttest SSRS Social Skills, Problem Behavior, and Academic Competence scores of MST students are presented in Figure 3.4. Inspection of Figure 3.4 reveals that all of the pre- and posttest scores of students departed substantially from the standardized mean score ($M = 100$, $SD = 15$). Students showed small increases (mean pre–post change scores) in their academic competence following the intervention period ($M = 5.1$, $SD = 5.34$). Students essentially evidenced no changes in their social skills and levels of problem behavior. Positive changes in parent ratings (CBCL) of the behavioral adjustment of students were inconsistent with those of teachers (SSRS).

### Reading Skills

Positive changes in teachers' ratings of student academic competence were consistent with changes in their pre- and posttest WRMT-R/NU Total Reading Scale scores. The pre- and posttest WRMT-R/NU Total Reading Scale scores of students were 92.0 ($SD = 18.17$) versus 100.33 ($SD = 7.5$). Students showed moderate increases (mean pre–post change scores) in their Total Reading Scale scores following the intervention period ($M$ = 8.3, $SD$ = 7.45).

## CONCLUSION

The prevalence of emotional and behavioral problems in school-age students have increased significantly over the past several years, challenging the patience and skills of families, schools, and communities. School-based, three-tiered behavior prevention programs have been developed to reduce the large number of students with emotional and behavioral problems that present within a school population. Three-tiered behavior programs consist of primary, secondary, and tertiary forms of prevention each directed at a specific type of student. Primary prevention programs are schoolwide and directed at typical students not yet at risk for problems. Secondary prevention programs are designed for students who do not respond to schoolwide efforts and are at risk for developing emotional or behavior problems. Tertiary prevention programs are provided students who show signs of life-course-persistent behavior patterns and very likely will require intensive, long-term programs, including special education services.

In this chapter we present a three-tiered behavior prevention approach that was based on a risk factor conceptual model. The individual programs were selected because they targeted one or more known risk factors, were appropriate for use in school settings, were manualized, and had documented empirical evidence of promoting appropriate behavior in students. The three programs were Behavior and Academic Support and Enhancement (BASE) (primary), First Step to Success (secondary), and MultiSystemic Therapy (MST) (tertiary). The programs were offered along a continuum based on the developmental level of the student, individual data on the student's functioning and the needs and desires of the family.

The three-tiered behavior prevention model was implemented in seven elementary schools in a mid-sized city in the Midwest. The implementation procedures and data from one of the schools were presented as a case study in this chapter. The Roosevelt Elementary School findings are partially supportive of the model. For the primary prevention tier (BASE) the students in the school increased their reading scores on the MAT from a mean NCE score of 53.9 to 59.9. However, about the time that BASE was implemented a new primary reading program was adopted for use in the school and the independent effects of BASE and the reading program could not be determined. For the students who received the secondary prevention program the effects on behavior were quite positive. First Step students evidenced dramatic improvements on the SSRS when compared to a criterion sample of students (see Table 3.1) and were rated by their parents as improved on the CBCL (see Figure 3.2). For the students who received the tertiary prevention program, the results were less clear. Specifically, parents of the students who received MST services rated their students as significantly improved, whereas the teachers of these students recorded no changes in school functioning (see Figures 3.3 and 3.4).

Throughout the implementation of the three-tiered program information on its use and outcomes were shared among the leadership team, teachers, related staff, and support staff. Regular meetings were held with staff where implementation information was solicited. Feedback was received and shared by all participants and strengths, and limitations of the model were identified. Indeed, much was learned in the implementation of the three-tiered model in Roosevelt Elementary School. Although we did not conduct a formal qualitative analysis of program implementation, based on experience and feedback from staff we learned four lessons. First, before such programs are implemented in schools the principal, leadership team, teachers, and related staff need to completely understand and fully commit to the model. Second, the leadership team needs to design and monitor a staff development plan that includes initial scaling activities for year 1 and maintenance activities for subsequent years to reinforce previously implemented strategies and to introduce new staff to the overall program. Third, in the secondary prevention program used in our model, paraprofessionals were the major staff that implemented the program with parents and teachers. The use of paraprofessionals required a significant of effort by project staff in (1) training and supervision of the paraprofessionals and (2) developing communication strategies so paraprofessionals, parents, and teachers could share important information on First Step students. Finally, the lack of improved functioning of school behavior for the tertiary students indicates that the change agents (i.e., therapists) for these students need to work closer with school staff in planning and implementing behavior change plans.

## REFERENCES

Achenbach, T. M. (1991). *Manual for the Child Behavior Checklist/4–18 and 1991 profile*. Burlington: University of Vermont, Department of Psychiatry.

American Psychiatric Association. (1994). *Diagnostic and statistical manual of mental disorders* (4th ed.) Washington, DC: Author.

Baum, D. D., Duffelmeyer, F. A., & Geelan, M. (1988). Resource teacher perceptions of the prevalence of social dysfunction among students with learning disabilities. *Journal of Learning Disabilities, 21*, 380–381.

Bourdin, C. M., Henggeler, S. W., Blaske, D. M., & Stein, T. (1990). Multisystemic treatment of adolescent sexual offenders. *International Journal of Offender Therapy and Comparative Criminology, 35,* 105–114.

Borduin, C. M., Mann, B. J., Cone, L. T., Henggeler, S. W., Fucci, B. R., Blaske, D. M., et al.. (1995). Multisystemic treatment of serious juvenile offenders: Long-term prevention of criminology and violence. *Journal of Consulting and Clinical Psychology, 63,* 569–578.

Brunk, M., Henggeler, S. W., & Whelan, J. P. (1987). A comparison of multisystem therapy and parent training in the brief treatment of child abuse and neglect. *Journal of Consulting and Clinical Psychology, 55,* 311–318.

Cicchetti, D., & Nurcombe, B. (Eds.). (1993). Toward a developmental perspective on conduct disorder [Special issue]. *Development and Psychopathology, 5*(1/2).

Department of Health and Human Services. (2000). *Surgeon general's report on children and mental health.* Washington, DC: Centers for Disease Control and Prevention.

Elliott, S., & Gresham, F. (1991). *Social skills intervention guide: Practical strategies for social skills training.* Circle Pines, MN: American Guidance Service.

Furlong, M. J., Morrison, G. M., & Dear, J. D. (1994). Addressing school violence as part of schools' educational mission. *Preventing School Failure, 38*(3), 10–17.

Golly, A. M., Stiller, B., & Walker, H. M. (1998). First Step To Success: Replication and social validation of an early intervention program. *Journal of Emotional and Behavioral Disorders, 4,* 243–249.

Greenburg M. (2000). *Preventing mental disorders in school-age children: A review of the effectiveness of prevention programs.* Available at www.psu/edu/dept/prevention.

Hawkins, J. D., VonCleve, E., & Catalano, R. F., Jr. (1991). Reducing early childhood aggression: Results of a primary prevention program. *Journal of the American Academy of Child and Adolescent Psychiatry, 30,* 208–217.

Henggeler, S. W., Borduin, C. M., Melton, G. B., Mann, B. J., Smith, L., Hall, J. A., et al. (1991). Effects of multisystemic therapy on drug use and abuse in serious juvenile offenders: A progress report from two outcome studies. *Family Dynamics of Addiction Quarterly, 1,* 40–51.

Henggeler, S. W., Melton, G. B., & Smith, L. A. (1992). Family preservation using multisystemic therapy: An effective alternative to incarcerating serious juvenile offenders. *Journal of Consulting and Clinical Psychology, 60,* 953–961.

Henggeler, S. W., Pickrel, S. G., & Borduin, M. J. (1999). Multisystemic treatment of substance abusing and dependent delinquents: Outcomes, treatment fidelity, and transportability. *Mental Health Services Research, 1,* 171–184.

Henggeler, S. W., Rodick, J. D., Borduin, C. M., Hanson, C. L., Watson, S. M., & Urey, J. R. (1986). Multisystemic treatment of juvenile offenders: Effects on adolescent behavior and family interactions. *Developmental Psychology, 22,* 132–141.

Henggeler, S. W., Schoenwald, S. K., Borduin, C. M., Rowland, M. D., & Cunningham, P. B. (1998). *Multisystemic treatment of antisocial behavior in children and adolescents.* New York: Guilford Press.

Hops, H., & Walker, H. M. (1988). *CLASS: Contingencies for Learning Academic and Social Skills.* Seattle, WA: Educational Achievement Systems.

Houghton Mifflin. (2003). *Houghton Mifflin reading: The nations' choice.* Boston: Author.

Lowry, R., Sleet, D., Duncan, C., Powell, K., & Kolbe, L. (1995). Adolescents at risk for violence. *Educational Psychology Review, 7*(1), 7–39.

Lynam, D. (1996). Early identification of chronic offenders: Who is the fledgling psychopath? *Psychological Bulletin, 120,* 209–234.

Nelson, J. R. (1996). Designing schools to meet the needs of students who exhibit disruptive behavior. *Journal of Emotional and Behavioral Disorders, 4,* 147–161.

Nelson, J. R., Benner, G. J., Lane, K., & Smith, B. (2004). Academic skills of K–12 students with emotional and behavioral disorders. *Exceptional Children, 71,* 59–74.

Nelson, J. R., & Carr, B. A. (2000). *The Think Time Strategy for schools.* Denver, CO: Sopris West.

Nelson, J. R., Martella, R. C., & Marchand-Martella, N. E. (2002). Maximizing student learning: The effects of a comprehensive school-based program for preventing disruptive behaviors. *Journal of Emotional and Behavioral Disorders, 10,* 136–148.

Nelson, J. R., Martella, R., & Galand, B. (1998). The effects of teaching school expectations and establishing consistent consequences on formal office disciplinary actions. *Journal of Emotional and Behavioral Disorders, 6,* 153–161.

Patterson, G. R., Reid, J. B., & Dishon, T. J. (1992). *A social interactional approach: Antisocial boys.* Eugene, OR: Castalia.

Rose, L. C., & Gallup, A. M. (1998). The 30th annual Phi Delta Kappa/Gallup Poll of the public's attitudes toward the public schools. *Phi Delta Kappan, 80,* 41–56.

Sugai, G., Sprague, J. R., Horner, R. H., & Walker, H. M. (2000). Preventing school violence: The use of office discipline referrals to assess and monitor school wide discipline intervention. *Journal of Emotional and Behavioral Disorders, 8,* 94–112.

Walker, H. M., Horner, R. H., Sugai, G., Bullis, M., Sprague, J. R., Bricker, D., et al. (1996). Integrated approaches to preventing antisocial behavior patterns among school-age children and youth. *Journal of Emotional and Behavioral Disorders, 4,* 193–256.

Walker, H. M., Kavanagh, K., Stiller, B., Golly, A., Severson, R. H., & Feil, E. G. (1998). First Step to Success: An early intervention approach for preventing school antisocial behavior. *Journal of Emotional and Behavioral Disorders, 6,* 66–80.

Walker, H., & Severson, H. (1990). *Systematic screening for behavior disorders (SSBD).* Longmont, CO: Sopris West.

Walker, H., Severson, H., & Feil, E. G. (1995). *Early Screening Project (ESP).* Longmont, CO: Sopris West.

Walker, H., Stiller, B., Golly, A., Kavanagh, K., Severson, H., & Feil, E. (1998). *First Step to Success: Helping young children overcome antisocial behavior* (An early intervention program for grades K–3). Longmont, CO: Sopris West.

Walker, H. M., Stiller, B., Severson, H. H., Feil, E. G., & Golly, A. (1998). First Step to Success: Intervening at the point of school entry to prevent antisocial behavior patterns. *Psychology in the Schools, 35*(3), 259–269.

Woodcock, R. W. (1998). *Woodcock Reading Mastery Tests–Revised.* Circle Pines, MN: AGS.

# CHAPTER 4

# Comprehensive Implementation of the Three-Tiered Prevention Approach to Schoolwide Behavioral Support

## An Oregon Case Study

TARY J. TOBIN, CELESTE ROSSETTO DICKEY, ROBERT H. HORNER, *and* GEORGE SUGAI

In this chapter we describe Barkley Elementary School's (a pseudonym) implementation of schoolwide positive behavior support (SWPBS) following the content and professional development procedures described in the *Positive Behavior Support Team Training Manual* (Sugai, Horner, Lewis-Palmer, & Todd, 2005). The purposes of this chapter are to provide a description of how SWPBS practices were implemented at Barkley during the four academic years between 2002 and 2006 and the impact of these procedures on student outcomes. SWPBS is a three-tiered prevention approach, with integrated, but separate, practices for *universal* (all students) prevention, *targeted* (at-risk students) prevention, and *intensive individual* prevention interventions (Horner, Sugai, Todd, & Lewis-Palmer, 1999–2000, 2005; Sugai & Horner, 2002). Most schools adopting this approach focus initially on implementation of the universal systems, with secondary and tertiary prevention systems added later (see Crone & Horner, 2003; Crone, Horner, & Hawken, 2004; Tobin, Lewis-Palmer, & Sugai, 2002; Tobin & Sugai, 2005; Todd, Horner, & Sugai, 1999).

Barkley was one of seven Oregon schools participating in an evaluation of SWPBS as a means of primary, secondary, and tertiary prevention of behavior problems in early elementary school. In each of these seven schools we identified a sample of students in kindergarten and grade 1 who were at risk for behavior disorders as part of the evaluation of the model's impact on student outcomes. We did this each year for each new kindergarten grade cohort, creating a sequential cohort design for the evaluation. Students in these at risk cohorts were known as the "tracking sample" (TS) because their progress was tracked for several years and the evaluation was known as the TS study. The kindergarten students who entered the study in the first year, if they remained enrolled, were tracked for 4 years. Those who entered in the second year were tracked for 3 years, and so on, as illustrated in Figure 4.1.

Two related larger research projects provided the foundation for the Oregon Behavior TS study. First, it was part of a national study of six centers implementing schoolwide behavior and/or reading interventions using a set of common measures (Coordination, Consultation, and Evaluation Center, 2004) to answer common questions (Coordination, Consultation, and Evaluation Center, 2002) about schoolwide interventions using a three-tiered approach. Second, one of those centers was the Research and Demonstration Center on School-Wide Behavior Support (Sugai & Horner, 2001b), which started with a design that included 30 sustaining schools with well-established primary prevention SWBPS interventions in place and 60 schools new to SWPBS that were randomly assigned either an initial treatment group to receive training the first year

| Grade | Year 1 2002–2003 | Year 2 2003–2004 | Year 3 2004–2005 | Year 4 2005–2006 |
|---|---|---|---|---|
| K | Year 1 K cohort | Year 2 K cohort | | |
| 1st | Year 1 1st cohort | Year 1 K cohort | Year 2 K cohort | |
| 2nd | | Year 1 1st cohort | Year 1 K cohort | Year 2 K cohort |
| 3rd | | | Year 1 1st cohort | Year 1 K cohort |

**FIGURE 4.1.** Sequential cohort design.

or to a delayed start control group that received training the second year (Horner et al., 2006). Barkley was one of the 30 sustaining schools.

Sustaining schools had demonstrated effective and sustained implementation of the primary prevention component of SWPBS and were in an excellent position to turn their attention to the development and implementation of systematic secondary and tertiary interventions for students who needed additional support. The seven sustaining schools selected for the TS study were in districts that had previously worked with the University of Oregon in providing opportunities for staff development, consultation, and inservice training related to the types of secondary and tertiary behavioral interventions used in SWPBS as a three-tiered approach (e.g., Crone & Horner, 2003; Crone, et al., 2004; Tobin et al., 2002; Todd et al., 1999).

This case study highlights Barkley, a school working to maintain, expand, and improve its implementation of SWPBS several years after first being introduced to this approach. Implementation tends to occur in four phases (See Figure 4.2) (Sugai & Horner, 2007). First, schools identify a need and agree to adopt SWPBS and assess outcomes. During this phase, training often involves working with outside experts. During the second phase, schools become more independent and local demonstrations of implementation with fidelity occur. Schools have reached the third phase when capacity is sustained, elaborated, and replicated. This can be a challenge over time, especially if a school experiences high staff turnover. The fourth phase involves scaling up to adopt systems that support continuous regeneration. At Barkley, the three tiers of SWPBS (primary, secondary, and tertiary prevention interventions) were not all

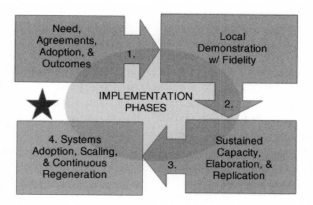

**FIGURE 4.2.** Four phases of implementation of SWPBS. From Sugai and Horner (2007).

fully implemented at once. Tier 1, primary prevention (universal, school-wide strategies) had been in place longer, and with greater fidelity of implementation, than Tiers 2 and 3 (SWPBS strategies for targeted and intensive individual interventions). Barkley was in the process of moving from the second to the third implementation phase. This case study illustrates effectiveness, in the sense of "Does it work in the real world?" rather than efficacy, in the sense of "Can this treatment work under ideal conditions?" (Winstein & Lewthwaite, 2004, p. 6).

## SCHOOL SELECTION

Barkley was selected for the case study out of the seven schools in the area participating in the TS study because it (1) demonstrated high-quality implementation and use of the model, (2) was typical of schools served by the Oregon Behavior Center, and (3) produced results indicating that prevention goals were being met with local resources. When the TS study started, Barkley had been using SWPBS and was experienced in accurate implementation of the primary prevention level, as measured by the School-wide Evaluation Tool (SET; Sugai, Lewis-Palmer, Horner, & Todd, 2001). It had previously received training in SWPBS from university researchers and was in a district that provided continuing support for SWPBS at the primary prevention level and opportunities for staff development relevant to secondary and tertiary prevention levels of SWPBS. However, responsibility for implementing the full three-tiered model rested with the school, not with the district or the university that provided the original training in SWPBS.

## SCHOOL DESCRIPTION

Barkley Elementary School is located in what the National Center for Education Statistics (NCES) would classify as "midsize Central City" in the northwestern part of the United States. It is a Title I school with an enrollment ranging from 325 to 345 students, in grades K–5, with non-white ethnicity/racial groups represented in the student body at about 12%. Latino students comprised the largest single minority group. About 65 to 70% of the students qualified for either free or reduced lunch.

The teacher-to-student ratio at this school was usually about 1 to 19 or 20. The average class size at Barkley for K–3 was approximately 25 students. Most of the teachers were certified for general education although a few also are certified for special education. Most had a bachelor's degree and a few also have a master's degree. The average number of years of (1) teaching experience was 17 or 18 (*SD* = 23); (2) teaching at this school was 7 (*SD* = 8); and at the current grade level, also was 7 (*SD* = 8). The primary language of most of the teachers was English, and most did not have a second language.

## SCHOOL THREE-TIERED RISK ASSESSMENT

In this section, we first describe the types of risk assessments that Barkley normally used and then describe additional risk assessment procedures introduced for the evaluation based on outcomes for TS students.

### Behavioral Assessments Barkley Normally Used

All students in the school received the primary prevention approach, the universal intervention part of SWPBS. Assessment of risk related to a students' needs for secondary- or tertiary-level behavior support interventions was completed by teachers as a part of their day-to-day instructional efforts, using a Response-to-Intervention (RTI) logic (Sugai & Horner, 2007), although not formalized. That is, if a teacher observed that a student appeared to be unresponsive or inadequately responsive, in the teacher's professional judgment, to universal behavioral support at the schoolwide and classroom level, then the teacher could initiate efforts to provide additional support. If needed, the school and/or the district would provide that teacher with resources and assistance, including teacher assistance team (TAT) meetings and/or school and district-level behavior support team meetings, and/or assistance from a school counselor or a district behavior specialist. In addition, like other elementary schools interested in using information on disruptive behavior even among young children to inform prevention interventions (Rusby, Taylor, & Foster, 2007), the school PBS team used data from the School-Wide Information System (SWIS; *http://www.swis.org*) on a regular basis, at least once a month, to monitor office disciplinary referrals. Barkley's PBS Team used school office discipline referral data to make decisions about adjusting action plans. In addition to the overall rate, reviews typically included specific information relevant to ongoing efforts to improve the school climate, such as when and where behavioral infractions were occurring, types of behavior problem, and frequency and duration of out-of-school suspensions (Horner & Sugai, 2001). Table 4.1 is an example of the type of specific information studied, using SWIS data, during the 2003–2004 school year.

**TABLE 4.1. Percent of Office Discipline Referrals
by Grade Level**

| Grade level | Percent of school's office disciplinary referrals |
|---|---|
| Kindergarteners | 3 |
| First graders | 8 |
| Second graders | 21 |
| Third graders | 26 |
| Fourth graders | 19 |
| Fifth graders | 23 |

## Risk Assessments to Identify Students for the Evaluation

For the evaluation using TS students, only risks for behavior disorders were assessed. The first step was to identify students qualified to be in the TS and to participate in the evaluation process. Modified versions of the Systematic Screening for Behavior Disorders (SSBD; Walker & Severson, 1990), for students in first grade, and the Early Screening Project (ESP, Walker, Severson, & Feil, 1995), for students in kindergarten, were used to identify students at risk for behavior disorders. The modifications were that only the Adaptive and Maladaptive Scales from the SSBD and ESP were used (described in more detail below), rather than all the scales and assessment procedures these tools provide. The goal was to identify students in the top 30th percentile on the Maladaptive Scale and/or the bottom 30th percentile on the Adaptive Scale, which would indicate that these students were "at risk" for internalizing or externalizing behavior problems, yet would be a broad enough range that some at-risk students might not need secondary- or tertiary-level interventions (Coordination, Consultation, and Evaluation Center, 2002). Percentile rank was based on normative benchmarks by grade level and gender. The scales are made up of questions that teachers answer about the following types of behaviors:

*Adaptive behaviors*

- Follows established classroom routines.
- Gains other children's attention in an appropriate manner.
- Expresses anger appropriately (without becoming violent or destructive)
- Gains teacher attention in appropriate ways.
- Participates well in group activities.
- Follows teacher's directions.
- Initiates positive social contact with peers.

*Maladaptive behaviors*

- Refuses to participate in games or activities with other children.
- Behaves inappropriately in class when directed (e.g., shouts, defies teacher).
- Responds inappropriately when other children try to interact socially.
- Tests or challenges teacher's limits/rules.
- Creates disturbance during class activities (noisy, bothers other children, etc.).
- Is very demanding of teacher attention.
- Pouts or sulks.
- Needs redirection, removal, or threat of punishment before he or she will stop an inappropriate behavior.
- Is overly affectionate with others (touching, hugging, kissing, hanging on, etc.).

The SSBD/ESP screening assessments were used to decide if students were eligible to participate in the evaluation as part of the TS, if parental permission was given, but they were not used to determine placement in primary, secondary, or tertiary prevention-level interventions. In fact, the evaluation was designed, in part, to show the extent to which students identified as at risk for behavior disorders would (1) need, (2) receive, and (3) benefit from, secondary and/or tertiary interventions. To assess benefit over time, a measure of particular interest, given that the TS students were identified as at risk in part on the basis of their percentile rank on the SSBD Maladaptive scale, was a very similar scale, the Problem Behavior Scale, on the Social Skills Rating Scale (SSRS; Gresham & Elliott, 1990). Grade-based percentile ranks on the Problem Behavior Scale of the SSRS were monitored every year for TS students. The SSRS Problem Behavior Scale includes internalizing, externalizing, and hyperactive problem behaviors, and teachers rank behaviors for this scale that are very similar to behavior listed on the Maladaptive Scale on the SSBD (described above).

## CORE PROCEDURES:
## COMMON AND CRITICAL THREE-TIERED FEATURES

### Early, Frequent Screening and Progress Monitoring with Decision Making

Barkley used the modified versions of the SSBD/ESP (described above) when it participated in the evaluation using outcomes for students. Table

4.2 presents the number of at-risk TS students at Barkley each year by cohort. Students who left the study did so because they moved away. The students who remained in the study had similar behavioral and demographic characteristics to the students who moved away. The use of office disciplinary referral data from SWIS and the use of teacher observations of behavior and progress in daily activities continued to be an important part of early, frequent, and ongoing screening, progress monitoring, and decision making for the school.

## Primary Prevention: Schoolwide Systems of Support

Barkley uses the schoolwide (primary prevention) systems of support that constitute PBS as described in the *Positive Behavior Support Team Training Manual* (Sugai et al., 2005). The common and critical features of SWPBS, are listed below, as described in *School Climate and Discipline: Going to Scale* (Sugai & Horner, 2001c):

• All students and staff members are taught the schoolwide expectations and received regular and frequent opportunities to practice them and to be positively acknowledged when they use them. Barkley's schoolwide expectations are "Be Safe, Be Responsible, Be Respectful, Be Kind." Underneath the umbrella of the schoolwide expectations, the school also emphasizes the Pillars of Character (Josephson, 2002).

• A majority (> 80%) of students, staff, and families can state the schoolwide positive expectations and give a specific behavioral example for each. Students, staff, and families can identify behavioral examples of the schoolwide expectations in the various school settings (e.g., classroom, hallway, playground).

• Positive schoolwide behavioral expectations are defined, taught, and encouraged for all students using a range of positive and negative examples. Barkley focuses on teaching the expectations at the beginning of the year and prior to and after breaks. The PBS team also provides booster lessons when data demonstrates the need.

**TABLE 4.2. Number of Students in the Tracking Sample Cohorts at Barkley**

|                        | 2002–2003 | 2003–2004 | 2004–2005 | 2005–2006 |
| ---------------------- | --------- | --------- | --------- | --------- |
| Year 1—kindergarten    | 5         | 5         | 3         | 0         |
| Year 1—first grade     | 8         | 8         | 8         | 4         |
| Year 2—kindergarten    | 0         | 12        | 12        | 9         |
| Total                  | 13        | 25        | 23        | 13        |

- Most contacts between teachers and students are prosocial (positive and preventive) rather than corrective and punishing (i.e., 5–8 positives for every negative interaction). Barkley uses "Pillars of Character" awards to acknowledge students who demonstrate positive behaviors.
- A full continuum of PBS is available for all students at the school and district levels.
- Behaviorally competent personnel are readily available.
- A function-based approach serves as the foundation for addressing problem behaviors.
- All staff members actively participate in the implementation of SWPBS.
- Accurate and consistent implementation of PBS practices by all staff members is emphasized.
- The school administrator is an active participant and leader in the PBS effort.
- A schoolwide leadership team guides the systemic adoption and sustained use of research-validated practices.
- School data (particularly data related to behavioral expectations) are reviewed at least monthly to guide decision making and planning.

### Classwide Systems

At Barkley the classwide system of support is an extension of the schoolwide system of support. For example, classroom teachers develop positive and negative examples of how the schoolwide rules and expectations apply in their classroom and use these examples to teach the students, often with role-plays. The secondary level used at Barkley is not a "classwide" system. It is part of the Individual Student System of support, which includes secondary and tertiary interventions.

## Primary Plus Secondary and Tertiary Prevention: Individual Student Systems of Support

Although some PBS schools use other secondary interventions, such as First Step to Success (Walker et al., 1997), Barkley used check-in/check-out (CICO) for secondary prevention. Also known as the Behavior Education Program (Crone et al., 2004), CICO is a type of secondary prevention or targeted behavioral support that is widely used in various forms with students whose behavior problems do not respond sufficiently to primary prevention in the form of universal SWPBS. Key features of the CICO intervention are (1) being readily available, (2) increasing monitoring and adult contact, (3) providing contingent and frequent feed-

back, and (4) increasing coordination between school and home support. After a brief, initial meeting of a behavior support team or a
teachers' assistance team, to clarify the nature of the behavioral issues
for this student, students participating in CICO typically follow a rou-
tine, described by Crone et al. (2004) as follows:

• Each morning the student will check-in with an adult at school
(e.g., the classroom teacher, a counselor, educational assistant). The
check-in will determine if the student has materials needed for class and
if the student is physically prepared to attend classes. The student is
given a form (e.g., point sheet or card) to use throughout the day that
lists the student's behavioral goals and a matrix showing classes or time
periods. The check-in usually takes less than 5 minutes and includes verbal prompts and encouragement. At Barkley, the counselor coordinates
the CICO program. Family communication is an important component
of Barkley's CICO intervention.

• A key feature of CICO is that the teachers continually monitor
the behavior of the student throughout the day. Each class period (or at
other designated times), the student brings the form to the teacher, who
marks a rating of how well the student met his or her behavioral goals.
In some cases, the student also self-monitors.

• At the end of the school day, the student takes the form back to
the person who conducted the morning check-in, for the afternoon
check-out, which consists of a quick review of the form, verbal feedback,
and, in some cases, small reinforcers if certain goals have been met (e.g.,
80% of possible points on the teachers' ratings). The afternoon check-
out typically takes fewer than 5 minutes.

• Students take the form (sometimes called a daily behavior report
card) home to show their parents, who will sign it. It will be returned to
school the next day.

• The school staff member who is monitoring the child maintains a
record of progress, which can be charted and used to make decisions
about maintaining, fading, or strengthening the intervention over time.

At the tertiary level, Barkley used function-based support, which starts
with a functional behavioral assessment (FBA) that is used to develop intensive, individualized, positive behavior interventions that address the
identified function of the behavior (Crone, Hawken, & Bergstrom,
2007; Crone & Horner, 2003; Sugai, Horner, & Lewis-Palmer, 2001;
Sugai et al., 2000). In some cases, teachers include elements of CICO
within a multicomponent intervention based on an FBA (e.g., Condon &
Tobin, 2001). FBAs vary according to individual needs. Elements of FBA
may include student, teacher, and/or parent interviews; rating scales; di-

rect observations; and archival reviews. At Barkley, the FBA process started with the Functional Assessment Checklist–Teachers and Staff (FACTS; March et al., 2000, McIntosh et al., 2008), typically followed by direct observations of behavioral sequences in settings where the problem behavior was most and least likely to occur, and a review of school records, including an Individual Student Report from SWIS providing information about the student's office discipline referrals, if any.

To link the FBA to a comprehensive Behavior Intervention Program (Crone & Horner, 2003; Repp & Horner, 1999), the concept of "competing behaviors" (Horner & Billingsley, 1988) and the Competing Behavior Pathway diagram (Crone & Horner, 2003; O'Neill et al., 1997) were used. The Competing Behavior Pathway diagram summarizes the sequences of events surrounding (1) desired behaviors, (2) problem behaviors, and (3) appropriate alternative behaviors. Function-based support begins with a problem-solving process to find an alternative behavior that will lead to the type of positive reinforcement powerful enough to maintain the appropriate behavior for this student. Concurrently, plans are made to minimize or eliminate reinforcement that has been (unintentionally) following problem behaviors. Steps toward generalization and maintenance include planning for ways to reinforce appropriate behavior that will be available in the natural environment when the individualized intervention is faded. The desired appropriate behavior, the behavior that is normally expected in the situation is the long-term goal. The alternative appropriate behavior is a short-term goal. There may be a series of short-term goals as behavior improves and the support can gradually be faded.

## Implementation Approach

### Leadership Team

Barkley began implementing schoolwide positive behavior support (SWPBS) in 1997. Since 2000, the faculty and staff have maintained a representative PBS leadership team, which includes the administrator, teacher representation, specialists (counselor, speech therapist), educational assistants, and the PBS district coordinator. The team meets monthly and monitors the goals of their annual action plan.

### Commitment to Support Systems Defined

Barkley's current administrator and PBS Team are committed to the three-tiered prevention model for SWPBS and to maintaining its essential support systems. Although this school has had three administrators since 1999, it has steadfastly implemented SWPBS. This commitment can be defined as following through, over the years, on providing organized ways for school staff to establish working relationships and to obtain needed information and resources. This commitment is expressed most clearly in the PBS leadership team meetings and in meetings of related committees with specific responsibilities. In addition to the school's PBS leadership team, the following subgroups of the PBS team are responsible for individual student support:

*Teacher Assistance Team.* The Teacher Assistance Team (TAT) includes the counselor, special education teacher, speech therapist, administrator, and teachers of students referred to TAT. Teachers refer students to TAT for behavioral and academic support when classroom interventions have not been effective. The TAT team works with the classroom teacher to develop a plan for behavioral and academic improvement.

*Student Study Team.* The student study team (SST) meets to determine if students may be eligible for special education services, or if a student already has an individualized education plan (IEP) and needs revisions for increased student academic success.

*District Individual Student Systems Cadre.* Since 2002, the district has trained staff on the elements of functional behavior assessment and function-based behavior intervention plans using a district-level team, the Individual Student Systems Cadre, to work in combination with school-level individual student behavior support teams. Barkley has an individual student behavior support team that includes members who have behavioral expertise and that coordinates classroom, building level, and district level support for individual students who need more support than can be provided by universal interventions. The individual student behavior support team meets monthly to determine individual student progress, and to ascertain whether students need more support or revisions to their individual plans. Students who are monitored by this team include students in CICO, students with more than three office disciplinary referrals, students with behavioral goals in their IEP, students diagnosed with Autism Spectrum Disorder, and students with function-based Behavior Intervention Plans. If students are not making adequate monthly progress, the team works with the classroom teacher to revise the student's plan, implement further behavioral supports, and to ensure the appropriate placement of students. Members of the individual student support team also attend monthly meetings of the District Individual Student Systems Cadre where they have opportunities to share with and learn from colleagues from other schools and district level personnel.

*Action Plans, Monitoring, Evaluating, and Adjusting*

Barkley's PBS team developed, monitored, evaluated, and adjusted, as needed, an annual action plan based on data collected through the School-wide Evaluative Tool (SET), the PBS Self-Assessment Survey, Team Implementation Checklist (TIC), and student data (office disciplinary referrals, attendance, and academics). Table 4.3 indicates action plans and monitoring, evaluation, and adjustments to action plans at Barkley over the past few years.

*Deviations from Core Procedures or Innovations*

Barkley, while putting its own stamp on SWPBS, did not deviate radically from core procedures or introduce unusual innovations. Barkley included character education under the umbrella of PBS, which gave teaching behavioral expectations and providing incentives a distinctive flavor that might be slightly different from the incentives or lessons used in another PBS school. However, use of SWPBS is not a rigidly imposed model where all schools are expected to look alike in all aspects. Rather, it is an approach that combines (1) essential principles and basic guidelines for data-based decision making and procedures for systematic organization, which do need to be followed well in every school seeking successful implementation, with (2) flexibility needed to accommodate differences from one school to another and changes in needs from one year to another within a school. That is, many details, such as the specific percentage of students receiving different levels of support, action plans, wording of mission statements and school rules or expectations, and types of incentives and training used are expected to vary to some extent from school to school and from year to year within a school, in response to local conditions. This combination of solid foundational guidelines with flexibility in response to varying needs enhances ownership, creativity, and responsibility at the school and district level.

## PROFESSIONAL DEVELOPMENT APPROACH

During this study, Barkley participated in professional development activities provided by the district, including PBS district team training (held 3 times each year), PBS facilitator training (3 times/year), supervision training, new staff member/ PBS team member trainings, reading and math trainings, and PBS team reports at each staff meeting. PBS team facilitators also are funded by the district to attend a state PBS conference. This school already had SWPBS in place to a large extent when the study

**TABLE 4.3. Barkley's Action Plans**

| School year | Action plan goals | Evaluation/measurement |
|---|---|---|
| 2002–2003 | 1. Continue to establish and strengthen SW PBS team<br>2. Develop effective targeted interventions for students.<br>3. Establish functional based assessment (FBA) team | 1. SET, Self Assessment Survey, TIC scores<br>2. List of targeted interventions and students participating. Review data for student improvement.<br>3. Establishment of FBA Team and training dates. |
| 2003–2004 | 1. Improve school emergency procedures<br>2. Focus on systematic targeted intervention (CICO)<br>3. Establish functional based assessment team. | 1. Review safety plans and develop timeline for drills/staff development.<br>2. Establish CICO and review student data.<br>3. Establishment of FBA Team and training dates. |
| 2004–2005 | 1. Provide staff supervision training to all staff members.<br>2. Create a "substitute packet" with information and resources for guest teachers/substitutes.<br>3. Offer alternative recess opportunities in the library (game room). | 1. Schedule supervision training and monitor data of students in non-classroom settings.<br>2. Develop substitute packet.<br>3. Alternative recess time activity implementation. |
| 2005–2006 | 1. Improve recess behavior.<br>2. Create a PBS brochure for parents and revise the PBS staff handbook.<br>3. Improve student dismissal procedures for safe home arrival. | 1. Schedule teaching of expected recess behaviors. Monitor data at recess. Reteach as necessary.<br>2. Creation of PBS brochure and staff handbook.<br>3. Reteach dismissal procedures, review in parent newsletter and survey parents pre–post. |

started so no "start-up" professional development took place during the study. Previously, the school had participated in "start-up" professional development at the primary tier level, involving approximately six or seven 1.5- to 2.0-day events for school-level leadership teams, with ongoing professional development events taking place during at least three or four events per year. Some (about six) of the teachers at this school had previously (before this study started) taken courses or participated in inservice training in functional behavioral assessment. Also, professional development at Barkley has involved additional training for school and district personnel to provide coaching and facilitation support, along the lines of the type of training described in the *Positive Behavior Support Team Training Manual* (Sugai et al., 2005; see *pbismanual. uoecs.org*) and the SWPBS blueprint (*pbis.org*).

## KEY OUTCOME DATA
### Number of Students Receiving Interventions in the Model

All students in the entire school received the primary intervention. The nature of SWPBS is that it is a universal intervention, therefore it is not possible to compare students receiving this intervention "in the model" with students receiving this intervention in "no model." However, for the TS students, we were able to determine the number and percentages who received secondary and tertiary interventions in the model. Slightly more than half of the at-risk sample received secondary interventions the first year. The second year, only about one-fourth of the at-risk sample received secondary interventions, but about 40% did in the following years. Tertiary interventions were used with less than 5% of the TS students. The primary prevention intervention was provided to all the TS students, with 14 (74%) of the TS students at Barkley receiving no additional intervention. Five TS students received the targeted intervention, CICO in addition to the universal intervention, and one student received a tertiary-level intervention, an intensive, individualized, behavioral intervention based on a functional behavioral assessment, also known as *function-based support*.

### Key Fidelity of Implementation Indicators (Measures)

The question involved in evaluating quality of implementation of SWPBS was, Did the school implement each of the three tiers to a criterion that would be expected to affect student behavior?

*Measure of Quality of Implementation of Primary Prevention*

The key measure for the primary prevention tier was the SET (Horner et al., 2004; Sugai et al., 2001). The SET measures key elements of the universal intervention, including the extent to which schoolwide behavioral expectations are (1) defined, (2) taught, and (3) positively reinforced; systems for (4) responding to violations and (5) monitoring and evaluating problem behavior patterns; (6) management, including leadership and use of data for making decisions and plans; and (7) district support. With the SET, to be ranked as "excellent" or "5" on primary prevention, using the Common Evidence Scale (CES) Transformation Ratings, the score for teaching expectations and the total score must be 85% or higher.

### Measure of Quality of Implementation of Secondary and Tertiary Prevention

The key measure for secondary and tertiary prevention tiers was the Individual Student Systems Evaluation Tool (I-SSET; Lewis-Palmer, Todd, Palmer, Sugai, & Sampson, 2005). The I-SSET is a paper-and-pencil research instrument that includes records of observations on-site visits; interviews with administrators, a person the administrator designates as the school's "behavior specialist" (typically a counselor or special education teacher with expertise in behavior disorders), and five randomly selected teachers or other school staff members; and examination of written documents related to behavior support (e.g., functional behavioral assessments, behavior intervention plans and results, request for assistance forms, minutes of team meetings). It yields three scores: (1) Foundations (commitment to behavioral support for all students, team-based planning, student identification, and monitoring and evaluating); (2) Targeted Interventions (connection to foundations, implementation and monitoring of targeted interventions) and (3) Intensive Individualized Interventions (functional behavioral assessments and function-based support). For the tracking sample study, for a school to achieve a CES rating of "excellent" for secondary prevention, I-SSET scores of 85 or higher on the Foundations and Targeted Interventions scales were necessary. For a CES rating of "excellent" on tertiary prevention, I-SSET scores of 85 or higher on the Foundations and Intensive Individualized Interventions scales were necessary.

### Other Measures of Quality of Implementation of SWPBS

Other measures of quality of implementation of SWPBS as a three-tiered prevention approach included the frequency of use and results of recommended internal, formative evaluation tools, including (1) the Staff Self-Assessment PBS Survey (www.pbssurveys.org/pages/TeamChecklist. aspx), (2) the Team Implementation Checklist (TIC; Sugai, Horner, & Lewis-Palmer, 2001, see pbis.org/tools.htm), and (3) SWIS, (see www. swis.org/). SWIS facilitates formative evaluation and development of action plans based on data-based decisions (Sugai & Horner, 2001a; Irvin et al., 2006). The PBS Self-Assessment Survey was used to assess implementation status and need for improvement of four behavior support systems: (1) schoolwide discipline systems, (2) nonclassroom management systems (e.g., in cafeteria, hallway, on playground), (3) classroom management systems, and (4) systems for individual students engaging in chronic problem behaviors. The criteria for effective implementation is 50% or more on "in place" scores. The TIC was completed by the PBS team several times a year and is similar to the SET in terms of the features of interest, although the TIC includes other information also, such as information on the use of individualized function-based support. The criteria for effective implementation is 80% or more of possible points in each area.

## Key Behavior Outcome Indicators (Measures)

The questions involved in evaluating outcomes for the at-risk students included questions about the types of interventions they received and the outcomes of those interventions, their adaptive behaviors (social and academic skills) and their problem behaviors, and time spent in special education. Did the school's use of SWPBS as a three-tiered model result in some of the at-risk sample receiving secondary or tertiary behavior support interventions? Were the at-risk students able to reduce their problem behaviors and increase their social skills? How did they do academically? Given that 100% of the TS students were identified as above the 70th percentile on the Maladaptive Behavior Scale of the SSBD when they entered the study, what percentage will be above the 70th percentile on the Problem Behavior Scale of the SSRS throughout the study? What were the outcomes of secondary and tertiary interventions, as recorded by teachers? How much time did TS students spend in special education classes, and did that change during the evaluation? The measures used to study these questions are described below.

### SSRS Problem Behavior Scale

The percentile rank on the SSRS Problem Behavior Scale was of particular interest because the students were identified as eligible for the tracking sample study on the basis of percentile rank on similar problem behaviors on the Maladaptive Scale of the SSBD (discussed above). By using grade-based percentiles, we were able to control differences in the children's grade levels and to combine across-grade levels and across cohorts. We also used the standard score for traditional comparisons.

### Student Intervention Record and Other Student Outcome Records

The Student Intervention Record was a tool provided by the University of Wisconsin's Coordination, Consultation, and Evaluation Center (2003) that included, among other items, questions about the outcomes of secondary and tertiary interventions and recorded perceptions of the school staff members most closely involved with the interventions. For the TS study, other records of student experiences and outcomes were collected, including amount of time in special education classes.

## Key School Level Findings from Indicators

### Fidelity of Implementation Results

Although the TS study was concerned with K–3 students identified as at risk for behavior disorders, Barkley was a K–5 school, and measures of fidelity of implementation of SWPBS involve whole-school assessments of each of the three tiers and of overall use of recommended practices for SWPBS. This section answers the question, "Did Barkley implement each of the three tiers to a criterion that would be expected to affect student behavior?" As shown below, the answer was "Yes."

Evidence of fidelity of implementation at the primary tier was found in Barkley's SET scores over the past three years: (1) 2005–2006, Teaching = 100%, Total = 89%; (2) 2004–2005, Teaching = 90%, Total = 90%; and (3) 2003–2004, Teaching = 100%, Total = 96%. These scores exceed the CES criteria for excellence. Although initially Barkley's scores on the I-SSET for Targeted and Intensive Individual systems were relatively low, steady progress was shown on the I-SSET in the last 3 years, with scores that meet the CES criteria for excellence achieved in 2005–2006 (Table 4.4). During the time period when Barkley's Targeted and Intensive Individual systems were improving the most (from 2003–2004 to 2004–2005), a 41% reduction in office disciplinary referrals for the fighting and aggression at Barkley occurred. Barkley's PBS team systematically used the recommended internal, formative evaluation tools. Results for the Individual Student System from the Staff Self-Assessment PBS Survey over a period of 5 years are shown in Table 4.5. Recall that the criteria for this measure is that at least 50% of the staff report the system is "in place." Recent results from the TIC at Barkley are shown in Table 4.6. As described above, the criteria for this measure is 80% of possible points in each area.

**TABLE 4.4. Steady Progress on the Individual Student Systems Evaluation Tool**

|                     | 2003–2004 | 2004–2005 | 2005–2006 |
|---------------------|-----------|-----------|-----------|
| Foundation          | 89%       | 94%       | 100%      |
| Targeted            | 63%       | 81%       | 88%       |
| Intensive individual | 70%      | 86%       | 88%       |

**TABLE 4.5. Percentage of Staff Reporting the Individual System Is "In Place" or "Partially In Place"**

| School year | In place | Partially in place | Combined "in place" or "partially in place" |
|---|---|---|---|
| 2000–2001 | 39 | 37 | 76 |
| 2001–2002 | 42 | 48 | 90 |
| 2002–2003 | 66 | 27 | 93 |
| 2003–2004 | 77 | 20 | 97 |
| 2004–2005 | 70 | 25 | 95 |

## Key Behavior Outcomes

### Pre- to Postintervention Changes on the SSRS Scales

The most important evaluation questions related to behavioral outcomes for students were answered by pre- to postintervention changes as measured by SSRS scales. The at-risk students, in general, were able to reduce their problem behaviors and increase their social and academic skills. Although 100% of the TS students were identified as above the 70th percentile on the Maladaptive Behavior Scale of the SSBD when they entered the study, a much lower percentage of the TS students were above the 70th percentile on the Problem Behavior Scale of the SSRS at the end of the study. Across all cohorts, Barkley had 19 TS students with data that could be used in this pre- to post-intervention analysis of average changes over time on the grade-based Problem Behavior Percentile Ranking from the SSRS. Barkley's TS students' average grade-based percentile ranking on the Problem Behavior Scale the first year they were as-

**TABLE 4.6. Formative Evaluation at the School Level Using the Team Implementation Checklist**

| Feature | Team implementation checklist date and percentage of possible points | | |
|---|---|---|---|
| | Sept. 29, 2004 | Jan. 28, 2005 | May 2, 2005 |
| Commitment | 100 | 100 | 100 |
| Team | 100 | 100 | 100 |
| Self-assessment | 83 | 100 | 100 |
| Define expectations | 100 | 100 | 100 |
| Teach expectations | 100 | 100 | 100 |
| Rewards system | 50 | 100 | 100 |
| Violations system | 100 | 100 | 100 |
| Information system | 100 | 100 | 100 |
| Function-based support | 100 | 100 | 100 |

sessed on the SSRS was at the 86th percentile, well above the 70th percentile. When the Barkley TS students were assessed in their second year of participation, their average ranking was at the 59th grade-based percentile, well below the 70th percentile and a drop of 27 percentile points. The TS students also improved average standard scores on SSRS scales. Figure 4.3 shows average changes over time for the Barkley TS students, using standard scores, for all three scales: Social Skills, Problem Behavior, and Academic Competence. Social skills and academic competence increased and problem behavior decreased.

### Outcomes and Perceptions Reported on the Student Intervention Record

A general response to the question, "What were the outcomes of secondary and tertiary interventions, as recorded by teachers?" would be "acceptable although, for many, extra support will continue to be needed for some time." With the cohorts combined, Table 4.7 shows the percentages of TS students receiving each level of support (primary only vs. primary plus secondary or tertiary). For students receiving extra support, secondary or tertiary, results recorded on the Student Intervention Record (Coordination, Consultation, and Evaluation Center, 2003) were key indicators of student outcomes and of teachers' satisfaction and parent involvement. We examined the results from the Student Intervention Record for students who remained in the study and found the following patterns:

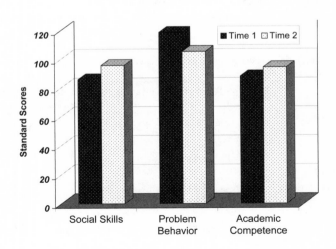

**FIGURE 4.3.** Standard scores on SSRS scales improve over time.

- When teachers were asked to estimate the degree to which the intervention was implemented as planned, all responded, "very high" or "high."
- When teachers were asked, "How familiar were you with this intervention?," all said "High" or "More than moderately familiar."
- When asked, "to what extent did you like the intervention?," one teacher marked "Neutral" and all the rest indicated "Acceptable" or "Very acceptable."
- When asked, "how likely are you to use this intervention with another student with similar problems?," Most teachers marked "Very likely" or "Likely" and two marked "Somewhat likely."
- In response to the request "Please indicate what role parents played in the implementation of the intervention," with a list of possible responses (e.g., not involved by design, home–school communication, homework support, home-based contingency program, generalization training opportunities, other), teachers reported that all of the parents were involved with home–school communication. A home-based contingency program was used by one family and generalization training opportunities were provided by two families.
- The most common response to the question "To what extent were parents involved in the implementation of the intervention?" was "Highly involved," and the next most common response was "Moderately involved." Only twice was "Not involved" marked. The involvement of the parents did not appear to be directly related to the student's outcome. For most of the students, the outcome was a recommendation that the extra support be continued the following year. Of the four students with the outcome of "Met exit criteria, no additional secondary or tertiary intervention anticipated," two had parents who were highly involved, one had a parent who was minimally involved, and one had a parent who was moderately involved.

**TABLE 4.7. Percentages of At-Risk Study Students by Level of Support at Barkley**

| Level of support | 2002–2003 | 2003–2004 | 2004–2005 | 2005–2006 |
|---|---|---|---|---|
| Primary only | 45.45 | 72.00 | 56.52 | 58.33 |
| Additional support: Primary plus secondary (+S) or tertiary (+T) | | | | |
| +S | 54.55 | 24.00 | 39.13 | 41.67 |
| +T | 0 | 4.00 | 4.35 | 0.00 |

The following patterns were found between the length of time that extra support was provided and outcomes in the last year for students who remained in the study:

1. For two students extra support was provided throughout the school year for 3 years; continued extra support was recommended for both.

2. For four students, extra support was provided for several years—not for the entire year every year but each year, for more months than the last year. For three of those students, continued extra support was recommended and for one, no further extra support was anticipated.

3. For two students, extra support for 6 months of the year was provided for 2 years, and continued extra support was recommended.

4. For three students extra support was provided all year for 1 year. For two of those students, no further extra support was anticipated and for one, continued extra support was recommended.

5. One student received extra support for only 2 months, and no further extra support was recommended.

Overall, the Student Intervention Record outcomes indicate that students in need of extra support received varying and individualized interventions that the teachers found to be acceptable and useful for making it possible for students at risk for, or identified with, behavior disorders to be educated in inclusive settings.

### Students with Disabilities and Time in Special Education

We wondered about how much time the TS students would spend in special education classes and if that would change during the evaluation. We found that eight TS students (35%) were spending some time in special education (SPED) settings by the end of the study. Half of these students also received extra behavior support in the form of secondary or tertiary prevention interventions. Time in SPED classes for the students who received only the primary prevention intervention of SWPBS averaged 40 minutes per day ($SD = 53$, range = 15 to 120) initially and increased over time to an average of 113 ($SD = 57$, range = 30 to 150). Time in SPED classes for students who received the primary prevention intervention of SWPBS plus extra support from secondary or tertiary interventions was zero minutes per day for all initially and increased over time to an average of 146 ($SD = 143$, range = 60 to 360). Type of disability did not seem to be associated with receiving extra support as the same three types of disabilities were identified for students with and without extra support: autistic, speech, and learning disabilities.

## Sustainability Events

Barkley benefited from "sustainability" events taking place at the district level that made it possible to continue to implement the universal PBS intervention well, long after the initial training, while devoting staff time and energy into expanding and refining the secondary-and tertiary-level interventions of the full three-tiered model of PBS. This approach began in District 1 in the late 80s with Project Prepare (Colvin, Kame'enui, & Sugai, 1993), a program that led to effective behavior support (Lewis & Sugai, 1999), and is now known as positive behavior support (Sugai & Horner, 2002). Two District 1 schools were involved in Project Prepare, and a few other schools joined in to participate in the EBS pilot project in the mid 90s. In 2000, District 1 received a Safe Schools Healthy Students (SSHS) grant through the U.S. Department of Education. The grant included PBS as an emphasis, and District 1 hired a full-time PBS coordinator to further PBS efforts. Beginning in 2000, all District 1 schools started implementing PBS and established PBS school teams. When the SSHS grant was completed, the district decided to continue funding PBS implementation. The components of PBS Implementation that have assisted the district to sustain PBS efforts include:

1. *Establishment of a district PBS Leadership Team.* The team includes the director of instruction, the director of special services, the multicultural coordinator, the district behavior specialist, a counselor representative, University of Oregon consultants and the PBS district coordinator. The team reviews PBS implementation data, organizes district training, coordinates the PBS budget and focuses on annual and long range action planning.

2. *PBS District Coordinator.* The district has invested in hiring a PBS coordinator to monitor, coordinate and provide training/resources to school PBS teams. From 2000–2005, the coordinator was a full-time position, Since 2005, the PBS coordinator position is a half-time position.

3. *Professional development.* The district provides three PBS team trainings during the school year and PBS facilitator training. The district also coordinates trainings with Lane County and the State of Oregon in PBS.

4. *School PBS team support and resources.* Each team is provided with $1000 per year to assist with action plan implementation. The PBS coordinator is also available to meet with teams, and assist schools with PBS initiatives.

5. *PBS newsletter.* The PBS coordinator publishes a district PBS newsletter three to four times per year. School reports, training events,

research updates and conference information are included in the news-letter.

6. *County and state involvement.* The district participates in PBS county and state efforts. The PBS coordinator serves on the state PBS network and encourages district staff involvement in an annual state level PBS conference.

## SUMMARY AND CONCLUSIONS

### Unique Benefits and Challenges of the SWPBS Approach as a Three-Tiered Prevention Model

Perhaps the most important benefit of the three-tiered model of SWPBS is efficiency in providing needed support to young students who are at risk for behavior disorders. When the universal schoolwide intervention is well implemented, most students, even young students considered "at risk" for behavior disorders, will respond to it and will not need extra support. For the nonresponders, targeted interventions, such as CICO, provide sufficient extra support for the student to benefit from the educational program, yet are practical for schools to implement. Efficiency is extremely important in most schools. Effective and efficient primary and secondary prevention interventions keep to a minimum the need for time and labor-intensive tertiary interventions. However, SWPBS enables staff to systematically plan in advance to have resources and procedures ready when tertiary-level interventions are needed. Providing compre-hensive, individualized, function-based support, which was the intensive tertiary-level intervention used, is difficult. It is necessary to change the behaviors of teachers and others who are involved in creating the exist-ing school environment that is providing the antecedents and conse-quences for the problem behaviors. Multicomponent interventions are needed that must be powerful initially and build skills for self-manage-ment over time that will make it possible to fade the initial intervention later. Staff may need training on how to develop, implement, monitor, evaluate, and adjust strategies over time. School district personnel and resources may be needed to supplement building-level efforts. This will not come as a surprise at a time of crisis if support systems, included training for district-level PBS coaches, were developed when the three-tiered approach to SWPBS was introduced to the school and have been maintained, as was the case at Barkley.

Other important benefits that can be expected from the SWPBS ap-proach to three-tiered prevention of problem behaviors include (1) in-creasing the school's capacity to educate students at risk for, or identified with, behavior disorders in general education settings; (2) increasing early identification when special education is needed; and (3) reducing reliance on aversive and exclusionary reactions to problem behaviors, a change in adult behavior that can be expected to improve children's health, well-being, and social adjustment (American Academy of Pediatrics, 2003; Horner et al., 1990; Sugai et al., 2000).

## Lessons, Challenges, and Solutions Illustrated by This School Exemplar

Barkley has had three different principals in the past 7 years. With changes of administration, concern always arises about sustaining programs. Barkley's commitment to PBS has been strengthened over the 7 years, and this is due to the staff's commitment and focus. With 70% of the students receiving free/reduced lunches, a growing homeless population, and a growing number of incarcerated parents, Barkley has focused on positive school environments, consistent behavioral expectations, and family communication. This has assisted Barkley in maintaining high behavioral and academic expectations in the midst of societal challenges. Barkley maintained quality implementation of SWPBS and improved support systems for secondary and tertiary prevention efforts. For most of the TS students who needed extra support, teachers chose to use the efficient, targeted, secondary prevention-level intervention, CICO. For students who required tertiary-level, intensive, function-based, individualized interventions, school and district-level support systems were in place for teacher and student. In this case, the challenge of bolstering school-level resources with district-level support to facilitate secondary- and tertiary-level prevention efforts was met.

## Future Outlook for This School

Barkley has a strong PBS team, a dedicated staff, and a supportive and effective principal. The CICO program is strong, and staff development continues as more staff are involved in function based assessment and behavior support planning. Barkley is committed to reviewing and maintaining systems that support schoolwide, targeted, and individual interventions and will continue to make progress in realizing its mission of assisting all students be successful academically and behaviorally.

## REFERENCES

American Academy of Pediatrics Committee on School Health. (2003). Out-of-school suspension and expulsion. *Pediatrics, 112,* 1206-1209. Retrieved November 17, 2006, from *www.pediatrics.aappublications.org/cgi/content/full/112/5/1206.*
Coordination, Consultation, & Evaluation Center. (2002). *Common research questions,*

*samples, measures, and data analysis: K–3 reading and behavior intervention projects.*
Madison: Wisconsin Center for Education Research.

Coordination, Consultation, & Evaluation Center. (2003). *Student Intervention Record.*
Madison: Wisconsin Center for Education Research.

Coordination, Consultation, & Evaluation Center. (2004). *Tracking sample data guidebook: 2005–2005.* Madison: Wisconsin Center for Education Research. Retrieved September 9, 2007, from *www.wcer.wisc.edu/cce/documents/TSDG04_05.pdf.*

Colvin, G., Kame'enui, E. J., & Sugai, G. (1993). School-wide and classroom management: Reconceptualizing the integration and management of students with behavior problems in general education. *Education and Treatment of Children, 16,* 361–381.

Condon, K. A., & Tubin, T. J. (2001). Using electronic and other new ways to help students improve their behavior. *Teaching Exceptional Children, 34,* 44–51.

Crone, D. A., Hawken, L. S., & Bergstrom, M. K. (2007). A demonstration of training, implementing, and using functional behavioral assessment in 10 elementary and middle school settings. *Journal of Positive Behavior Interventions, 9,* 15–29.

Crone, D. A., & Horner, R. H. (2003). *Building positive behavior support systems in schools: Functional behavioral assessment.* New York: Guilford Press.

Crone, D. A., Horner, R. H., & Hawken, L. S. (2004). *Responding to problem behavior in schools: The Behavior Education Program.* New York: Guilford Press.

Gresham, F. M., & Elliott, S. N. (1990). *Social skills rating system.* Circle Pines, MN: American Guidance Service.

Horner, R. H., & Billingsley, F. F. (1988). The effect of competing behavior in the generalization and maintenance of adaptive behavior in applied settings. In R. H. Horner, G. Dunlap, & R. L. Koegel (Eds.), *Generalization and maintenance: Life-style changes in applied settings* (pp. 197–220). Baltimore: Paul H. Brookes.

Horner, R. H., Dunlap, G., Koegel, R. L., Carr, E. G., Sailor, W., Anderson, J., et al. (1990). Toward a technology of "nonaversive" behavioral support. *Journal of the Association for Persons with Severe Handicaps, 15*(3), 125–132.

Horner, R. H., & Sugai, G. (2001). "Data" need not be a four-letter word: Using data to improve schoolwide discipline. *Beyond Behavior, 11*(1), 20–22.

Horner, R., Sugai, G., Smolkowski, K., Eber, L., Nakasato, J., Todd, A., et al. (2006, July). *Research brief: A randomized controlled trial assessing schoolwide positive behavior support.* Eugene: University of Oregon, College of Education, Educational and Community Supports.

Horner, R. H., Sugai, G., Todd, A., & Lewis-Palmer, T. (1999–2000). Elements of behavior support plans: A technical brief. *Exceptionality, 8*(3), 205–215.

Horner, R. H., Sugai, G., Todd, A. W., & Lewis-Palmer, T. (2005). School-wide positive behavior support. In L. Bambara & L. Kern (Eds.), *Individualized supports for students with problem behaviors: Designing positive behavior support plans* (pp. 359–390). New York: Guilford Press.

Horner, R. H., Todd, A. W., Lewis-Palmer, T., Irvin, L., Sugai, G., & Boland, J. (2004). The School-wide Evaluation Tool (SET): A research instrument for assessing schoolwide positive behavior support. *Journal of Positive Behavior Interventions, 6,* 3–12.

Irvin, L. K., Horner, R. H., Ingram, K., Todd, A. W., Sugai, G., Sampson, N. K., et al. (2006). Using office discipline referral data for decision making about student behavior in elementary and middle schools: An empirical evaluation of validity. *Journal of Positive Behavior Interventions, 8,* 10–23.

Josephson, M. (2002). *Making ethical decisions.* Los Angeles: Josephson Institute of Ethics. Retrieved November 19, 2006, from *www.charactercounts.org.*

Lewis, T. J., & Sugai, G. (1999). Effective behavior support: A systems approach to proactive schoolwide management. *Focus on Exceptional Children, 31,* 1–24.

Lewis-Palmer, T., Todd, A., Horner, R., Sugai, G., & Sampson, N. (2005). *Individual student system systems evaluation tool*. Eugene: University of Oregon, College of Education, Educational and Community Supports.

March, R. E., Horner, R. H., Lewis-Palmer, T., Brown, D., Crone, D., Todd, A. W., et al. (2000). *Functional Assessment Checklist—Teachers and Staff (FACTS)*. Eugene, OR: Author.

McIntosh, K., Borgmeier, C. J., Anderson, C. M., Horner, R. H., Rodriguez, B. J., & Tobin, T. J. (2008). Technical adequacy of the Functional Assessment Checklist—Teachers and Staff (FACTS) FBA interview measure. *Journal of Positive Behavior Interventions, 10*, 33–45.

O'Neill, R. E., Horner, R. H., Albin, R. W., Storey, K., Sprague, J. R., & Newton, M. (1997). *Functional assessment and program development for problem behavior: A practical handbook* (2nd ed.). Pacific Grove, CA: Brooks/Cole.

Repp, A. C., & Horner, R. H. (1999). *Functional analysis of problem behavior: From effective assessment to effective support*. Belmont, CA : Wadsworth.

Rusby, J. C., Taylor, T. K., & Foster, E. M. (2007). A descriptive study of school discipline referrals in first grade. *Psychology in the Schools, 44*, 333-350. Retrieved September 9, 2007, from *www.pubmedcentral.nih.gov/picrender.fcgi? artid=1828691&blobtype=pdf*.

Sugai, G., & Horner, R. H. (2001a). Features of effective behavior support at the district level. *Beyond Behavior, 11*(1), 16–19.

Sugai, G., & Horner, R. H. (2001b). *Research and demonstration center on schoolwide behavior support* [Funded grant proposal submitted to the Office of Special Education Programs, U.S. Department of Education, No. H324X01005]. Eugene: University of Oregon, College of Education, Educational and Community Supports.

Sugai, G., & Horner, R. (2001c, June 23). *School climate and discipline: Going to scale*. Paper presented at the National Summit on the Shared Implementation of IDEA, Washington, D.C.

Sugai, G., & Horner, R. (2002). The evolution of discipline practices: School-wide positive behavior supports. *Child and Family Behavior Therapy, 24*, 23–50.

Sugai, G., & Horner, R. (2007). *Response to intervention logic and positive behavior support* [PowerPoint Presentation]. Retrieved September 9, 2007, from *www.pbis.org/main.htm*.

Sugai, G., Horner, R. H., Dunlap, G., Hieneman, M., Nelson, C. M., Scott, T., et al. (2000). Applying positive behavior support and functional behavioral assessment in schools. *Journal of Positive Behavior Interventions, 2*(3), 131–143. Retrieved April 8, 2002, from *pbis.org*.

Sugai, G., Horner, R., & Lewis-Palmer, T. (2001). *Effective behavior suppost team implementation checklists*. University of Oregon, Eugene. Retrieved March 4, 2008, from *pbis.org/tools.htm*.

Sugai, G., Horner, R. H., Lewis-Palmer, T., & Todd, A. W. (2005). *Positive behavior support team Training Manual*. Eugene: University of Oregon. Retrieved March 19, 2006, from *pbismanual.uoecs.org*.

Sugai, G., Lewis-Palmer, T., Horner, R. H., & Todd, A. W. (2001). *School-wide evaluation tool*. Eugene: University of Oregon. Retrieved August 1, 2007, from *pbis.org*.

SWIS, School Wide Information System. Retrieved May 20, 2008, from *http://www.swis.org*.

Tobin, T. J., Lewis-Palmer, T., & Sugai, G. (2002). School-wide and individualized effective behavior support: An explanation and an example. *Behavior Analysis Today, 3*(1), 51–75.

Tobin, T. J., & Sugai, G. (2005). Preventing problem behaviors: Primary, secondary, and tertiary level prevention interventions for young children. *Journal of Early Intensive Behavior Intervention, 2*(3), 115–124.

Todd, A. W., Horner, R. H., & Sugai, G. (1999). Self-monitoring and self-recruited praise: Effects on problem behavior, academic engagement, and work completion in a typical classroom. *Journal of Positive Behavior Interventions, 1,* 66–76.

Walker, H. M., & Severson, H. H. (1990). *Systematic Screening for Behavior Disorders: User's guide and administration manual.* Longmont, CO: Sopris West.

Walker, H. M., Severson, H. H., & Feil, E. G. (1995). *Early Screening Project: A proven child-find process.* Longmont, CO: Sopris West.

Walker, H. M., Stiller, B., Golly, A., Kavanagh, K., Severson, H. H., & Feil, E. G. (1997). *First Step to Success.* Longmont, CO: Sopris West.

Winstein, C. J., & Lewthwaite, R. (2004). *Efficacy and effectiveness: Issues for physical therapy practice and research: Examples from PTClinResNet.* Nashville, TN: Eugene Michele Forum. Retrieved September 9, 2007, from *pt.usc.edu/clinresnet/CSM04/Eugene%20Michels%20pdf%20files/Winstein%20EM%202004.pdf.*

CHAPTER 5

# Effects of Professional Development on Improving At-Risk Students' Performance in Reading

SHARON VAUGHN, SYLVIA LINAN-THOMPSON, ALTHEA L. WOODRUFF, CHRISTY S. MURRAY, JEANNE WANZEK, NANCY SCAMMACCA, GREG ROBERTS, *and* BATYA ELBAUM

For the past century researchers have examined what does and does not work in reading instruction, particularly for students with reading difficulties. Numerous consensus reports (Adams, 1990; Donovan & Cross, 2002; National Reading Panel, 2000; Perkins-Gough, 2002; Snow, Burns, & Griffin, 1998; Swanson, Hoskyn, & Lee, 1999) providing syntheses on the efficacy of instructional practices in reading for students with reading difficulties converge on the following conclusions:

- A teacher with high content and procedural knowledge will effect more positive student outcomes.
- Key instructional elements are associated with the development of reading success (e.g., foundation skills such as phonemic awareness and phonics early in the development of reading with the early and ongoing integration of word reading, fluency, vocabulary, and comprehension).
- Understanding and learning from text requires knowledge of words (how to read them and what they mean), interesting and

115

engaging text, and opportunities to discuss texts with peers and adults.

- Practices associated with improved outcomes include differentiated instruction for students with special needs, enhanced or modified instruction for students at risk, application of explicit and systematic instructional practices, and screening and ongoing progress monitoring to ensure appropriate students are identified and provided with interventions.

In addition, laws and other government actions such as the National Commission of Excellence in Education (1983); the Individuals with Disabilities Education Improvement Act (IDEA, 2004); the GOALS 2000: Educate America Act (1994), and the No Child Left Behind Act of 2001 (2002) have encouraged and even mandated improvements in instruction in general and in reading instruction specifically.

Despite these efforts, the percentage of fourth graders unable to read on grade level continues to remain high (Perie, Grigg, & Donahue, 2005). Thus, the present study sought to determine whether a systematic change at the school and teacher level through a districtwide change model would be associated with improved reading outcomes for struggling students.

## THE RESEARCH QUESTION

This longitudinal study addressed numerous other research questions related to intervening with Tiers 2 and 3 using more intensive interventions. However, for the purpose of reporting in this chapter, the study addresses only the following research question that is related to the influence of professional development on reading outcomes: What is the impact of primary instruction (Tier 1), including ongoing professional development for teachers and screening and progress monitoring for students, on reading outcomes for at-risk students as measured at the end of first grade? Furthermore, we provide a case study of a principal of one of the participating schools to reflect the role of contextual factors such as school leadership on successful implementation of the practices.

## RESPONSE TO INTERVENTION

As discussed in Chapter 1, response to intervention (RTI) provides a prevention and remediation framework for early screening, intervention, and progress monitoring of at-risk students with the ultimate goal of preventing the number of students inappropriately referred and identified as learning disabled and preventing academic difficulties. Although conceptualized in various ways, what most RTI approaches have in common is the utilization of increasingly more intensive interventions along with universal screening. Primary instruction (also referred to as Tier 1) using a research-based instructional program and/or curriculum is a critical step in implementing an effective RTI prevention program in reading. Teachers are often engaged in ongoing professional development to improve their instruction, and typically screening assessments are administered at the beginning, middle, and end of the school year to all students combined with frequent progress monitoring one to two times a month for students identified as at risk for reading problems.

The many variations on RTI approaches (Marston, Muyskens, Lau, & Canter, 2003; O'Conner, Fulmer, Harty, & Bell, 2005; Simmons, Kuykendall, King, Cornachione, & Kame'enui, 2000; Speece, Case, & Molloy, 2003; Vaughn & Chard, 2006) contrast with the traditional IQ–achievement discrepancy model and represent a more systematic orientation toward using increasingly more intensive layers of intervention to provide information for identifying students with reading delays/disabilities and preventing reading difficulties. Hence, these approaches are more appropriate for screening for students with reading difficulties and providing intervention (Fletcher et al., 1994). Of high importance within all RTI frameworks is a well-informed general education teacher who has the knowledge and skills to provide high-quality research-based reading instruction to all students.

## Levels of Intervention

Much of the research related to RTI has examined the effect that secondary and tertiary interventions (Tier 2 and Tier 3) have on struggling students' reading performance and progress. For example, Torgesen and colleagues (Torgesen et al., 2001) provided 50 minutes of one-on-one reading instruction twice a day for 8 weeks to a group of older elementary students with very significant reading problems. Students made significant gains, and many of them improved to the extent that they were reading within the average range. Vellutino and colleagues (Vellutino, Scanlon, & Jaccard, 2003) also provided intensive tutoring to at-risk first graders with positive results at the end of first grade that were maintained through third grade for all but a few of the lowest readers. Research embedding secondary and tertiary interventions for at-risk students in kindergarten through third grade reports consistently positive effects for programs that address foundation skills (e.g., phonemic awareness, phonics) and higher level skills (reading text fluently and understanding and appreciating multiple text types). These findings are consistently associated with students who are provided instruction in relatively small groups or one-on-one and use direct, explicit, and systematic instructional practices. These findings contrast markedly with typical reading remediation (i.e., special education reading classes), which is known to consist of instruction that is relatively less intense (Hanushek, Kain, & Rivkin, 1998; Moody, Vaughn, Hughes, & Fischer, 2000; Vaughn, Moody, & Schumm, 1998).

Focusing on effective interventions for struggling readers remains an important goal of reading research; however, given that most students, including those participating in secondary or tertiary intervention, take part in the reading lessons offered as primary instruction within the general education classrooms, an emphasis must also be placed on maximizing the effectiveness of the primary instruction. Ensuring that instruction is as effective as possible in general education reading classrooms is especially important considering that many schools do not have the resources necessary for providing additional intervention to large numbers of students. Fundamentally, effective Tier 1 instruction is expected to reduce the number of students who require Tier 2 and Tier 3 interventions.

## PRIMARY INSTRUCTION (TIER 1)

Although much research has focused on the more intensive reading interventions within RTI models, some research has examined the effects of improved reading instruction (Tier 1) on student performance and progress (e.g., Baker & Smith, 1999; Greenwood & Delquadri, 1993; O'Connor, 1999). Specifically, researchers have analyzed the impact of professional development and support (Clement & Vandenberghe, 2001; Gersten, Morvant, & Brengelman, 1995; Newmann, King, & Youngs, 2000; Renyi, 1998) and the impact of using data collected from student assessments (Baker & Smith, 2001; Fuchs & Fuchs, 2003) on teacher practice and student outcomes. Although few in number, the existing studies that have examined student outcomes in relation to teacher professional development suggest that improved teacher knowledge is associated with improved student outcomes. Interestingly, relatively few studies focused on beginning reading, and most were conducted more than 20 years ago (professional development for first-grade teachers— Anderson, Evertson, & Brophy, 1979; Stallings & Krasavage, 1986; Stallings, Robbins, Presbrey, & Scott, 1986; Streeter, 1986). Two studies have focused specifically on kindergarten teachers and their students (Baker & Smith, 2001) and kindergarten and first-grade teachers and their students (McCutchen et al., 2002), again reporting positive outcomes for students from professional development.

From the descriptive literature on professional development, several critical factors have emerged as necessary for teachers to gain new knowledge and implement effective instructional practices: (1) collaborative environments in which teachers have input in decision making and problem solving (Gersten et al., 1995; Newmann et al., 2000; Renyi, 1998), (2) providing teachers with feedback as new methods are integrated into their current teaching practices (Clement & Vandenberghe, 2001; Gersten et al., 1995; Newmann et al., 2000; Renyi, 1998), (3) using student data to examine the effects of implementing new teaching methods (Baker & Smith, 2001; Fuchs & Fuchs, 2003), and (4) engaging teachers as active learners who provide support and feedback to each other about new literacy practices (e.g., Greenwood & Delquadri, 1993; O'Connor, 1999).

## SCHOOL SELECTION AND PARTICIPATION

The overarching questions addressed in this research were related to the effects of enhancing Tier 1 instruction for students at risk for failure in learning to read. This study measured the reading performance over time of at-risk K–1 students in six schools. All K–1 teachers and their at-risk students participated in this study for 3 years. In the first year of the study (cohort 1), kindergarten students were screened, and those identified as at risk were tested in May of kindergarten, and September and May of first grade. Neither teachers nor their students were provided intervention; hence, we refer to this group as the historical control group.

During year 2 of the study (cohort 2), kindergarten students were again screened and those identified as at risk were tested. The K–1 teachers participated in a year-long professional development program (Tier 1) while these students were in their classes. In year 3 (cohort 3), a third cohort of at-risk kindergarten students was identified and tested. The K–1 teachers were provided with additional professional development while these students were in their classes. Although this large-scale study is also addressing issues related to effectiveness of secondary and tertiary interventions, for the purpose of this chapter, effects related to primary instruction (Tier 1) are isolated and reported.

The design provided a historical control group and two experimental comparison groups of students in the same schools from the same classrooms but subsequent academic years. This design enabled comparisons of different groups of students receiving different instructional experiences at the same point in their school experience. The instructional experiences of students in the experimental cohorts were manipulated by the provision of Tier 1 instruction enhanced by professional development in research-based strategies as described below. This allowed comparison of students in the experimental groups to students in the historical control group and to one another. Additionally, a case study of one of the schools is provided to illustrate the important role educational leadership played in effective school change.

This study was conducted in six Title I elementary schools in one near-urban district in the Southwest. Of the students in this district, 74.2% are economically disadvantaged and 22.9% are limited English proficient. Demographic information for all students is provided in Table 5.1. Three sequential K–1 grade cohorts of students from all six elementary schools were the focus of this study. We followed each cohort of students from kindergarten through the end of first grade. The initial cohort of students (2001–2003) and their kindergarten and first-grade teachers were the historical control group; the teachers did not receive any Tier 1 intervention (professional development). The second cohort of students began kindergarten in 2002. The third cohort of students began kindergarten in 2003. Tier 1 intervention was implemented with cohorts 2 and 3. The kindergarten and first-grade teachers of the students in cohorts 2 and 3 participated in ongoing professional development, occasional in-class support, and progress monitoring of at-risk students to strengthen the core curriculum.

Sixteen kindergarten teachers and 13 first-grade teachers were present all 3 years of the study. Twenty-eight of these teachers were certified to teach general education, one teacher was certified to teach special education, and one teacher was certified in reading. All teachers had a bachelor's degree, and three had a master's degree. On average, these teachers had 13 years of teaching experience. All teachers were female, and English was their primary language. There were approximately 19 students per class in each grade.

During the time we were implementing the three-tiered interventions in the schools, the special education personnel provided special services to students using primarily a resource-room, pull-out approach. Since the project data collection was completed, the schools have transitioned to using a special education inclusion model whereby the special education teachers work with general education teachers in a pull-in approach.

## Criteria for Selection of At-Risk Students

Students were identified as at risk in January of kindergarten if they scored below 27 on the Letter Naming Fluency (LNF) subtest of the Dynamic Indicators of Basic Early Literacy Skills (DIBELS; Good & Kaminski, 2002). We selected this criteria because it represented stu-

**TABLE 5.1. Student Demographics**

| Cohort | N | Gender | | Ethnicity | | | | | SES | Home language | | |
|---|---|---|---|---|---|---|---|---|---|---|---|---|
| | | M | F | H | W | AA | A/PI | NA | Receiving free or reduced lunch | E | S | OL |
| Cohort 1 | 76 | 42 (55%) | 34 (45%) | 46 (61%) | 14 (18%) | 14 (18%) | 1 (1%) | 1 (1%) | 55 (72%) | 67 (88%) | 9 (12%) | 0 (0%) |
| Cohort 2 | 51 | 29 (57%) | 22 (43%) | 37 (73%) | 11 (22%) | 2 (4%) | 1 (2%) | 0 (0%) | 42 (82%) | 39 (76%) | 12 (24%) | 0 (0%) |
| Cohort 3 | 35 | 20 (57%) | 15 (43%) | 24 (69%) | 5 (14%) | 3 (9%) | 3 (9%) | 0 (0%) | 28 (80%) | 29 (83%) | 4 (11%) | 2 (6%) |
| Total | 162 | 91 (56%) | 71 (44%) | 107 (66%) | 30 (19%) | 19 (12%) | 5 (3%) | 1 (1%) | 125 (77%) | 135 (83%) | 25 (15%) | 2 (2%) |

*Note.* M, male; F, female; H, Hispanic; W, white; AA, African American; A/PI, Asian/Pacific Islander; NA, Native American; E, English; S, Spanish; OL, other language.

dents who were "at risk" for later reading difficulties and provided a cut-off that would represent more false positives than false negatives ensuring that students received intervention that needed it. Chall (2000) identified letter naming as a predictor of later reading development, and research continues to support this position. Speed and accuracy of letter naming has been used as a predictor of accurate word reading ability (Compton, 2003; Neuhaus & Swank, 2002). Kindergarten measures of letter naming fluency predicted first-grade students' oral reading fluency scores (Stage, Sheppard, Davidson, & Browning, 2001), and letter-naming fluency in kindergarten is a primary discriminator of reading difficulty in kindergarten and first grade (O'Connor & Jenkins, 1999).

The final sample of students used in analyses consisted of all students who remained in the study through the end of first grade and included (1) 76 at-risk students in the historical control group (cohort 1), (2) 51 at-risk students in cohort 2, and (3) 35 at-risk students in cohort 3.

## SCHOOL READING RISK ASSESSMENTS

The following outcomes were used for screening all students to determine students who were at risk for reading problems and then to assess these students to determine student progress.

### Screening: LNF Subtest of the DIBELS

The DIBELS (Good & Kaminski, 2002) targets early literacy skills and includes subtests of letter recognition and tasks related to phonological awareness and the alphabetic principle. In this study, the LNF subtest was administered as a screening measure in January of kindergarten to identify students at risk for reading problems. This is a brief, individually administered, standardized, timed assessment. During LNF administration, students are asked to name as many letters as they can in a minute when presented a page of random upper- and lowercase letters. The 1-month, alternate-form reliability for LNF is reported as 0.88 (Good et al., 2004). The predictive validity of kindergarten LNF with first grade Woodcock–Johnson Psycho-Educational Battery–Revised Reading Cluster standard score is 0.65.

### Assessment: WRMT-R and PPVT-III

The Word Identification, Word Attack, and Passage Comprehension subtests of the Woodcock Reading Mastery Tests–Revised (WRMT-R;

Woodcock, 1987) were administered. The Word Identification subtest determines word reading skills. The Word Attack subtest measures a student's ability to decode nonsense words. The Word Identification and Word Attack subtests were administered in the winter of kindergarten (cohorts 2 and 3), spring of kindergarten, fall of first grade, and spring of first grade. The Passage Comprehension subtest asks students to read sentences and passages, supplying the correct word through a close procedure. The Passage Comprehension measure was administered in the fall and spring of first grade. A median split-half reliability coefficient of 0.97 to 0.98 is reported for the Word Identification subtest in the standard sample. For the Word Attack subtest, the split-half reliability coefficient is reported as ranging from 0.87 to 0.94, and a median split-half coefficient of 0.92 to 0.96 is reported for the Passage Comprehension subtest. Concurrent validity ranges for the subtests of the WRMT-R are reported to be from 0.63 to 0.82 when compared to the Total Reading score of the Woodcock–Johnson Psycho-Educational Battery (Woodcock & Johnson, 1977).

The third edition of the Peabody Picture Vocabulary Test (PPVT-III, Dunn & Dunn, 1997) is an individually administered, untimed, norm-referenced test available in two parallel forms. It is designed to measure a student's receptive vocabulary as well as screen for overall verbal ability. Students are asked to identify (by either pointing or verbalizing) the picture that best represents the meaning of a stimulus word presented orally by the examiner. The PPVT was administered in the spring of first grade to each cohort of students.

Test–retest reliability coefficients for the PPVT-III are estimated to be between 0.93 and 0.94 for 6- to 10-year-old students. Alternate-forms reliability coefficients range from 0.88 to 0.96. Content validity was established through a critical evaluation (using statistical and opinion data) and extensive field testing of the stimulus words selected for both forms of the test.

## Testing Procedure

Trained graduate students and research associates administered all measures; all testers were blind to conditions. Practice sessions for each measure were held prior to each round of testing. Scoring was checked and, if discrepancies were found, testers completed a second practice on that measure. All testers completed practice administrations successfully prior to testing. Validity checks were conducted for each tester to assure high reliability of testing and scoring procedures.

## CORE PROCEDURES:
## PROFESSIONAL DEVELOPMENT FOR TEACHERS

Kindergarten and first-grade teachers were provided with ongoing professional development, including use of progress monitoring, and in-class support from the research team as part of Tier 1. The professional development provided to teachers was selected based on the high-priority skills needed for improving outcomes in reading for students at each grade level (for review, see University of Oregon website: *idea.uoregon.edu/presentations/presentations.html*). For example, in kindergarten, high-priority skills are oral language and vocabulary, letter naming, mapping sounds to print (alphabetic principle), and word reading. In first grade, students who have not adequately accomplished high-priority skills in kindergarten need additional support on these skills as well as reading connected text fluently and listening comprehension. In addition to addressing these high-priority skills, teachers participated in ongoing professional development to enhance their knowledge and skills about implementing a multi-tiered intervention including appropriate use of core reading materials, linking progress monitoring to instructional decision making and grouping practices, and providing intensive instruction interventions to students falling behind.

### Professional Development Sessions

Researchers provided teachers with seven professional development sessions in the course of each school year. One to two sessions were conducted before the start of each school year. These beginning of the year sessions were 6 hours each; subsequent sessions throughout the school year were 2.5 hours each. The initial training sessions focused on adjusting the curriculum for at-risk readers and the use of progress monitoring. The remaining topics included peer-pairing practices, managing classrooms for small-group instruction, using progress monitoring data to make instructional decisions, strategies for word reading, increasing student vocabulary, reading comprehension practices, advanced word study, and effective instructional practices. The final session each year consisted of focus group discussions and planning for the next school year. Members of the research team and consultants conducted all professional development sessions. The beginning of the year sessions, and the phonological awareness, behavior management, word recognition, and comprehension sessions were held with all teachers together, whereas the remaining sessions were held in smaller groups with teachers from two schools meeting at one elementary school to allow for more teacher interaction.

- *Curriculum development (August 2003).* Teachers were provided with information on the effective features of reading instruction. Teachers worked in small groups with members of the research staff to analyze their core instructional program and identify strengths of their curriculum as well as areas in need of supplements.
- *Progress monitoring (August 2002, August 2003, August 2004).* Kindergarten and first-grade teachers were provided instruction on administering DIBELS progress monitoring measures. Each of the appropriate measures for kindergarten and first grade were discussed and practiced. Refresher sessions were provided for teachers in their second year of implementation.
- *Behavior management (September 2002).* Kindergarten teachers examined the link between behavior management and instruction and were provided with strategies for managing classroom behavior to maximize instruction. A review of LNF progress monitoring administration was also provided.
- *Phonological awareness (September 2002).* Kindergarten teachers were provided with background information on phonological awareness skills and the link to reading acquisition. Multiple phonological awareness activities were demonstrated, and teachers were provided with sample activities to use as resources for enhancing core instruction in this area.
- *Peer-pairing practices (January 2003, August 2003, November 2004).* Teachers were instructed on the implementation of the Kindergarten Peer-Assisted Learning Strategies (K-PALS) (Mathes, Clancy-Menchetti, & Torgesen, 2001) or PALS (Mathes, Torgesen, & Allor, 2001) program, and presenters modeled portions of the lessons. Teachers practiced lessons and used data from the fall DIBELS benchmark assessments to pair the students in their classroom.
- *Managing your classroom for small-group instruction (October 2002, September 2003).* Kindergarten and first-grade teachers were provided assistance in using progress monitoring data to plan instruction to meet students' instructional needs. Management plans for teaching small groups were shared with teachers and sample activities were modeled.
- *Using progress monitoring to make instructional decisions (November 2003, October 2004).* Kindergarten and first-grade teachers were provided with instruction in graphing student progress monitoring data and determining trend lines. Teachers worked with their classroom data sets to determine students making sufficient progress and students making insufficient progress. Teachers were provided support to establish intervention plans for students making insufficient progress.
- *Strategies for improving word recognition and reading fluency*

*(January 2004).* Kindergarten and first-grade teachers were presented with activities for targeting word recognition and reading fluency in the classroom. Teachers worked in groups to analyze student progress monitoring assessments and determine appropriate instructional activities to target.

• *Increasing student vocabulary (February 2004, September 2004).* The sessions focused on selecting appropriate vocabulary words and effective vocabulary instruction and using literature read-alouds for increasing students' oral vocabulary. During the September 2004 session, first-grade teachers reviewed the selection of appropriate vocabulary words, were introduced to more strategies for teaching meaning of words, and practiced teaching a vocabulary word to other teachers in the session.

• *Reading comprehension strategies (August 2004).* First-grade teachers were instructed on the importance of effective comprehension instruction and were guided through the implementation of using comprehension practices to teach listening and reading comprehension to first-grade students.

• *Advanced word study (January 2005).* First-grade teachers were instructed on systematic methods of teaching students to decode words, as well as read sight words. Instructional activities that could be incorporated into word study instruction were shared.

• *Structuring classroom reading instruction (February 2003, February 2005).* The 2003 session with kindergarten teachers consisted of a discussion on organizing instruction and incorporating all of the previous professional development topics into core instruction. Teachers also set goals for the remainder of the year and the following year. In addition, teachers were given the opportunity to share successful activities they had implemented during the year related to each component of reading. The 2005 session for first-grade teachers consisted of centers led by research team members. Each center focused on ways to increase academic engaged time during reading instruction. Teachers were divided into small groups and rotated among the centers consisting of word wall activities, word and phrase fluency activities, and discussions on how to make smoother transitions during the school day and increase the effectiveness of time for reading instruction.

## IMPLEMENTATION APPROACH: IN-CLASS SUPPORT

Members of the research team were designated as primary intervention coordinators and were assigned to each school to coordinate the professional development for kindergarten and first-grade teachers at the school, hold monthly grade-level meetings, conduct biweekly classroom observations (observations with teachers were less frequent during their second year of implementation [cohort 3 students]), and provide ongoing support. As a follow-up to professional development sessions, the primary intervention coordinator provided demonstration lessons of specific reading content and/or features of effective instruction; assistance with implementing specific content or grouping; and assistance with planning and implementation of progress monitoring. Primary intervention coordinators met with teachers 3 times per year (fall, winter, spring) to share classroom data. At-risk students were identified for progress monitoring, and instructional implications were discussed. The coordinators also assisted teachers in interpreting progress monitoring data throughout the year for students falling below benchmarks. Primary intervention coordinators spent approximately 10 hours every 2 weeks at each school.

## CASE STUDY: TEACHER AND PRINCIPAL INTERVIEWS, CLASSROOM OBSERVATIONS, AND ONGOING NOTES

The purpose of this section is to describe one principal's effect on her school through her leadership and commitment to implementing an RTI-type approach to instruction. During the 3 years in which this study was conducted, we worked at least 1 day per week in one of the six elementary schools providing in-class coaching and ongoing professional development, and engaged in informal classroom observations and ongoing discussion with teachers and the school principal. We selected the principal of this school as our illustrative case study because we had the same person working in the school for all 3 years. The data gathered over this 3-year period were transcribed and recorded yielding information about the importance of school leadership in change in reading instruction and student outcomes. Information from these interviews and observations is summarized in our principal case study in the results section that follows.

### The Principal: Linda Baker

The central phenomenon arising from the interview data with the principal, Linda Baker (pseudonym), is *meeting teachers' needs* (see Figure 5.1). The themes related to this phenomenon include *instruction as a top priority*, *leadership beliefs and actions*, and *time and student needs*. Explanations of the central phenomenon and each of the themes follow.

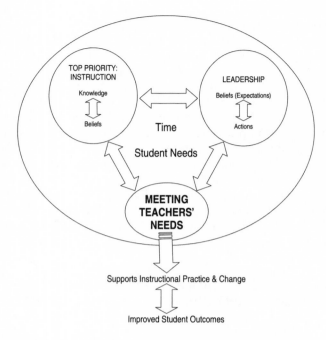

**FIGURE 5.1.** Principal as instructional leader in reading.

### Meeting Teachers' Needs

Central to the principal's view of her role as the administrator was meeting the teachers' needs for providing the effective instruction to students.
Throughout discussions with Dr. Baker and teachers over the course of
our project, the principal's focus on supporting teachers and providing
them with the resources and knowledge that they need to then meet students' needs became clear. As Dr. Baker explained:

> "What I think helps with teachers is to give them information. To be-
> lieve in them. To believe they can do a good job and to let them figure
> out by using information if they can get a better result. And then
> have them let you know and let them have complete ownership of
> the success. That's the best way."

The principal met teachers' needs through several important means, including:

- Stating her expectations.
- Giving teachers' choices and providing autonomy.

- Making sure that teachers knew she was "involved."
- Giving them "an out" (letting them know they did not have to be "perfect").
- Supporting teachers in their collaborations with each other.
- Giving them credit and attention when they demonstrated success.

In providing this support, however, Dr. Baker also understood the importance of not allowing teachers to make excuses for students' lack of success. She described teachers as needing to be knowledgeable and flexible and expressed her view of teachers' needing to provide "planful instruction." As she stated:

> "It's not a happen stance thing . . . it shouldn't be. Often it is. . . . That's the difference between knowing what children need and just teaching reading and hoping they get it."

And she continued later:

> "All subjects should be taught the same way, and that is knowing exactly what the child needs, exactly what you're going to teach, how children learn it best, and then using data and making sure that you don't waste your time."

To help teachers gain such an understanding of meeting students' needs, Dr. Baker talked about how teachers struggle with being "aware" of the difficulties they have in teaching reading, and again she mentioned using student data to help build this awareness:

> "I think it will be impossible for the teachers to forget the results that happen when they do a good job of teaching reading. I think that their level of consciousness will be different, so it will be really hard for teachers who now know that they can do better to not do better."

### Instruction as a Top Priority

When asked about her most important roles as an administrator, Dr. Baker's first response was instruction, and throughout our discussions, her knowledge of and expressed beliefs about reading instruction clearly supported the priority she placed on being her school's instructional leader. Although she has almost 30 years of experience in education, including much training specifically in reading and working with students with disabilities, this principal focused much of her energy on continuing to learn as much as she could about instruction. When asked about her training and background knowledge, Dr. Baker described her college and graduate learning and then stated:

> "The rest has been since I've become a leader and just my own need to know about reading instruction, and I've learned a lot through the reading, [and] the three-tiered reading staff development that I've attended."

Not only did Dr. Baker attend almost every professional development, at least for part of the time, but she also met with her primary intervention coordinator at least every month to discuss instruction and what the teachers should be doing based on this training. She described her beliefs about her role as instructional leader in this way:

> "Everything I do revolves around setting up the environment for the best possible instruction. Everything from scheduling to the lack of [staff] meetings that we have. I purposely don't have meetings all the time so that people can meet . . . with their teams. I schedule alignment meetings among grade levels and within grade levels to discuss instruction. We have a framework, kind of an environment where everything is structured to help them have time to talk about instruction."

Her theoretical framework underlying this emphasis included beliefs such as "whatever it takes for each child to help them learn to read" and "your reading program is as good as the teacher that's doing it."

### Leadership Beliefs and Actions

Along with a focus on instruction, Dr. Baker demonstrated leadership beliefs and actions that supported her meeting teachers' needs, including:

- High but reasonable expectations and standards.
- Providing teachers with opportunities but not overwhelming them.
- Modeling behavior ("practice what I preach").
- Using "peer pressure" among teachers to meet expectations.
- Providing trust and support through consultation and coaching.

As an example of her modeling for teachers, Dr. Baker was known to cover a teacher's class, including special education classes, when a substitute was not available and work with individual students or groups of students when she conducted her walk-through visits. In the interview, she summed up her leadership philosophy as follows:

> "Hire really good people and make sure they understand what I want. Provide those resources whether it's training or materials or whatever it is they need and then give them a lot of freedom within that framework . . . I don't have to know all the things that they (the teachers) know . . . [but] I know enough about the latest in reading instruction to provide support for them."

### Sense of Urgency and Specific Students' Needs

Underlying all of her knowledge, beliefs, and actions related to meeting teachers' needs, making instruction a priority, and providing effective leadership are a real sense of urgency (not wasting time) and a focus on student needs. Dr. Baker used phrases such as "minutes available for instruction," "not waste their (students') time," "no day can be wasted," and being "productive" to meet the needs of "every single child" throughout our discussions of reading instruction on her campus.

## KEY OUTCOME DATA

The effect of primary instruction (Tier 1) was assessed by comparing the spring of first-grade performance of at-risk students in cohorts 2 and 3 to the performance of students in the historical control group (cohort 1). Students in the sample were those who were identified as at risk in winter of kindergarten and assigned to a condition of Tier 1 intervention only. Descriptive and multilevel modeling analyses (Bryk & Raudenbush, 1992; Kreft & de Leeuw, 1998; Snijders & Bosker, 1999) were conducted to evaluate the effect of Tier 1 intervention on at-risk students.

### Descriptive Results by Cohort and Group

Descriptive results for the kindergarten and first-grade administration of the WRMT-R and PPVT for students with complete data are presented by cohort in Table 5.2. There were 76 at-risk students in cohort 1, 51 in cohort 2, and 35 in cohort 3. Thirty of the 51 students in cohort 2 were not administered the Passage Comprehension measure in first grade because the administration was initially intended only to obtain follow-up data on students who qualified for secondary intervention in winter of kindergarten.

Inspection of the WRMT-R data indicates a positive trend across cohorts, with cohort 3 showing higher scores at spring of first grade than earlier cohorts. To evaluate whether differences in scores of the three cohorts of students were statistically significant, a series of multilevel models were estimated.

## Multilevel Modeling of Student Outcomes

Multilevel modeling provides a framework for dealing with the hierarchical data structures that are common in the social and behavioral sciences. In this study, it was assumed that student performance in the spring of first grade was a product of person-level attributes and participation in Tier 1 intervention, which was nested within and influenced by teacher and/or school-level factors.

## Primary Instruction: Tier 1 Effects

The effect of Tier 1 only intervention (professional development) was examined in terms of differences in spring of first-grade performance for

**TABLE 5.2. Means and Standard Deviations for WRMT-R Standard Scores by Cohort**

|  | Cohort 1 (*n* = 76) | Cohort 2 (*n* = 51 for WA and WID; *n* = 21 for PC) | Cohort 3 (*n* = 35) |
|---|---|---|---|
| WRMT-R Word Identification (WID) |  |  |  |
| Winter, grade K | N/A | 88.25 (10.03) | 90.83 (9.95) |
| Spring, grade K | 92.70 (11.87) | 100.25 (11.99) | 103.34 (11.77) |
| Fall, grade 1 | 92.91 (10.66) | 96.16 (10.92) | 102.23 (11.15) |
| Spring, grade 1 | 101.59 (13.00) | 103.98 (11.66) | 109.66 (9.69) |
| WRMT-R Word Attack (WA) |  |  |  |
| Winter, grade K | N/A | 93.49 (5.67) | 96.97 (6.42) |
| Spring, grade K | 96.09 (10.14) | 99.14 (10.10) | 105.66 (9.51) |
| Fall, grade 1 | 94.64 (11.83) | 99.67 (12.43) | 103.06 (13.45) |
| Spring, grade 1 | 101.29 (13.29) | 104.63 (10.45) | 110.60 (12.40) |
| WRMT-R Passage Comprehension (PC) |  |  |  |
| Fall, grade 1 | 88.25 (9.14) | 81.71 (9.16) | 91.91 (10.20) |
| Spring, grade 1 | 96.84 (10.67) | 95.24 (9.58) | 102.09 (7.39) |
| PPVT | 88.08 (9.89) | *n* = 51: 89.43 (12.30) *n* = 21: 86.24 (12.21) | 91.03 (12.69) |

*Note.* N/A, not available.

students in each of the three cohorts who were identified as being at risk and who were assigned to the comparison condition. Because the Tier 1 intervention is best conceptualized at the teacher level, teacher-level effects were of interest. A series of two-level models (student performance nested within teachers) was estimated for each WRMT-R measure. Fall of first-grade performance and PPVT scores were included in the models to account for the effect of these person-level factors. Kindergarten data are provided for descriptive purposes but were not used in the analysis. Models were estimated using cohort 2 as the reference group and then using cohort 3 as the reference group to allow for the comparison of all three cohorts.

Results are summarized in Table 5.3. On Word Attack, students in cohort 3 outperformed students in cohort 1, $t(157) = 2.92, p = .004$, and cohort 2 $t(157) = 2.65, p = .009$. No significant differences were found between the performance of students in cohort 1 and cohort 2, $t(157) = 0.33, p = 0.74$. Variance around the slope estimate was significant (variance = 39.35, $p = .000$) suggesting that factors in addition to Tier 1 intervention are likely related to group differences in student performance.

On Passage Comprehension, students in cohort 3 performed significantly better than students in cohort 1, $t(127) = 3.22, p = 0.002$. However, no significant differences were found in the performance of students in cohort 1 and cohort 2, $t(127) = 0.74$ $p = 0.46$ or in cohort 2 and cohort 3, $t(127) = 1.56, p = 0.12$. Again, the variance around the slope estimate was significant (variance = 11.41, $p = 0.007$), indicating that unspecified factors in addition to Tier 1 intervention may have contributed to group differences in student performance.

On Word Identification, no significant differences were found in average spring performance of cohort 1 compared to cohort 2, $t(157) = 0.05, p = 0.96$, cohort 1 compared to cohort 3, $t(157) = 0.92, p = 0.36$, or cohort 2 compared to cohort 3, $t(157) = 0.77, p = 0.44$. However, variance around the slope estimate was significant (variance = 30.14, $p = 0.000$), suggesting that unspecified factors may have contributed to group differences in student performance.

## Effect Size Estimates

Standardized mean difference effect sizes were calculated using the means reported in Table 5.4. The procedure for calculating unbiased effect size estimates for Cohen's $d$ provided by Hedges (1981) was used. Effect size estimates were computed to compare cohort 1 and cohort 2, cohort 1 and cohort 3, and cohort 2 and cohort 3 at the end of first grade. Effect sizes for cohort 3 (when compared to cohorts 2 or 1) were in the moderate to large range. Effect size estimates in terms of percent-

**TABLE 5.3. Spring of First Grade Comparison of Students by Cohort**

| Parameter | Coefficient | SE | t-ratio | p-value | df |
|---|---|---|---|---|---|
| | | | Fixed effects | | |

Using cohort 2 as the reference group (compares C1 to C2 and C3 to C2)

Word Identification

| Parameter | Coefficient | SE | t-ratio | p-value | df |
|---|---|---|---|---|---|
| Intercept | 102.98 | 1.69 | 60.99 | 0.000 | 34 |
| Effect of C1 | −0.10 | 1.88 | −0.05 | 0.96 | 157 |
| Effect of C3 | 1.57 | 2.04 | 0.77 | 0.44 | 157 |

Word Attack

| Parameter | Coefficient | SE | t-ratio | p-value | df |
|---|---|---|---|---|---|
| Intercept | 102.57 | 1.48 | 69.09 | 0.000 | 34 |
| Effect of C1 | −0.65 | 1.99 | −0.33 | 0.74 | 157 |
| Effect of C3 | 5.90 | 2.23 | 2.65 | 0.009 | 157 |

Passage Comprehension

| Parameter | Coefficient | SE | t-ratio | p-value | df |
|---|---|---|---|---|---|
| Intercept | 97.88 | 1.68 | 58.25 | 0.000 | 34 |
| Effect of C1 | −1.42 | 1.91 | −0.74 | 0.46 | 127 |
| Effect of C3 | 2.52 | 1.61 | 1.56 | 0.12 | 127 |

Using cohort 3 as the reference group (compares C1 to C3 and C2 to C3)

Word Identification

| Parameter | Coefficient | SE | t-ratio | p-value | df |
|---|---|---|---|---|---|
| Intercept | 104.55 | 1.73 | 60.43 | 0.000 | 34 |
| Effect of C1 | −1.66 | 1.81 | −0.92 | 0.36 | 157 |
| Effect of C2 | −1.57 | 2.04 | −0.77 | 0.44 | 157 |

Word Attack

| Parameter | Coefficient | SE | t-ratio | p-value | df |
|---|---|---|---|---|---|
| Intercept | 108.47 | 2.10 | 51.61 | 0.000 | 34 |
| Effect of C1 | −6.55 | 2.24 | −2.92 | 0.004 | 157 |
| Effect of C2 | −5.90 | 2.23 | −2.65 | 0.009 | 157 |

Passage Comprehension

| Parameter | Coefficient | SE | t-ratio | p-value | df |
|---|---|---|---|---|---|
| Intercept | 100.40 | 1.11 | 90.27 | 0.000 | 34 |
| Effect of C1 | −3.94 | 1.23 | −3.22 | 0.002 | 127 |
| Effect of C2 | −2.52 | 1.61 | −1.56 | 0.12 | 127 |

Random effects

| | Intercept | Slope |
|---|---|---|
| Word Identification | 30.14 | 66.01 |
| Word Attack | 39.35 | 103.23 |
| Passage Comprehension | 11.41 | 64.83 |

**TABLE 5.4. Effect Size Estimates and Confidence Intervals for End of First Grade**

|  | C1 vs. C2 | 95% CI | C1 vs. C3 | 95% CI | C2 vs. C3 | 95% CI |
|---|---|---|---|---|---|---|
| Word Identification | ES = 0.19 | −0.16, 0.55 | ES = 0.67 | 0.26, 1.08 | ES = 0.52 | 0.09, 0.96 |
| Word Attack | ES = 0.27 | −0.08, 0.63 | ES = 0.72 | 0.30, 1.13 | ES = 0.53 | 0.09, 0.97 |
| Passage Comprehension | ES = −0.15 | −0.64, 0.33 | ES = 0.54 | 0.14, 0.95 | ES = 0.84 | 0.27, 1.40 |

*Note.* C, cohort; CI, confidence interval; ES, effect size.

age of total variance accounted for (eta-squared) are reported in Table 5.5. Eta-squared effect sizes for Word Identification and Word Attack are in the medium range, whereas the effect for Passage Comprehension is small to medium (Cohen, 1988).

## SUMMARY AND CONCLUSIONS

A premise and goal in multi-tiered models is that Tier 1 instruction be as effective as possible to prevent the need for more costly Tier 2 and Tier 3 intervention, including special education. The purpose of this study was to evaluate the effects of a professional development program for teachers that specifically addressed practices identified in the literature as highly effective and considered by teachers as desirable and feasible to implement. To strengthen Tier 1 instruction that teachers provided, we integrated the following components of effective professional development: (1) the professional development occurred over time and in small units with ample opportunity for follow-up, (2) grade-level teams at each school participated in the professional development with other schools and across all schools so that many opportunities to interact with colleagues were provided, and (3) teachers were provided feedback and support at their request on any or all instructional practices. Teachers were engaged in communities that included high levels of content working with other teachers around topics of high utility to them, and using data to make instructional decisions. Overall participating

**TABLE 5.5. Eta-Squared Effect Size Estimates**

| Word Identification | 0.06 |
|---|---|
| Word Attack | 0.08 |
| Passage Comprehension | 0.04 |

teachers responded with high levels of interest and engagement that were sustained over 2 years (90% or higher attendance) and with requests for the professional development to continue.

Overall, how effective was the professional development for teachers in improving reading outcomes for students identified as having reading difficulties? Considering the amount of time invested by the teachers (approximately 25 hours per year), results for students after their teachers had participated for 2 years (cohort 3), totaling 50 hours of professional development, were sizeable. The 50 hours of professional development represent slightly more time than is typically allotted for a three-credit graduate class. Effect sizes for the students in cohort 3 compared to students in the historical control group ranged from 0.54 for passage comprehension to 0.72 for Word Attack; both were statistically significant. The findings from this study suggest that when teachers participated for 2 years versus 1 (cohort 3 compared with cohort 2), effect sizes for students were considerably higher (0.52 for Word Identification, 0.53 for Word Attack, and 0.84 for Comprehension). Overall, effects on critical indicators of student progress were in the moderate range for students. These effects were on standardized reading achievement tests and not teachers' perceptions of students' success, researcher-developed measures, progress monitoring measures, or other less rigorous methods of determining effectiveness. In addition, these effects were for students who were identified as at risk in reading.

Given students' outcomes, one might assume that other changes, such as adopting a new reading curriculum or teachers implementing some new intervention, may have co-occurred with the professional development being provided. It is important to note that the reading curriculum used by the teachers in these six schools did not change over the 3-year period. Although teachers may have selected different areas to emphasize and prioritized elements from their programs based on the professional development provided, the effects on student outcomes could not be attributed to a change in the reading program they used. Thus, the results of this study provide support for the specific benefits of improving the knowledge and practice of K–1 teachers. This investment in improving teachers' knowledge was associated with overall improved outcomes for their lowest performing students in reading.

Over the course of the study, notes from researchers indicated that teachers' practices changed as they became increasingly knowledgeable about teaching reading to at-risk students. Teachers reported that a significant influence on their instructional practice was the increased use of screening and progress monitoring data to make instructional decisions. Field notes by primary intervention coordinators indicated that three professional development sessions were perceived as having affected teachers' practice most: the use of progress monitoring, using data to make instructional decisions, and managing classrooms for small-group instruction. Teachers received professional development on these topics both years. When deciding on these and other topics for the professional development, the research team considered data from students' assessments and classroom observations. The primary intervention coordinators incorporated the information that they gleaned from these sources into the delivery of the professional development.

In addition to our using data to inform the professional development, teachers began to use screening and progress monitoring to identify students in need of additional instruction to monitor their own teaching. The use of screening measures led to an increased use of flexible grouping for instruction. In particular teachers used small-group instruction to provide targeted instruction during core reading and paired instruction to engage all students in peer-assisted learning activities. The use of small groups provided students more opportunities to engage in instructional activities in various reading components. In addition, teachers provided more individualized and differentiated instruction. This awareness of the relationship between the instructional decisions they made and student outcomes was evident in their grouping practices and in the increased use of data to determine what to teach. Emphasis on various reading components changed as the year progressed and students' skills improved.

This study reports very promising findings for the effects on students from teachers who participated in an ongoing professional group in which they continually engaged in the discussion and implementation of research-based practices associated with improved outcomes in reading. The students of these teachers benefited, and the benefits were greater when teachers participated for more than 1 year. Although we cannot "unpack" which element or combination of elements was associated with student outcomes, we think that the critical elements identified in previous research (e.g., Baker & Smith, 1999; Greenwood & Delquadri, 1993; O'Connor, 1999) were integrated in our professional development including ongoing professional development on topics of high importance to teachers that could be readily integrated into their classroom routines (e.g., partner reading), opportunities to share practices with grade-level teachers from their same school as well as other schools, feedback and support within their classroom on practices used, and progress monitoring data to inform decision making.

In addition to these elements, the primary intervention coordinators met with the principal individually to (1) provide updates on the professional development, (2) analyze student data, and (3) discuss the ongoing support that teachers were receiving. Combining these efforts with the incorporation of critical elements of professional development illustrates the importance of considering the content, process, and contextual variables that Guskey and Sparks (1996) identified as key to examining the effects of professional development on student outcomes. In this and other articles (e.g., Guskey, 1997; Guskey & Sparks, 2002), researchers have advocated the need for connecting staff development with student outcomes. Not only does this study provide an analysis of the effects that ongoing and integrated professional development for teachers can have on student outcomes, but it also provides evidence in support of the importance of primary instruction (Tier 1) particularly in the context of current legislation (reauthorization of IDEA, 2004) that encourages response to intervention as a data source in the identification process of students with learning disabilities. Essential to utilizing a response to intervention model is high-quality instruction that allows student response to be gauged through ongoing analyses of student data. A critical factor in determining whether students are responding to intervention is knowing that the quality of instruction they are receiving as part of their classroom instruction (Tier 1) is of "high quality" so that students who are struggling are doing so because they need additional instruction—not because the instruction that they are receiving is inadequate. To ensure that appropriate instruction occurs, however, teachers need the knowledge and skills (1) to understand and interpret student data, and (2) to provide the reading instruction that meets the needs of all students, including struggling readers.

As provided in this study, Joyce and Showers (1996) promoted a "job embedded, staff development system" (p. 2) that focuses on the individual, collective, and district levels. By working with teachers individually and in groups (e.g., at grade-level meetings) and with principals individually and in groups (e.g., at district meetings) and framing our professional development as one piece of a response to intervention model, we worked within the type of system that these and other researchers (Guskey & Sparks, 2002) have described as important to effective staff development. At the most basic level, this study shows that students' overall progress can be enhanced when teachers participate in sustained professional development and use ongoing progress monitoring to inform their instructional decision making. At a more sophisticated level and for those implementing a response to intervention model, this study evidences the need for allocating time and resources to improve primary instruction before placing an overemphasis on the more intensive interventions provided at the secondary and tertiary levels.

Given the success that such an allocation of time and resources at the Tier 1 level demonstrated for students at risk for reading difficulties, we were interested in how the leadership at these schools played a role in their success. As stated earlier, the primary intervention coordinators met with each school's principal on a regular basis to discuss data and instruction. In our field notes, we observed one principal in particular who was especially active in the instructional processes and improvements that were noted throughout the observations. To enlighten our study further, we interviewed this principal about her perspectives of her role as the school's leader and analyzed these data along with data from field notes to develop a principal case study.

In summary, this 3-year study indicates the benefits for students at risk for reading problems when Tier 1 instruction is improved by the infusion of evidence-based practices due to teachers' engagement in ongoing and research-based professional development in reading, ongoing use of progress monitoring as data sources to inform instruction, and with strong leadership in their school supporting their efforts. We recognize that there are many challenges to maintaining these gains in future years as well as ensuring that these gains continue in older grades where more complex reading tasks make improving reading instruction for at-risk readers even more challenging.

## REFERENCES

Adams, M. J. (1990). *Beginning to read: Thinking and learning about print.* Cambridge, MA: MIT Press.

Anderson, L. M., Evertson, C. M., & Brophy, J. E. (1979). An experimental study of effective teaching in first grade reading groups. *Elementary School Journal, 79,* 193–222.

Baker, S., & Smith, S. (1999). Starting off on the right foot: The influence of four principles of professional development in improving literacy instruction in two kindergarten programs. *Learning Disabilities Research & Practice, 14,* 239–253.

Baker, S., & Smith, S. (2001). Linking school assessments to research-based practices in beginning reading: Improving programs and outcomes for students with and without disabilities. *Teacher Education and Special Education, 24*(4), 315–332.

Bryk, A., & Raudenbush, S. W. (1992). *Hierarchical linear models for social and behavioral research: Applications and data analysis methods.* Newbury Park, CA: Sage.

Chall, J. S. (2000). *The academic achievement challenge: What really works in the classroom?* New York: Guilford Press.

Clement, M., & Vandenberghe, R. (2001). How school leaders can promote teachers' professional development: An account from the field. *School Leadership and Management, 21,* 43–57.

Cohen, J. (1988). *Statistical power analysis for the behavioral sciences* (2nd ed.). Hillsdale, NJ: Elbaum.

Compton, D. L. (2003). The influence of item composition on ran letter performance in first-grade children. *Journal of Special Education, 37,* 81–94.

Donovan, M. S., & Cross, C. T. (Eds.). (2002). *Minority students in special and gifted education.* Washington, DC: National Academies Press.

Dunn, L. M., & Dunn, L. M. (1997). *Peabody Picture Vocabulary Test* (3rd ed.). Circle Pines, MN: American Guidance Service.

Fletcher, J. M., Shaywitz, S. E., Shankweiler, D. P., Katz, L., Liberman, I. Y., Stuebing, K. K., et al. (1994). Cognitive profiles of reading disability: Comparisons of discrepancy and low achievement definitions. *Journal of Educational Psychology, 86,* 6–23.

Fuchs, L. S., & Fuchs, D. (2003). Can diagnostic reading assessment enhance general educators' instructional differentiation and student learning? In B. R. Foorman (Ed.), *Preventing and remediating reading difficulties: Bringing science to scale* (pp. 325–351). Parkton, MD: York Press.

Gersten, R., Morvant, M., & Brengelman, S. (1995). Close to the classroom is close to the bone: Coaching as a means to translate research into classroom practice. *Exceptional Children, 62,* 52–66.

*GOALS 2000: Educate America Act of 1994*, 20 U.S.C.A. § 5811, 5812 (1994).

Good, R. H., & Kaminski, R. A. (Eds.). (2002). *Dynamic indicators of basic early literacy skills* (6th ed.). Eugene, OR: Institute for the Development of Education Achievement. Available at *dibels.uoregon.edu/*.

Good, R. H., Kaminski, R. A., Shinn, M., Bratten, J., Shinn, M., Laimon, L., et al. (2004). *Technical adequacy and decision making utility of DIBELS* (Technical Report No. 7). Eugene: University of Oregon.

Greenwood, C. R., & Delquadri, J. (1993). Current challenges to behavioral technology in the reform of schooling: Large-scale, high-quality implementation and sustained use of effective educational practices. *Education and Treatment of Children, 16*(4), 401–440.

Guskey, T. R. (1997). Research needs to link professional development and student learning. *Journal of Staff Development, 18*(2), 36–40.

Guskey, T. R., & Sparks, D. (1996). Exploring the relationship between staff development and improvements in student learning. *Journal of Staff Development, 17*(4), 34–38.

Guskey, T. R., & Sparks, D. (2002, April). *Linking professional development to improvements in students learning.* Paper presented at the annual meeting of the American Educational Research Association, New Orleans, LA.

Hanushek, E. A., Kain, J. F., & Rivkin, S. G. (1998). *Does special education raise academic achievement for students with disabilities?* (Working Paper No. 6690). Cambridge, MA: National Bureau of Economic Research.

Hedges, L. V. (1981). Distribution theory for Glass's estimator of effect size and related estimators. *Journal of Education Statistics, 6,* 107–128.

*Individuals with Disabilities Education Improvement Act*, 20 U.S.C. § 1400 (2004).

Joyce, B., & Showers, B. (1996). Staff development as a comprehensive service organization. *Journal of Staff Development, 17*(1), 2–6.

Kreft, I., & de Leeuw, J. (1998). *Introducing multilevel modeling.* London: Sage.

Marston, D., Muyskens, P., Lau, M., & Canter, A. (2003). Problem-solving model for decision making with high-incidence disabilities: The Minneapolis experience. *Learning Disabilities Research and Practice, 18,* 187–200.

Mathes, P. G., Clancy-Menchetti, J., & Torgesen, J. K. (2001). *Kindergarten peer-assisted literacy strategies.* Longmont, CO: Sopris West.

Mathes, P. G., Torgesen, J. K., & Allor, J. H. (2001). The effects of peer-assisted literacy strategies for first-grade readers with and without additional computer-assisted instruction in phonological awareness. *American Educational Research Journal, 38,* 371–410.

McCutchen, D., Abbott, R. D., Green, L. B., Beretvas, S. N., Cox, S., Potter, N. S., et al. (2002). Beginning literacy: Links among teacher knowledge, teacher practice, and student learning. *Journal of Learning Disabilities, 35,* 69–86.

Moody, S. W., Vaughn, S., Hughes, M. T., & Fischer, M. (2000). Reading instruction in the resource room: Set up for failure. *Exceptional Children, 66,* 305–316.

National Commission on Excellence in Education. (1983). *A nation at risk: The imperative*

*for educational reform* (Stock No. 065-000-00177-2). Washington, DC: U.S. Department of Education.

National Reading Panel. (2000). *Teaching children to read: An evidence-based assessment of the scientific research literature on reading and its implications for reading instruction: Reports of the subgroups* (NIH Publication No. 00-4754). Washington, DC: National Institute of Child Health and Human Development.

Neuhaus, G. F., & Swank, P. R. (2002). Understanding the relations between ran letter subtest components and word reading in first-grade students. *Journal of Learning Disabilities, 35*, 158–174.

Newmann, F. M., King, M. B., & Youngs, P. (2000). Professional development that addresses school capacity: Lessons from urban elementary schools. *American Journal of Education, 108*, 259–299.

*No Child Left Behind Act of 2001*, P.L. 107–110, 20 USC § 6301 (2002).

O'Connor, R. E. (1999). Teachers learning ladders to literacy. *Learning Disabilities Research and Practice, 14*, 203–214.

O'Connor, R. E., Fulmer, D., Harty, K. R., & Bell, K. M. (2005). Layers of reading intervention in kindergarten through third grade: Changes in teaching and student outcomes. *Journal of Learning Disabilities, 38*, 440–455.

O'Connor, R. E., & Jenkins, J. R. (1999). Prediction of reading disabilities in kindergarten and first grade. *Scientific Studies of Reading, 3*, 159–197.

Perie, M., Grigg, W., & Donahue, P. (2005). *The nation's report card: Reading 2005* (NCES 2006-451). Washington, DC: U.S. Government Printing Office.

Perkins-Gough, D. (2002). RAND report on reading comprehension. *Educational Leadership, 60*(3), 92.

Renyi, J. (1998). Building learning into the teaching job. *Educational Leadership, 55*(5), 70–74.

Simmons, D. C., Kuykendall, K., King, K., Cornachione, C., & Kame'enui, E. J. (2000). Implementation of a schoolwide reading improvement model: "No one ever told us it would be this hard!" *Learning Disabilities Research and Practice, 15*, 92–100.

Snijders, T. A., & Bosker, R. J. (1999). *Multilevel analysis: An introduction to basic and advanced multilevel modeling*. Thousand Oaks, CA: Sage.

Snow, C. E., Burns, M. S., & Griffin, P. (Eds.). (1998). *Preventing reading difficulties in young children*. Washington, DC: National Academic Press.

Speece, D. L., Case, L. P., & Molloy, D. E. (2003). Responsiveness to general education instruction as the first gate to learning disabilities identification. *Learning Disabilities Research and Practice, 18*, 147–156.

Stage, S. A., Sheppard, J., Davidson, M. M., & Browning, M. M. (2001). Prediction of first-graders' growth in oral reading fluency using kindergarten letter fluency. *Journal of School Psychology, 39*, 225–237.

Stallings, J., & Krasavage, E. M. (1986). Program implementation and student achievement in a four-year Madeline Hunter follow through project. *Elementary School Journal, 87*, 117–138.

Stallings, J., Robbins, P., Presbrey, L., & Scott, J. (1986). Effects of instruction based on the Madeline Hunter model on students' achievement: Findings from a follow-through project. *Elementary School Journal, 86*, 571–587.

Streeter, B. B. (1986). The effects of training experienced teachers in enthusiasm on students' attitudes toward reading. *Reading Psychology, 7*, 249–259.

Swanson, H. L., Hoskyn, M., & Lee, C. (1999). *Interventions for students with learning disabilities: A meta-analysis of treatment outcomes*. New York: Guilford Press.

Torgesen, J. K., Alexander, A. W., Wagner, R. K., Rashotte, C. A., Voeller, K. S., Conway, T., et al. (2001). Intensive remedial instruction for children with severe reading disabilities: Immediate and long-term outcomes from two instructional approaches. *Journal of Learning Disabilities, 34*, 33–58.

Vaughn, S., & Chard, D. (2006). Three-tier intervention research studies: Descriptions of two related projects. *Perspectives, 32*(1), 29–34.

Vaughn, S., Moody, S. W., & Schumm, J. S. (1998). Broken promises: Reading instruction in the resource room. *Exceptional Children, 64,* 211–225.

Vellutino, F. R., Scanlon, D. M., & Jaccard, J. (2003). Toward distinguishing between cognitive and experiential deficits as primary sources of difficulty in learning to read: A two year follow-up of difficult to remediate and readily remediated poor readers. In B. R. Foorman (Ed.), *Preventing and remediating reading difficulties: Bringing science to scale* (pp. 73–120). Parkton, MD: York Press.

Woodcock, R. W. (1987). *Woodcock Reading Mastery Test–Revised.* Circle Pines, MN: American Guidance Service.

Woodcock, R. W., & Johnson, M. B. (1977). *Woodcock–Johnson Psycho-Educational Battery.* Chicago: Riverside.

# CHAPTER 6

# Project CIRCUITS

*Center for Improving Reading Competence
Using Intensive Treatments Schoolwide*

DAVID J. CHARD *and* BETH A. HARN

$S$everal years before the conception of the project described in this chapter, two school districts, Bethel School District in Eugene, Oregon, and Tigard–Tualatin School District on the outskirts of Portland, Oregon, embarked separately on paths to implementation of a multi-tiered model of reading intervention. Both were laying the foundation for the project we describe in this chapter. Both districts were experiencing major challenges in academic achievement such that referrals to special education were inordinately high. Despite flagging state support for educational improvement, leadership in both districts were committed to securing external grant support through a university–school partnership with the University of Oregon. Districts were seeking to build a prevention model of reading instruction and behavioral support designed to build the capacity within each school and district to independently implement and sustain effective practices within a prevention model that is responsive to the range of students.

Because of the commitment made by both districts and the professional and compassionate efforts made daily by administrators, teachers, paraprofessionals, and parents to make sure this system was sustained, these two districts have since become state, regional, and national models. They demonstrate the potential impact that the components of multi-tiered models can have on student achievement when sustained implementation is achieved (Kame'enui, Good, & Harn, 2005). The accomplishments of these two school districts can not be overstated, for example, over 90% of students passed state-level assessments, annual yearly progress was maintained across schools, both experienced high graduation rates, and schools' were acknowledged by the state for closing the achievement gap for students from minority backgrounds.

In this chapter, we describe the combined efforts of the Project CIRCUITS (Center for Improving Reading Competence Using Intensive Treatments Schoolwide) team and school district partners to study and improve the features of the multi-tiered system in place in each district. Our description is of a formative research study in which we observed existing practices developed from a multiyear researcher–practitioner partnership between the participating school districts and the University of Oregon dating back nearly 10 years before the start of Project CIRCUITS. We used the findings of our observations to inform further professional development, refinement of practices and procedures, and further evaluation. We believe this design, though inadequate to provide definitive findings pointing to evidence-based practices, may increase our understanding of schoolwide practices that are likely to be sustained by teachers and schools after the completion of the project. Project CIRCUITS set out with two primary purposes: (1) to describe features of instruction in classrooms implementing research-based core reading programs that are associated with student success, and (2) to develop and evaluate procedures and practices to implement a systemic, preventive approach to reading instruction that would address the needs of all children K–3. The overarching research questions addressed in this project were

1. What was the state of three-tiered model practices in place in schools in both districts?
2. What aspects needed improvement?
3. What were the outcomes based on these improvements?

Below, we describe the specific instructional supports that were in place and the process and procedures for modifying practices to create instructional efficiencies that maximize instructional resources. We describe how we conceptualized and implemented a coordinated instructional support system in year 2 of the study for students needing Tier 2 and 3 instructional supports. Next, we provide a specific example of how data from screening, progress monitoring, and outcome measures were used in designing an instructional support plan in second grade for both Tier 2 and Tier 3 students. Finally, we discuss the lessons we have learned as a result of our work and the work of our district partners and how these lessons might guide future implementation of multi-tiered models of reading instruction.

## PARTICIPATING DISTRICTS AND SCHOOL DEMOGRAPHICS

### Bethel

The Bethel School District is a fast-growing district located in a midsize city in Lane County, Oregon, and serves approximately 3,000 elementary school students. According to the 2005 U.S. Census American Community Survey, 16% of children aged 5 to 17 in the county are living below the poverty level. According to the 2004–2005 Common Core of Data public school data, students in this district are primarily white (85%), followed by Latino (9%), with students of other races accounting for the remaining 6% of the student population (National Center on Educational Statistics, 2005a). The case study school presented within this chapter is Danebo Elementary School.

Danebo Elementary School is a Title I school located in the Bethel School District. The current enrollment at this school is 316 students in Kindergarten through fifth grade. According to 2004–2005 data (National Center on Educational Statistics, 2005a), students in this school are primarily white (71%), followed by Latino (17%), with students of other races accounting for the remaining 11% of the student population. Fifty-five percent of the students at this school qualify for free or reduced lunch, and seven students at this school qualify for services under the Migrant Education program.

### Tigard–Tualatin

The Tigard–Tualatin School District is located in Washington County (Oregon) on the urban fringe of a large city and serves over 5,500 elementary school students. According to the U.S. Census Bureau, 2005 American Community Survey, 12% of children aged 5 to 17 in the county are living below the poverty level (U.S. Census Bureau, 2005). According to the 2004–2005 CCD public school data, students in this district are primarily White (83%), followed by Latino (13%), with students of other races accounting for the remaining 4% of the student population. The case example school described here is Durham Elementary School.

Durham Elementary School is a Title I school located in the Tigard–Tualatin School District. The current enrollment at this school is 563 students in Kindergarten through fifth grade. According to the 2004–2005 CCD public school data students in this school are primarily white (67%), followed by Latino (19%), and Asian (9%), with students of other races accounting for the remaining 5% of the student population. Thirty-one percent of the students at this school qualify for free or reduced lunch. Table 6.1 provides some descriptive characteristics of teachers in both school districts.

## YEAR 1: IDENTIFYING FEATURES OF EFFECTIVE MULTI-TIERED SYSTEMS OF SUPPORT

Because Bethel and Tigard–Tualatin had been implementing a multi-tiered model of reading instruction several years before the inception of Project CIRCUITS in year 1, we conducted an observational study designed to identify features of established Tier 1 and Tier 2 instruction as discussed in Chapter 2 that were currently established, in place, and well implemented. This descriptive study used the Instructional Content Emphasis–Revised (ICE-R) instrument (Edmonds & Briggs, 2003). The ICE-R was developed to systematically categorize and code the content of reading and language arts instruction. Dimensions of instruction that were recorded included main instructional categories (e.g., phonemic awareness, fluency, comprehension), instructional focus, student grouping, and materials. These dimensions reflect instructional practices described as evidence-based by the National Institute of Child Health and Human Development (2000) and reviews of research focused on struggling learners (Vaughn, Gersten, & Chard, 2000). Observers, including

**TABLE 6.1. Descriptive Characteristics of Teachers in the Two Participating School Districts**

| | Districts | |
|---|---|---|
| Characteristics | 1 | 2 |
| No. of participating schools | 5 | 5 |
| No. of general education teachers (grades K–3) | 53 | 69 |
| No. of Title I teachers (grades K–3) | 8.5 | 10.2 |
| No. of special education teachers (grades K–3) | 5 | 2.5 |
| No. of teachers providing both special education and Title I services (grades K–3) | 0 | 7 |
| No. of teachers providing English language learner instruction (grades K–3) | 2 | 5.5 |

the principal investigators, graduate students, and school-based research staff, were trained to use the ICE-R using videotaped lessons. During the course of data collection, interobserver reliability was monitored on approximately 20% of observations in Tier 1 (primary) and Tier 2 (secondary) settings. Reliabilities were calculated on two dimensions of reading activities, a categorical dimension (e.g, phonemic awareness, reading comprehension) and an activity dimension (e.g., blending, summarizing) using the number of minutes each observer coded a particular activity occurring in the classroom. Kappa coefficients were calculated by both types of dimensions to identify agreements and disagreements. A kappa of .60 is a generally accepted criterion for observational data. The kappa coefficients for observations of Tier 1 classrooms across both dimensions averaged .65 ($SD$ = 0.07). In Tier 2 settings, the kappa coefficients averaged .76 ($SD$ = 0.11). In addition, as an indicator for student academic engagement, the total number of individual and group responses to instructional requests (teacher questions, prompts) as well as the total seconds of student oral reading time were recorded for each observation. The total numbers for each pair of reliability observations were compared. Percent agreement was calculated by dividing the smaller value by the larger value. Percent agreement for individual responses, group responses, and student reading time were 88.3%, 95.8%, and 98.8%, respectively.

Two rounds of observations were completed (winter and spring) during year 1 of Project CIRCUITS. Each classroom and teacher across primary, secondary, and tertiary instructional settings were observed by trained observers in winter and spring. The participating schools provided a time frame for reading instruction, the program, who was teaching, and the students that were to be present in each instructional group. However, because of limited resources, not every instructional group could be observed. For Tier 1, every general education teacher was observed. If a class was divided into small groups during Tier 1 instruction, the small group with whom the general education teacher worked was observed if it contained a targeted struggling student. Each teacher that provided Tier 2 and 3 instruction was also observed when working with a targeted student.

Descriptive statistics were calculated on the observation data and are available in detail from the authors. We summarize some of the key findings below. The maximum time limit for kindergarten instruction was 60 minutes and 90 minutes for first grade. Because some first-grade reading periods lasted longer than 90 minutes, observations were limited to 60 minutes of whole-group instruction and 30 minutes of small-group instruction. For secondary and tertiary reading groups, every interventionist was observed once. The maximum time limit for an observation was 60 minutes. We discuss these results within the next section of the chapter.

## Background Contexts: School District Similarities

Bethel and Tigard–Tualatin school districts shared many features that contributed to their successful implementation of multi-tiered instructional support in reading. These similarities included district-level leadership and support for a schoolwide approach to reading improvement; a sophisticated data collection system used for screening, diagnosis, progress monitoring, and evaluation; and an integrated approach to reading and behavioral support. Two particular features of the districts' reading programs set them apart from other districts with which we've worked. First, both districts implemented and sustained a professional development program designed to ensure that all educators (all teachers and paraprofessionals) were knowledgeable, skillful, and successful in their role in implementing a multi-tiered system of support. Second, both districts encouraged the adoption and use of instructional programs (core, supplemental, intervention) that focused on evidence-based instructional practices in teaching early reading. Although the features we listed are often found in other schools, the nature of the professional development and core program implementation in our partner districts are distinctive and are detailed below.

### Sustained Model of Professional Development

Little is known about the precise nature of professional development that promotes inservice teachers' sustained use of effective practices (Denton, Vaughn, & Fletcher, 2003). Still several researchers have pointed out that we are not without some guidance on the topic. For example, Showers, Joyce, and Bennett (1987) recommended that professional development programs include inservice opportunities that explain to teachers the how and why to implement new practices with supportive and specific feedback when teachers implement the new practices in their own classrooms. Relatedly, Gersten, Chard, and Baker (2000) noted that ongoing monitoring with feedback is an essential component of professional development because it leads to practice mastery, a degree of competence that makes teachers more likely to continue using a particular practice (Huberman & Miles, 1984).

The Bethel and Tigard–Tualatin school districts had developed and implemented efforts that reflected these research-based professional development practices. Specifically, both districts conceptualize professional development as a multifaceted system with multiple objectives that ensure that new and veteran teachers (1) have sufficient knowledge and skills to teach the core instructional program to address the state standards, (2) understand the needs of struggling readers and how to employ intervention materials to accelerate student learning, and (3) understand the system of early reading assessments and how to use these assessments to evaluate instructional effectiveness and make instructional changes to maximize student learning.

In addition to the content of the professional development, the format of professional development in both districts is rather unique. Both districts have developed internal capacity by developing a cadre of teachers who serve as instructional and assessment experts who can deliver professional development to new and veteran teachers to minimize the need for hiring outside consultants and make the support more timely and contextually relevant. Both districts schedule annual professional development opportunities before the school year begins that focus on introducing new teachers to the core program and interventions, the assessment systems, and the overall multi-tiered support model. Additionally, the districts schedule "refresher" professional development for teachers who want opportunities to improve their knowledge and skills as they relate to their classroom practice. During the school year, each school utilizes their Title I teachers to provide classroom teachers and intervention specialists with monitoring and feedback designed to support practice mastery and sound instructional decision making. These features of professional development are combined with teachers' and principals' close monitoring of student data to gauge instructional effectiveness. The combination of these professional development features has been a powerful tool in encouraging teachers to sustain their focus on the multi-tiered model of support and improving the quality of their instruction and improve student outcomes.

## Core Program Implemented with Fidelity

Many elementary classrooms in the United States are influenced by commercially published instructional materials. Core instructional programs are one way that school districts can facilitate the use of innovative practices across multiple classrooms (Ball & Cohen, 1996). However, it would be naïve to think that adoption of a core reading program would result in improved reading outcomes without the concomitant professional development and support needed to effectively use the core program with the range of readers in most classrooms. Indeed, the program is simply a tool, if not shown how to use it effectively, the outcome may not be what was intended. High-quality, research-based curriculum materials paired with high-quality professional development and support are likely to lead to improved instructional practices (Chard, 2004; Denton et al., 2003).

The multi-tiered models developed in Bethel and Tigard–Tualatin schools have depended in part on the adoption of research-based core instructional programs. Unlike many districts that have elected to implement systemwide reading reforms and have insisted that a single core program be used in every school in the district, both partner districts have allowed their elementary schools to select a core program from a list of options. All of the programs that were identified as options were first reviewed by district-level leadership and reading instructional experts and were determined to address important grade-level reading standards. Once the list of optimal programs was developed, school principals were encouraged to have their teachers review the options and make a decision based on their professional knowledge and their knowledge and understanding of the community and the students with whom they work. Consequently, within each district there is a range of programs used. Rather than insist that every school use the same curricular materials, the districts focus on evidence-based practices and give local schools parameters about how best to implement those practices. This strategy is believed to have lead to greater "buy in" on the part of each school's teachers.

## Descriptive Findings: Instructional Variation between Schools and Districts

One of the most prominent findings of our year 1 observation work was the unexpected degree of variation documented in classroom reading instruction within and between tiers of support. Despite their many common features, there were striking differences documented during the course of observations. Table 6.2 provides detailed data on several classroom variables including total instructional minutes, minutes spent in each of four key areas (i.e., phonemic awareness, phonics, fluency, and vocabulary/comprehension), the number of group responses to instruction, and the number of individual responses to instruction for first grade across the two districts. The overall number of minutes spent in instruction, as well as the amount of time spent in each skill area, are generally equivalent within instructional tier across districts. Observations indicated that, in general, first-grade teachers in both districts appeared to spend much more time in phonics and vocabulary/comprehension instruction than in phonemic awareness and fluency. However, district 2 primary classrooms spent considerably more time in vocabulary and comprehension instruction. In general, observations in both districts documented that much more time was spent in Tier 1 than in Tier 2 instruction. The number of group responses

**TABLE 6.2. Selected Descriptive Results from Year 1 Observations of Instructional Contexts in Participating School Districts**

| Term | Setting | District | N | Total instructional minutes | | Minutes in PA | | Minutes in Ap | | Minutes in FL | | Minutes in VC | | Minutes I academic—other | | Individual responses | | Group responses | |
|---|---|---|---|---|---|---|---|---|---|---|---|---|---|---|---|---|---|---|---|
| | | | | M | SD | M | SD | M | SD | M | SD | M | SD | M | SD | M | SD | M | SD |
| Winter | Tier 1 | 1 | 17 | 75.8 | 17.4 | 1.7 | 3.2 | 31.1 | 17.2 | 9.8 | 10.6 | 6.1 | 5.1 | 27.1 | 17.1 | 19.8 | 37.9 | 118.1 | 69.3 |
| | | 2 | 22 | 77.3 | 14.1 | 1.9 | 3.5 | 25.9 | 10.9 | 15.2 | 11.4 | 22.7 | 15.5 | 11.6 | 8.2 | 18.7 | 23.1 | 104.7 | 85.1 |
| | Tiers 2/3 | 1 | 24 | 34.8 | 14.1 | 2.4 | 4.2 | 18.9 | 14.1 | 4.1 | 4.7 | 5.7 | 5.9 | 3.6 | 4.2 | 69.5 | 57.4 | 108.1 | 90.6 |
| | | 2 | 32 | 22.0 | 9.3 | 0.3 | 1.1 | 10.1 | 9.4 | 5.1 | 5.2 | 4.5 | 4.7 | 1.9 | 3.4 | 64.6 | 60.4 | 21.9 | 42.3 |
| Spring | Tier 1 | 1 | 17 | 77.7 | 11.2 | 0.3 | 1.3 | 28.6 | 11.3 | 13.4 | 12.1 | 11.5 | 10.5 | 23.9 | 13.6 | 15.1 | 15.3 | 104.4 | 82.6 |
| | | 2 | 22 | 71.9 | 19.5 | 0.3 | 1.1 | 19.8 | 16.9 | 8.5 | 7.9 | 25.9 | 21.8 | 17.3 | 11.0 | 13.7 | 20.2 | 58.5 | 50.6 |
| | Tiers 2/3 | 1 | 25 | 34.2 | 11.8 | 1.2 | 3.1 | 16.0 | 10.8 | 6.5 | 5.9 | 6.1 | 6.7 | 4.4 | 5.1 | 67.8 | 53.0 | 73.3 | 47.5 |
| | | 2 | 26 | 19.6 | 7.4 | 0.3 | 1.0 | 7.5 | 6.8 | 5.6 | 5.1 | 4.7 | 4.7 | 1.5 | 2.6 | 56.7 | 39.2 | 12.3 | 22.1 |

*Note.* PA, phonemic awareness; AP, alphabetic principles; FL, fluency; VC, vocabulary.

documented in Tier 1 and 2 instruction was consistently higher in district 1, suggesting that students in district 1 were more actively engaged in reading activities than those in district 2. In some cases, these differences were nearly fivefold. Despite considerable variation in these key instructional variables, the differences in group responses did not seem to matter relative to student achievement.

One general observation we noted across the observations we completed in year 1 was that students were being exposed to a number of different instructional programs and approaches across settings, especially the most at-risk readers. Additionally, observers noted that the programs often varied in the approach taken in how reading was taught, though each was teaching essential skills in reading, leaving the negotiation of how the differing instructional approaches were the same up to the students least likely to identify the commonalities (i.e., the most at-risk readers)

In summary, our observations in year 1 left us impressed with the progress Bethel and Tigard–Tualatin had made in developing multi-tiered systems of support. Rather than developing a new support model, we collaborated with district leadership to determine ways to enhance the instruction and support already being provided in Tiers 1 and 2 and to develop and implement effective Tier 3 intervention support for students who were not benefiting sufficiently from Tier 2 instruction. Creating efficiencies through instructional alignment and coordinating instructional support was the focus of year 2 of the project as we followed our identified at-risk kindergartners into first grade.

## YEAR 2: CAN TIER 2 AND 3 SUPPORTS LEAD TO IMPROVEMENTS IN LEARNING?

As part of implementing a three-tiered approach to supporting the range of learners, schools within the project created a continuum of instructional support. This continuum provides the general plan of how reading instruction will be provided at each grade level to allocate resources across settings and personnel as efficiently and effectively as possible while also being responsive to student instructional needs. The general features each school considered in creating the plan for each tier of instructional support included the following:

1. Program: Specifying which program or materials to be used with the group.
2. Time: The amount of time allocated to accelerate student learning.

3. Grouping: The grouping arrangements necessary for meeting student instructional needs.
4. Instructor: The instructor identified to provide or supervise the instructional delivery of the group.
5. Setting: The instructional setting or location of the group.
6. Evaluating progress: The frequency of how often a student's response to the instructional support will be collected for evaluation purposes.

The next section provides a general overview of the features and considerations when creating a continuum of instructional support, with general examples provided in Figure 6.1, and then we provide a more detailed example using two schools within this project for Grade 2.

## Tier 1

The purpose of Tier 1 instructional support is to deliver the instructional components necessary to meet the needs of the vast majority of students, and within this project this was accomplished by using a research-based core reading program. The goal of this tier is to continue to develop and expand the reading skills of all students through careful attention to teaching the essential skills in reading within multiple grouping arrangements with sufficient time that is prioritized, protected, and allocated to the topic. The time allocated is determined by each program, and the general education teacher typically assumes responsibility for meeting the needs of these students. To ensure students are continuing to make progress, students are screened at the beginning, middle, and end of the school year using the Dynamic Indicators of Basic Early Literacy Skills (DIBELS). The DIBELS are a set of standardized, individually administered measures designed to efficiently and effectively assess developing skills in phonological awareness, alphabetic principle, fluency in connected text, and letter knowledge. The specific data supporting the reliability and validity of these measures are addressed within this book as well as in the literature (Good & Kaminski, 2003).

## Tier 2

The purpose of Tier 2 instructional support is to systematically increase instructional support for students identified as at risk for long-term reading difficulty. As specified in Figure 6.2, students requiring Tier 2 instructional support are provided more reading instructional time and more of this time spent in smaller grouping arrangements. To maximize instructional days and be responsive to student needs, student progress is

| Instructional elements | Tier 1—primary instructional support | | | |
|---|---|---|---|---|
| | K | 1 | 2 | 3 |
| Program | Research-based core reading program | | | |
| Time allocated | 60 | 90 | 100 | 100 |
| Grouping | Large and small arrangements based on program and skill of students | | | |
| Instructor | General education teacher | | | |
| Setting | General education classroom | | | |
| Evaluating progress | Beginning, middle, & end of year | | | |
| Instructional elements | Tier 2—secondary instructional support | | | |
| | K | 1 | 2 | 3 |
| Program | Research-based core reading program + supplemental intervention | | | |
| Time allocated | 60 + 30 = 90 | 90 + 30 = 120 | 80 + 45 = 125 | 90 + 45 = 135 |
| Grouping | Large and small arrangements based on program and skill of students | | | |
| Instructor | GE + Title | GE + Title | GE + Title | GE + Title |
| Setting | General education classroom | GE + Title classroom | GE + Title classroom | GE + Title classroom |
| Evaluating progress | 2 x month | 2 x month | 2 x month | 2 x month |
| Instructional elements | Tier 3—tertiary instructional support | | | |
| | K | 1 | 2 | 3 |
| Program | Research-based core reading program | Research-based core + intervention program | Research-based core + intervention program | Research-Based Core + Intervention Programs |
| Time allocated | NA | 60 + 60 = 120 | 30 + 45 + 45 = 120 | 30 + 45 + 45 = 120 |
| Grouping | Large and small arrangements based on program and skill of students; mainly small skill groups | | | |
| Instructor | | GE + Title | GE + Title + SPED | GE + Title + SPED |
| Setting | NA | GE + Title classroom | GE + Title + SPED classroom | GE + Title + SPED classroom |
| Evaluating progress | | 4 x month | 4 x month | 4 x month |

*Note.* GE, general education; SPED, special education; NA, not applicable

**FIGURE 6.1.** Description of instructional variables for each level of support needed.

monitored at least twice a month using the DIBELS so educators know when/if a change in their instructional plan is warranted. The sensitivity of this type of progress monitoring has been documented to improve instructional decision making and improve outcomes for students (Fuchs, Deno, & Mirkin, 1984; Fuchs, Fuchs, Hosp, & Jenkins; 2001; Kaminski & Good, 1996). Because of individual child variation in learning to read, and the reality that a core reading program is not designed to meet the needs of all children, schools must select or develop and implement a range of reading programs to effectively target instructional needs. "One size does not fit all" is a pedagogical and instructional reality in schools (Harn, Kame'enui, & Simmons, 2007). Therefore, Tier 2 support involves selecting programs and procedures to systematically supplement, enhance, and/or support the core reading program. The goal of Tier 2 is to increase instructional support to accelerate learning by systematically targeting the instructional needs of students through coordinating instructional programs and personnel across settings. To maximize instructional time for at-risk readers, the following were considered in the selection process: verification of research-based results, alignment of program with the core reading program, and consistency of instructional language and delivery. Additionally, the number of instructional objectives taught within the supplemental program was also carefully considered in relation to the needs of the learner. For example, students in third grade may be low performing and needing Tier 2 support, but some may have instructional needs in building fluency in reading connected text whereas others also have needs in word reading instruction. These groups of students would be supported differentially through program selection, time, and/or setting of the group, yet all groups are coordinated at the grade level. The coordination at the grade level ensures that all instructional support personnel (general education, Title I, English language learning [ELL], special education, etc.) work with one another to assist in scheduling, increase communication of instructional focus, and allow for discussion of student progress in relation to the instructional plan.

## Tier 3

Students needing Tier 3 instructional support demonstrate either (1) significantly low skills, or (2) significantly low skills combined with limited progress when provided additional instructional support. Students needing this instructional support require significantly more instructional resources delivered with greater intensity and specificity than students receiving Tier 2 instructional support. To accelerate learning of the essential skills of reading upon which all other reading skills rest, pro-

Grade: 2     Time of Year: Fall–Winter     Instructional Area: Reading

Summary of Instructional Support Plan for Danebo Elementary School

| Level of instructional support | Who? (What skill level of students) | With What? (Which materials and activities) | What More? (Supplemental or additional support materials and activities) | How Are We Doing? (Determining effectiveness with progress monitoring) |
|---|---|---|---|---|
| Tier 1 / Primary: | Which students: Students on-track As measured by: ORF > 44 | Name of program / materials: Open Court Reading Program When: 8:45–10:15 Activities: All activities in core Group size: Large and some small group (5–8) | Name of program / materials: Not Applicable | Who to collect: Schoolwide team How Often: Quarterly Criteria: See DIBELS goals Determining fidelity of implementation (Who, With what, How often?): Literacy coach, district form, quarterly |
| Tier 2 / Secondary: | Which students: Students with difficulties in fluency, general decoding, and possibly comprehension As measured by: ORF 26–44 | Name of program / materials: Open Court Reading Program When: 8:45–10:15 Activities: All except independent writing Group size: Large and some small group (5–8) | Name of program / materials: Read Naturally and Phonics for Reading Program Combination Who to deliver: Title 1 staff When: In addition to typical time Specify time (minutes, days of week): 10:30–11 M–F Group size: 4–8 | Who to collect: Title 1 staff How often: 2 × month Criteria: Keeping pace with DIBELS aimline Determining fidelity of implementation (Who, With what, How often?): Title teacher, project developed form, monthly) |
| Tier 3 / Tertiary: | Which Students: Students with significant difficulties in fluency, decoding, and possibly comprehension As measured by: ORF < 25 | Name of Program / Materials: Open Court Reading Program When: 8:45–9:15 Activities: Vocabulary and oral comprehension Group size: Large group | Name of program / materials: Reading Mastery (RM); Read Naturally (RN) Who to deliver: Special Education (RM) and Title 1 (RN) When: Within typical and additional time Specify time (minutes, days of week): Reading Mastery: 9:15–10 M–F Read Naturally: 1–1:45 Group size: 4 or fewer | Who to collect: Special education team How often: Weekly Criteria: Keeping pace with DIBELS aimline Determining Fidelity of Implementation (Who, With what, How often?): Special education teacher, project developed form, monthly |

**FIGURE 6.2.** A summary of instructional support provided for second grade at Danebo Elementary School.

grams selected are typically highly focused on component skills. This narrow focus is purposeful to accelerate learning of the component skills as quickly as possible to catch students up as quickly as possible to transition them to a more balanced reading approach. The nature of such intervention, or acceleration program, has many delivery requirements that must be carefully considered before selection. The delivery requirements of these research-based programs include the expense of the materials, need for professional development, specified group size in delivery, skill level of the interventionists/teacher, as well as instructional time.

Because these students have the most to learn, they need to receive even more instructional time than students receiving Tier 2 instructional supports, and more of that time needs to be spent in small-group situations. Students requiring this intensive level of support need a plan of instruction that is specifically designed to meet the instructional needs of the students. Often the instruction is delivered by personnel with specialized training (e.g., Title I, special education, reading specialists) in coordination with the general education teacher. The scheduling of additional time in small-group arrangements necessitates careful coordination of resources and thoughtful discussion with parents/guardians and educational personnel. As indicated in Figure 6.2, students received far more instructional time then their peers, and with the finite amount of time in the instructional day, this means that students missed other instructional content. This was a joint conversation where all (parents, teachers, principals) carefully weighed the pros and cons of putting reading as the highest priority during the instructional day. All agreed that improving reading skills early in children's schooling was a necessary decision that would support the students' learning content (e.g., social studies, science) in later grades when students would be able to read the content successfully. The goal is to intensify in grades 1–3 sufficiently to actually change the child's future. This was approached as a temporary, short-term decision to reap the long-term benefit of adequate reading skills to support overall student learning. Team discussions also revolved around ways to address content standards through reading practices.

Considerations in creating an instructional plan differentiated to meet the needs of the range of learners primarily revolve around the selection and implementation of programs/materials. High-quality implementation of research-based programs is essential given the focus of the current IDEA—Response to Intervention legislation. Crucial to implementing programs as designed, or with fidelity, is the role of professional development. Schools approached the role of professional development to ensure delivery of the program with fidelity while also improving overall instructional skills. Areas also targeted for professional development included support in effectively differentiating instruction within and across programs as well as effective grouping arrangements across settings.

In summary, the general features of a three-tiered instructional delivery model include implementing a continuum of instructional support across grades, settings, and instructional personnel (ELL, special education, Title I, and general education). This continuum systematically increases support in response to student performance by carefully coordinating and attending the following features:

1. *Programs*: Careful selection of a continuum of research-based programs and materials that are aligned with one another as well as effective at targeting the range of instructional needs students display.

2. *Time*: Allocating sufficient time to improving student reading performance. The magnitude of the reading difficulty needs to be carefully considered in determining the amount of time necessary to change long-term reading skills.

3. *Grouping*: Teachers need to carefully consider the skills to be taught as well as the needs of the learner to determine the amount of time spent in more intensive grouping arrangements.

4. *Instructors*: Schools need to consider the needs of the learner in relation to the person best capable in meeting student learning needs.

5. *Setting*: Instructional resources need to be allocated and coordinated at the school/grade level to improve communication across settings as well as to maximize scheduling and personnel.

6. *Evaluation of progress*: To make timely instructional changes, students more at risk need their skills evaluated more often.

Evident in developing this continuum of instructional support is the need for a unified, team, and schoolwide approach to providing reading instruction. All essential personnel are necessary in creating the instructional schedule, selecting and implementing instruction, and reviewing student progress. This team approach to meeting the needs of students shares the awesome responsibility and challenge these schools accept in meeting the needs of each student through more effective and efficient resource allocation. The "lone arranger" approach to instruction of the recent past, although well intentioned and filled with many success stories, conflicts with current societal expectations and needs for each student to be a successful reader. Each teacher can be more successful with all students through the coordination of professional development, programs, and personnel in response to the instructional needs of the building or classroom of students.

Our question in year 2 was "Could we improve reading skills and growth in reading for students receiving Tiers 2 and 3 instructional supports by creating overt instructional alignment across settings/tiers? For example, for students requiring Tier 2 instructional supports, could we increase reading skills by using the same instructional materials and objectives from the core reading program, yet reteaching the priority skills (word reading, connected text reading) in smaller groups with a more explicit and consistent instructional delivery approach in a reteaching format? A similar, yet more intensive approach (smaller group size, more time, greater explicitness, additional practice) was used with students requiring Tier 3 instructional supports. Figure 6.3 provides a comparison of oral reading fluency (ORF) growth for students in first grade requiring additional supports (i.e., Tier 2 or Tier 3) at our two case example schools across year 1 and year 2 of the project. Remember the year 1 data are the results obtained by schools without project support and limited alignment in instructional materials and objectives across tiers, while year 2 was when the schools aligned supports. The box plots display how all the students receiving additional supports performed across time (winter and spring) as well as across year (year 1 and year 2) for each school. Results indicated a more beneficial effect for Danebo than Durham in aligning the instructional supports. At Danebo in year 1, the typical student (50th percentile) receiving additional supports read 30 words per minute at the end of year compared to 60 words per minute in year 2 for students who received aligned supports. Additionally, the entire distribution of at-risk students (between the 20th and 80th percentiles) demonstrated greater growth when compared to similar performing students the year before. At Durham, the differences in alignment demonstrated no discernable differences. There are many reasons needing further investigation as to why these schools displayed differential results (i.e., fidelity of implementation, possibly the materials used in one school prior to change were more/less aligned then the other, amount of instructional time spent teaching reading in general education). However, these results and collaboration with schools demonstrated a need for creating a broader continuum of instructional support to organize instructional efforts and allocate resources.

## PROJECT IMPLEMENTATION: CONTINUUM OF INSTRUCTIONAL SUPPORT FOR SECOND GRADE

In this section, we provide an example of how second grade implemented its instructional support plan to accelerate student learning for the case example schools described previously: Danebo and Durham Elementary Schools. See Figure 6.2 for the general features of how programs, time, and instructional resources were coordinated and allocated.

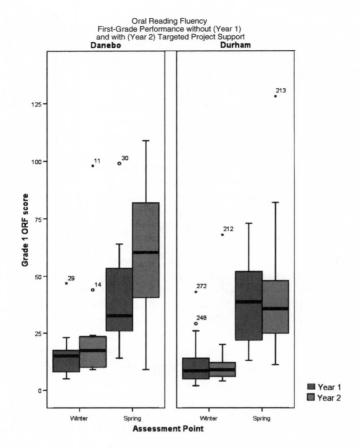

**FIGURE 6.3.** First-grade oral reading fluency (ORF) performance without (year 1) and with (year 2) targeted project support.

For the purposes of this example, we do specify the programs used; however, they are provided as an example and not used as an endorsement of them specifically. After discussing the specific instructional features, general results are provided from two schools.

## Tier 1

Both example schools within our project had previously adopted the Open Court Reading Program and had been using the program for over 3 years. To implement the program with fidelity, schools had allocated a minimum of 90 minutes each day to reading instruction. Teachers carefully considered the instructional objective to be taught (vocabulary, phonics, etc.) as well as skill level of students when determining grouping arrangements. Instructional objectives that were less challenging, reviewed, and/or required students to simply listen to the teacher were typically provided in large-group arrangements (e.g., listening comprehension, vocabulary). Objectives requiring students produce the taught skill as well as more challenging were selected to be taught in small homogenous groups (phonics, fluency). General education teachers carefully orchestrated the transition between activities, and students' progress was monitored quarterly. Students evaluated as on-track with their reading skills received all instructional support within the general education setting.

## Tier 2

For students identified at moderate risk on the DIBELS assessment (i.e., strategic), instructional support was systematically intensified. As specified in the instructional support plan, the core program was still the primary source of reading instruction. However, these students were identified as having instructional needs in improving word reading and fluency in connected text skills. These skills were addressed using an alternating schedule of Read Naturally (Ihnot, 2003) and Phonics for Reading (Archer, Flood, Lapp, and Lungren, 2002) during a 45-minute period in additional to the core reading instruction time. The groups were delivered within the Title I classroom setting in small-group arrangements (4–8). Students' progress was monitored twice a month using ORF. As part of the research project, schools implemented this instructional support plan for 14 weeks to determine the efficacy of this combination of programs. Although final results are pending, average words per week growth was 2.54 for Danebo and 1.76 for Durham, which is higher than the typical rate of 1.4 words per week reported by Fuchs, Fuchs, Hamlet, Walz, and German (1993). After the research portion of the school year, schools evaluated each student's progress to determine the level of instructional support necessary. Some students demonstrated they no longer needed instructional support beyond Tier 1, some displayed continued need for Tier 2 support, and a few demonstrated a need for increased instructional support.

## Tier 3

For students identified as at high risk (i.e., intensive) on the DIBELS assessment or displayed limited growth in response to additional instructional supports in Tier 2, instructional support was further intensified. For many of these students, the gap between the instructional objectives

of the core reading program in some reading areas (e.g., advanced pho-
nic elements) and student skill level (e.g., inconsistent letter–sound
knowledge) was so large that the school-level reading team and parents
determined that other instructional materials would be more appropriate. Careful decisions were made on what skills (e.g., vocabulary, listening comprehension) to teach during the time students were in the general
education classroom so that this time would be beneficial to all students.
Critical skills that needed to be taught with urgency (i.e., alphabetic
principle, word reading, reading connected text) were thought to be best
addressed by intervention and acceleration programs specifically designed with careful sequencing of skill introduction and development,
ample opportunities to practice and review, and explicit instructional
strategies to maximize instructional time and learning. To accelerate
learning, these students were provided with more than 90 minutes of
reading instruction each day, with the majority of it provided in small
groups by Title I and/or special education personnel. To improve the
quality of instructional decision making, progress monitoring was conducted every week so that instruction was maximally responsive to student learning.

Initially, the research-based program Reading Mastery was delivered in small groups (i.e., four or fewer) across two 45-minute sessions
each day. Instructors were explicitly trained to accelerate pace through
the program to fill students' skill gaps as quickly as possible. Progress
for the five students across both of the case example schools are presented in Figure 6.4. As the graph displays, progress from implementation of just the Reading Mastery program, even with an accelerated approach and implemented with high fidelity, demonstrated unsatisfactory
progress. We then considered the nature of the instructional objectives
taught within the program, rate of demonstrated progress, and general
instructional needs of the students. A decision was made to increase the
amount of time spent with students in fluency building, so students began receiving the Read Naturally program along with Reading Mastery
beginning approximately in March. So the 90 minutes of small-group instruction was split so that students received 60 minutes of instruction
within Reading Mastery and 30 minutes of Read Naturally each day. So
time, instructor, setting, and group size were not adjusted; only the nature of the instructional objectives taught within the time was modified.
This change in instructional focus appears to have a dramatic effect on
student performance. Table 6.3 illustrates the slopes of students before
and after the change of instructional focus and demonstrates that all but
one student more than doubled their rate of progress with this change.
Three of five students also improved to the point of moving from the intensive to the strategic instructional recommendation across the course

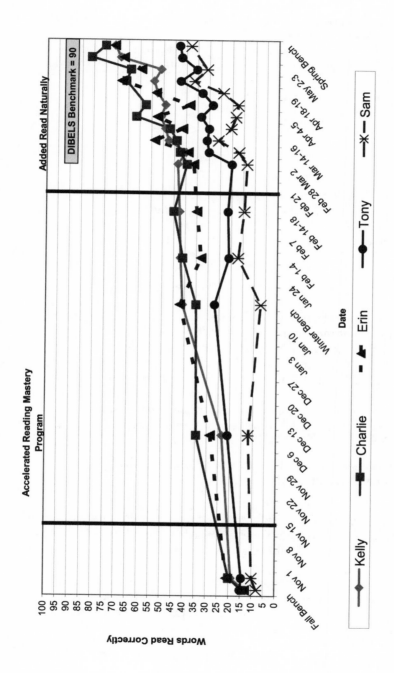

**FIGURE 6.4.** Oral reading fluency progress for students in second grade receiving Tier 3 supports across sample schools.

**TABLE 6.3. Words per Week Growth on Oral Reading Fluency for Sample Tier 3 Students across Both Schools**

| Student | Slopes from Nov.–Feb. (words per minute per week) | Slopes from March–May (words per minute per week) |
|---|---|---|
| Kelly | 1.58 | 2.49 |
| Charlie | 1.43 | 3.91 |
| Erin | 1.11 | 3.23 |
| Tony | 0.44 | 1.83 |
| Sam | 0.29 | 2.21 |

of the year. Although two of the students (both of which were identified as learning disabled) continue to display significantly low reading skills, it is important to emphasize the amount of individual growth these students made when provided this intensive level of instructional support.

## LESSONS LEARNED

Over the course of the past several years, we have had the opportunity to work with two of the finest school districts in the United States in building a sustainable system of supports intended to prevent reading difficulties in young children and to provide them with the skills and knowledge they need to be successful as they progress in school. As with any initiative of this sort, we have learned many lessons. In this section, we share some of these lessons in hopes that our insights may assist other school districts, researchers, and partnerships in similar efforts.

### Don't Underestimate the Importance of High-Quality Professional Development

Professional development as it relates to a multi-tiered model of support needs to be conceived as multifaceted and delivered through a variety of interdependent approaches. These approaches should include, but may not be limited to, the following: large-group in-service, small-group problem solving, ongoing coaching, and troubleshooting. Each of these delivery models has advantages. The large-group in-service provides for getting a common message to many people quickly. The small-group problem solving allows for teachers and support personnel to discuss a professional paper or discuss approaches they have tried and how they might modify their approach to achieve their goal. The troubleshooting sessions give participants an opportunity to focus on a specific identified issue (e.g., implementation of an intervention or new program) and to develop hypotheses on how to solve it.

In the initiative we've described in this chapter, we believe that the coaching model was of particular importance for several reasons. It was the role of the coach to be the additional eyes in the classroom as teachers implemented Tier 2 and 3 interventions. As such, the coach collected specific data on each child to provide the teacher with objective feedback about how students were responding during instruction. For example, coaches would frequently let teachers know if they had perceived that a child was not responding accurately to questions or was depending too much on a peer in their attempts to identify a particular letter–sound or word in text. Additionally, the coach provided specific feedback on the fidelity with which teachers were using the instructional materials and made suggestions to the teacher about how they might change how they were delivering the instruction to improve outcomes. The regularly scheduled fidelity observations were implemented as overt, targeted professional development opportunities. Interventionists were fully aware of the need for the observations, were provided good training for successful implementation of the intervention, were made aware of explicit "look fors" in implementation, and were provided additional support if the implementation was not considered adequate. The specificity of the coaching model was also noted by school district administrators as playing an important role in the quality of the interventions provided.

Another critical and unique feature of all aspects of the professional development component of the multi-tiered approach was its ongoing nature. We discussed this in great detail earlier in the chapter. At this point, we want to follow up by noting that teachers in both districts now expect that they will be engaged in focused opportunities to learn more about how to provide effective instruction to all their students. They also expect that this professional development will include regular evaluation of the work they are doing, differentiated professional development for teachers who need assistance or are new to the system, reminders of principles that form the foundation of the multi-tiered support system, and a constant focus and refocus the instruction in improving data-based outcomes.

## Ensure Clarity of and Maintain Expectations

Multi-tiered systems of support like those described in this book require a significant change in the way school personnel perceive of the challenges they face. Historically, when a student failed to meet expectations, it was often attributed to intra-individual problems experienced by the student. In contrast, the approach we describe here would view reading or behavior problems as problems in the environment that should be addressed by examining variables in the environment that can be altered to ensure success (Howell & Nolet, 2000; Kame'enui & Simmons, 1990). This shift empowers all educators in the building (teachers, administrators, and paraprofessionals) and highlights the critical role they play in improving outcomes through their instructional efforts. Moreover, these expectations need to be communicated clearly so that all personnel understand that when challenges arise within the system the challenges are addressed through changes in instruction or the instructional environment.

These expectations have been embraced and maintained by the districts participating with us. Each year, they are reinforced through district- and school-level meetings that focus on goal setting, planning, and determining the means of support necessary to assist schools to meet their goals. As noted earlier in the chapter, the expectations that are reinforced in these districts are maintained despite the significant variations with which schools implement the three tiers of support. To many people, this variation would suggest that some students must not be receiving high-quality support. We believe this variation is more a function of the specific approach to implementation taken by each school, grade, and class and does not preclude having similar high expectations. Finally, we think it is important to note that even in lean financial times, as we often find in Oregon schools, our partner districts maintain their priority on instructional and behavioral supports and the tools that schools need to help their students be successful.

## Create a Shared Vision among Critical Parties

Related to the clarity of expectations, schools that choose to embark on a multi-tiered system of support must develop a shared vision focused on student success. Foremost, this vision must be shared by personnel who will be working most closely with students in the classroom and intervention settings. We believe it is this vision that stimulates clear communication and an "esprit de corps" that helps school personnel overcome many of the challenges they will face as they implement similar models (Simmons, Kame'enui, Harn, Cole, & Braun, 2000). It is a bonus if this vision is also shared by principals and district leadership as it is in Bethel and Tigard–Tualatin schools. However, we believe that success in a multi-tiered model can be achieved even when principals and district leadership are distracted by other business (Denton et al., 2003). Although leadership support will certainly facilitate the hard work that must be done to develop and implement an effective multi-tiered model of instructional support, it is most important that leadership not stand in the way of implementation. When that happens, success will be much more difficult to achieve.

fluency), we feel certain that many of these students will need ongoing support as the reading and language arts demands increase from grade to grade.

Our aim with this chapter was to add to the growing number of reports of promising systemic results including decreased referral rates and higher achievement rates (Haager, Klinger, & Vaughn, 2007; Vaughn, Linan-Thompson, & Hickman, 2003). Additionally, we hope this chapter serves to illustrate some of the critical features necessary for multitiered models to be implemented in real classrooms in real schools including the extensive planning for differentiated support and the high degree of flexibility that may be a necessary part of implementation.

## REFERENCES

Archer, A., Flood, J., Lapp, D., & Lungren, L. (2002). *Phonics for reading.* North Billerica, MA: Curriculum Associates, Inc.

Ball, D. L., & Cohen, D. K. (1996). Reform by the book: What is—or might be—the role of curriculum materials in teacher learning and instructional reform? *Educational Researcher, 25*(9), 6–8,14.

Chard, D. J. (2004). Toward a science of professional development in early reading instruction. *Exceptionality, 12*(3), 175–191.

Denton, C. A., Vaughn, S., & Fletcher, J. M. (2003). Bringing research-based practice in reading intervention to scale. *Learning Disabilities: Research and Practice, 18*(3), 201–211.

Duke, N. K. (2004). The case for information text. *Educational Leadership, 61*(6), 40.

Edmonds., M. S., & Briggs, K. L. (2003). Instructional content emphasis instrument. In S. R. Vaughn & K. L. Briggs (Eds.), *Reading in the classroom: Systems for observing teaching and learning* (pp. 31–52). Baltimore: Brookes.

Ehri, L. C. (2005). Learning to read words: Theory, findings, and issues. *Scientific Studies of Reading, 9*(2), 167–188.

Foorman, B., & Torgesen, J. (2001). Critical elements of classroom and small-group instruction promote reading success in all children. *Learning Disabilities Research and Practice, 16*(4), 203–212.

Fuchs, L. S., Deno, S. L., & Mirkin, P. K. (1984). The effects offrequent curriculum-based measurement and evaluation on pedagogy, student achievement, and student awareness ofleaming. *American Educational Research Journal, 21*(2), 449–460.

Fuchs, L. S., Fuchs, D., Hamlet, C. L., Walz, L., & German, G. (1993). Formative evaluation of academic progress: How much growth can we expect? *School Psychology Review, 22*(1), 27–48.

Fuchs, L. S., Fuchs, D., Hosp, M. K., & Jenkins, J. (2001). Oral reading fluency as an indicator of reading competence: A theoretical, empirical, and historical analysis. *Scientific Studies of Reading, 5*(3), 239–256.

Gersten, R., Chard, D. J., & Baker, S. (2000). Factors enhancing sustained use of research-based instructional practices. *Journal of Learning Disabilities, 33,* 445–457.

Good, R. H., & Kaminski, R. A. (2003). *DIBELS: Dynamic Indicators of Basic Early Literacy Skills, sixth edition.* Longmont, CO: Sopris West.

Haager, D., Klinger, J., & Vaughn, S. (Eds.). (2007). *Evidenced-based reading practices for response to intervention.* Baltimore: Brookes.

Harn, B. A., Kame'enui, E. K., & Simmons, D. C. (2007). Essential features of interventions for kindergarten students most in need of accelerated learning: The nature and role of the third tier in a primary prevention model. In D. Haager, S. Vaughn, & J. Klingner (Eds.), *Evidenced-based reading practices for response to intervention*. Baltimore: Brookes.

Hoskyn, M., & Swanson, H. L. (2000). Cognitive processing of low achievers and children with reading disabilities: A selective meta-analytic review of the published literature. *School Psychology Review, 29*(1), 102–119.

Howell, K. W., & Nolet, V. (2000). *Curriculum-based evaluation: Teaching and decision making* (3rd ed.). Atlanta, GA: Wadsworth.

Huberman, A. M., & Miles, M. B. (1984). Rethinking the quest for school improvement: Some findings from the DESSI Study. *Teachers College Record, 86*(1), 34–54.

Ihnot, C. (2003). *Read naturally*. Saint Paul, MN: Read Naturally Inc.

Kame'enui, E. J., Good R. H. III, & Harn, B. A. (2004). Beginning reading failure and the quantification of risk. In H. L. Heward, T. E. Heron, N. A. Neef, S. M. Peterson, D. M. Sainato, G. Cartledge, et al. (Eds.), *Focus on behavior analysis in education: Achievements, challanges and opportunities* (pp. 69–89). Upper Saddle River, NJ: Pearson Education.

Kame'enui, E. J., & Simmons, D. C. (1990). *Designing instructional strategies: The prevention of academic learning problems*. Columbus, OH: Merrill.

Kaminski, R. A., & Good, R. H. (1996). Toward a technology in assessing basic early literacy skills. *School Psychology Review, 25*(2), 215–227.

Lyon, G. R., & Moats, L. C. (1997). Critical conceptual and methodological considerations in reading intervention research. *Journal of Learning Disabilities, 30*, 578–588.

National Center on Educational Statistics (2005a). Common core data. Available at *http://nces.ed.gov/ccd/schoolsearch/school_detail.asp?Search=1&InstName=Danebo&City =Eugene&State=41&SchoolType=1&SchoolType=2&SchoolType=3&SchoolType =4& SpecificSchlTypes=all&IncGrade=-1&LoGrade=-l&HiGrade=-1&ID=410204000617*.

National Center on Educational Statistics (2005b). Common core data. Available at *http://nces.ed.gov/ccd/schoolsearch/school_detail.asp?Search=1&InstName=Durham& City=Tigard&State=41&SchoolType=1&SchoolType=2&SchoolType=3& SchoolType=4&SpecificSchlTypes=all&IncGrade=-1&LoGrade=-l&HiGrade=-1&ID= 411224001191*.

National Institute of Child Health and Human Development. (2000). *Report ofthe National Reading Panel. Teaching children to read: An evidence-based assessment ofthe scientific research literature on reading and its implications for reading instruction* (NIH Publication No. 00-4769). Washington, DC: U.S. Government Printing Office.

Perfetti, C. A. (1999). Comprehending written language: A blueprint of the reader. In P. Hagoort & C. Brown (Eds.), *Neurocognition of language processing* (pp. 167–208). New York: Oxford University Press.

Showers, B., Joyce, B., & Bennett, C. (1987). Staff development and student learning: A synthesis of research on models of teaching. *Educational Leadership, 45*(2),11–23.

Simmons, D. C., Kame'enui, E. J., Good, R. H. III, Harn, B. A., Cole, C., & Braun, D. (2000). *Building, implementing, and sustaining a beginning reading model: School by school and lessons learned*. Eugene, Oregon School Study Council.

Stanovich, K. (1986). Matthew effects in reading: Some consequences of individual differences in the acquisition of literacy. *Reading Research Quarterly, 21*, 360–407.

U.S. Census Bureau (2005). *American Community Survey*. Available at *www.census.gov/acs/www/*.

Vaughn, S., Gersten, R., & Chard, D. J. (2000). The underlying message in LD intervention research: Findings from research syntheses. *Exceptional Children, 67*, 99–114.

Vaughn, S., Linan-Thompson, S., & Hickman, P. (2003). Response to instruction as a means of identifying students with reading/learning disabilities. *Exceptional Children, 69*, 391–409.

Williams, J. P. (2005). Instruction in reading comprehension for primary grade students: A focus on text structure. *Journal of Special Education, 39*(1), 6–18.

CHAPTER 7

# The North Carolina Reading and Behavior Center's K–3 Prevention Model

*Eastside Elementary School Case Study*

BOB ALGOZZINE, NANCY COOKE, RICHARD WHITE,
SHAWNNA HELF, KATE ALGOZZINE, *and* TINA MCCLANAHAN

The Behavior and Reading Improvement Center (BRIC) at the University of North Carolina at Charlotte, in collaboration with its partners in the Charlotte–Mecklenburg Schools (CMS), undertook an experimental study of the effects of the center's three-tiered reading and behavior model. Using a wait-list control group design, we examined the three-tiered model's impact on the academic and behavioral performance of students attending seven District elementary schools that enrolled high percentages of at-risk students. Eastside Elementary School was one of the four original treatment schools selected for intervention, and its efforts and outcomes are the focus of this chapter.

## SCHOOL SELECTION

The selection of participating BRIC schools was made by the CMS associate superintendent for Curriculum and Instruction. The BRIC leadership asked the associate superintendent to select schools that (1) were not receiving direct state intervention due to low performance; (2) were above 40% participation in the federal free and reduced lunch program; (3) demonstrated evidence of effective daily implementation of the core reading program for 90 minutes; (4) were willing to use project identified measures as evidence of reading and behavior improvement; and (5) had strong school principals who voiced enthusiasm for the project. Eastside Elementary met all of these criteria.

After the superintendent made the selection of schools, the center contracted with the CMS to release one employee from each selected school to serve as a center support coordinator (CSC). The CSCs worked with project personnel to support project personnel development, ensure procedural fidelity with intervention implementation, and ensure reliable collection of data on all reading and behavior dependent measures. Principals of the selected schools were requested to pick a well-respected employee among the teachers at the school to serve as CSC. Within the seven schools, one selected CSC was an assistant principal, one was a school psychologist, four were literacy facilitators, and one was a paraeducator. The literacy facilitator position was a CMS personnel allocation at every elementary school designated to promote reading effectiveness.

Tina McClanahan was the literacy facilitator at Eastside Elementary School prior to project implementation and was selected by the school principal to serve as the school's literacy facilitator for (K–2) and as CSC. Within the learning community of CSCs, Tina became an expert in the implementation of the BRIC three-tiered model in reading and behavior. The principal of the school has reallocated budget to retain Tina in her position providing behavior support to teachers even though the project contract with CMS has lapsed. Eastside Elementary was selected for this case study because it embraced the reading and behavior models with acceptable fidelity, whereas some of the other schools were not as strong in either or both areas. In addition, the school principal is a strong instructional leader and continuing supporter of the BRIC model.

## SCHOOL DESCRIPTION

Eastside Elementary School is located in the eastern-central section of the CMS district. The mission of Eastside Elementary is to achieve academic excellence in a positive, nurturing, culturally rich learning environment. In the 2005–2006 school year, Eastside served 685 students in grades kindergarten through fifth grade. Fifty-seven percent (57%) of the students were African American, 4% Asian, 25% Hispanic, 2% multiracial, 1% Native American, and 11% white. Seventy-six percent of the students were on free or reduced lunch. Eighteen percent of the students were identified as limited English proficient. Eastside's diverse population includes students from 17 countries speaking 13 languages. Eleven percent of the students at Eastside are students with disabilities, and because Eastside is a partial magnet for the gifted and talented program, 11% in third through fifth grades are identified as students with gifts and talents.

Fifty-nine teachers, 2 administrators, 23 paraeducators, and 6 other certified staff were employed at the school. Sixty-one percent of the teachers had a bachelor's degree, and 39% have advanced degrees. Twenty-four percent of the faculty had fewer than 3 years of experience, but over 30% of the faculty have 15 years of experience or more. The special education program at Eastside consisted of a mix of pull-out, inclusion, and self-contained programs. The program included two full-time and one half-day resource teachers, two full-time teachers of students with autism in self-contained classrooms, three preschool teachers, and three paraeducators. The program was served by a speech pathologist and a part-time preschool speech pathologist.

## SCHOOL BEHAVIOR AND READING RISK ASSESSMENT

Prior to participating in the project, 60–70% of Eastside students in third grade performed at or above mastery level in reading on the North Carolina end-of-grade achievement test (Figure 7.1). As seen in the figure, reading achievement for Eastside third graders was below that in the district, and African American and Hispanic students' performance was below that of their Eastside Caucasian peers. Over 90% of the students were from minority and diverse family backgrounds. Sixty-nine percent of the Eastside students participated in the federal free/reduced lunch program. These children came from families whose incomes place them just at or below the poverty line. At the beginning of the effort, Eastside was one of 33 elementary schools designated as an Equity Plus school by the CMS due to the diverse population and low socioeconomic status of the students enrolled.

## CORE PROCEDURES: COMMON AND CRITICAL
## THREE-TIERED FEATURES

The BRIC established a model for addressing the three tiers of reading and behavioral instruction with an emphasis on interventions for each

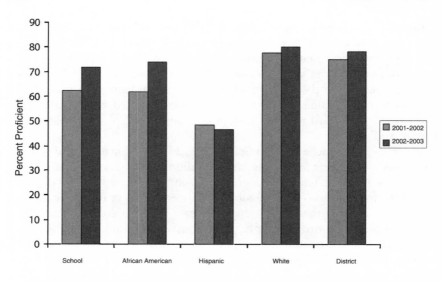

**FIGURE 7.1.** Eastside third-grade reading performance (2000–2002).

tier, systematic communication across school personnel, and data-based decision making. To understand how Eastside used our model, we describe interventions for each tier in reading and behavior, the progress monitoring and data-based decision-making components that systematized communication, and how the roles of personnel were used to support the model.

## Schoolwide or Universal Systems of Support

### Universal Reading Interventions

Charlotte–Mecklenburg Schools adopted Open Court Reading (Adams et al., 2000), as the core reading program for all elementary schools, therefore serving as the primary-level intervention for our project schools. Open Court was recognized by the National Reading Panel (National Institute of Child Health and Human Development, 2000) as an evidence-based curriculum, and the systemwide adoption of this curriculum was a great benefit to our center. Classroom teachers were responsible for providing the primary intervention with support from the literacy facilitator. This included Open Court instruction with differentiated instruction during a 40-minute segment of the 90-minute instructional block, referred to as Independent Work Time (IWT). Our project did not focus on teachers' implementation of Open Court. This was considered under the purview of the school system initiative and the responsibility of the literacy facilitator. The school district provided systemwide professional development through SRA/McGraw-Hill consultants, along with school-level consultations and further professional development when indicated. The school's literacy facilitator attended monthly meetings for additional training in how to support Open Court and had the responsibility of ensuring full implementation in their schools.

To enhance the strong primary level of reading instruction provided by districtwide implementation of Open Court, the project developed Basic Early Literacy Skills Activities (BELS; Algozzine, Marr, McClanahan, & Barnes, 2006). These universal-level activities were designed to provide kindergarten and first-grade teachers with minilessons and additional practice with key kindergarten skills needed for success in decoding. The collection of activities includes basic, targeted, and extension activities in these areas: phonemic awareness of sounds, phonemic segmentation, letter–name identification, and letter–sound associations. BELS was used in 8 of the 12 K–1 classrooms at Eastside during the last year of the project.

Additionally, a project-developed Fluency Practice Partner Program (FPPP) was implemented as a second-grade classroom-based intervention at the universal level to increase students' oral reading fluency using partners, repeated readings, and leveled passages (congruent with Open Court materials). It was used either prior to the 90-minute literacy period or during the independent work time IWT segment of the period. During FPPP, more skilled readers ("coaches") are paired with less skilled readers ("readers"). The readers practice reading a short passage (100–140 words) written at their independent reading level that allows them to focus on rapid word reading, intonation, and expression without the difficulty of decoding unfamiliar words. Students practice reading their passages a few times, with coach support as needed, and then the coach times the reader reading for 1 minute. The reader marks the passage at the 1-minute mark then counts the number of words read. The reader records her progress on charts in their fluency folders. When the student reaches the Dyanmic Indicators of Basic Early Lieracy Skills oral reading fluency benchmark for second grade (90 words per minute) or has read the passage for three timing sessions, the teacher then assigns another passage at the same reading level or at the next reading level. FPPP was used in all five of the second-grade classrooms in the last year of the project.

## Universal Behavior Intervention

The primary or universal-level intervention within the BRIC three-tiered behavior model is an operationally defined model of schoolwide positive behavior support termed *positive unified behavior support* (PUBS). When implementing PUBS, administrators, teachers, and other professionals teach behavior relentlessly by promoting similar attitudes toward instruction of behavior, reinforce school and class rules and expectations with high levels of praise and prompting, use a consistent correction procedure unified across personnel to address inappropriate behavior, and adopt mutually supportive roles. Within the PUBS model, threats to safety are addressed with a correction procedure that results in an immediate office referral, but disruptive events entail a different correction procedure. After three disruptive events, the student receives a class pass (a nonexclusionary time-out in another teacher's classroom for no more than 15–20 minutes). Chronic disruption was operationally defined as six disruptive events, and therefore an office referral was submitted after the sixth event.

The explicitness of the PUBS model also permitted direct assessment of procedural fidelity with the model. Two observation systems were developed that enabled direct assessment of procedural fidelity, a quick check form (Figure 7.2) and a more intensive observation form that provided for collection of direct measures of teacher behavior (Figure 7.3). Specifically, frequency of teacher reinforcement of school rule events, frequency of prompts or teaching events regarding school rules, and compliance with the PUBS correction procedures were recorded for analysis of procedural fidelity using the intensive form. The "quick check" procedural fidelity was done early in the academic year with all teachers in all classrooms and then selectively whenever there was a concern regarding fidelity of implementation. The more intensive procedural fidelity assessment was conducted once a year in the fall semester with all teachers and with a sample in the spring semester.

## Strategic or Secondary-Level Systems of Support

### Secondary Reading Intervention

Practice Court (Gibbs, Campbell, Helf, Cooke, & Algozzine, 2004), now published as *Early Reading Tutor* (Gibbs, Campbell, Helf, & Cooke, 2007), is a supplemental secondary or tertiary reading intervention designed to increase phonemic awareness, alphabetic understanding, decoding skills, and fluency of students who are not progressing at the expected rate for their grade level or through screening are shown at risk for failure in reading. This program was developed with scripted lessons that followed formats and a sequence of skills recommended in *Direct Instruction Reading* (Carnine, Silbert, Kame'enui, & Tarver, 2004), incorporated Simmons and Kame'enui's (1998) six principles of instructional design, and could be implemented during the IWT portion of the

| School _____ Teacher _____ Grade _____ | BRIC Check–Support–Connect |
|---|---|

| Provide a rating for each item using the following scale:<br>E = Exemplary, M = Mastery, N = Not Observed. | Week of<br>/   /   /   / |
|---|---|

1. Procedures are posted or evident as part of classroom practice.
2. Rules are posted so every child can see them.
3. Specific praise is being used to teach and reinforce behavior.
4. Rules are monitored during instructional presentations and/or independent practice.
   a. Supportive feedback is used to acknowledge and reward behavior.
   b. Corrective feedback is used to acknowledge and change behavior.
   c. Positive unified behavior support (PUBS) correction procedure is being used.
   d. Other correction procedure is being used.
5. Instruction is adjusted to account for individual differences.
6. Positive behavior is promoted.

| **Optional** | Overall grade for behavior instruction. (circle one) | A A A A A A<br>B B B B B B<br>C C C C C C |
|---|---|---|
| **Optional** | Overall grade for behavior of class. (circle one) | A A A A A A<br>B B B B B B<br>C C C C C C |

Use space below for dated comments and/or notes (use back of sheet for more space).

/    •
/    •
/    •

**FIGURE 7.2.** PUBS fidelity (quick check–support–connect) form.

literacy period, usually within the classroom. The lessons are brief (i.e., approximately 10 minutes) and designed to be taught to one to three students at a time. Practice Court provides instruction in the following areas: (1) auditory skills of blending and segmenting (i.e., phonemic awareness); (2) letter–sound correspondences (i.e., alphabetic under-standing); (3) reading phonetically regular words (i.e., decoding); (4) flu-ency building with connected text; and (5) sight word practice. The 110 lessons cover all of the decoding skills addressed through first grade. Practice Court serves as a secondary-level intervention for kindergarten and first grade and as a tertiary intervention for second-grade students. It was used during the IWT portion of the literacy period, usually within the classroom.

Observer _____ Grade ____ Start Time _____ Stop Time _____

Observation Recording for Positive Unified Behavior Support

|                                                                                                                                                                                                                                                 | Observation Period |
| --- | --- |
| I.  Teacher reinforces student behavior. (Event record every incidence of general or specific praise of desired behavior.) | |
| II. Teacher teaches rules. Event record every incidence of: <br>• Teacher provides examples/ nonexamples of behavior related to a rule or procedure. <br>• Teacher provides rule or procedure reminder. <br>• Teacher encourages rule or procedure compliance. <br>• Teacher models/directly teaches rule or procedure. | |
| III. Teacher teaches when correcting student misbehavior. <br>• Record a+ if teacher teaches when correcting misbehavior (Teacher directs child to perform correctly, reinforces self-correction, encourages future compliance) in adult voice. <br>• Record a– if teacher corrects without teaching and/or uses angry voice. | |

Summary/Analysis:

I.  Report teacher reinforcement/correction ratio. (_____ teacher reinforcement : teacher correction _____)

II. Report rule prompting (total number of cues or instances of teaching rules) =_____)

III. Report use of appropriate correction: ((____total +) / (____Total tallies)) * 100 =_____%

Summary/Conclusions:

Strengths:

Next Challenge:

**FIGURE 7.3.** PUBS fidelity observation form.

*Secondary Behavior Interventions*

If a student attained more than two office referrals in a year (School-wide Information System benchmark) or if the student received more than two class passes in a week (BRIC benchmark) for at least 2 weeks in the year, the Positive Behavior Support (PBS) team deliberated the need for more intensive (secondary) intervention. Within the BRIC model, teachers and the PBS team had access to a variety of evidenced-based secondary intervention alternatives that have a history of research support, could be implemented with fidelity by general education teachers, were aligned with the universal positive behavior support model, and aligned with other CMS adoptions. At the less intrusive level student contracting, teacher or student self-monitoring systems, and teacher or student self-evaluation systems were recommended for students deemed in need of extra support but not intensive support. More intrusive pull-out individual interventions and small group social skill interventions were available to the PBS team to recommend for students with greater targeted needs at the secondary level. The CMS with consultation from the OSEP Technical Assistance Center on Positive Behavior Interventions and Supports (PBIS), had adopted the Boys Town model as the preferred social skills model, and the BRIC aligned with that decision. The social-skill intervention procedural reliability checklists were derived from the Boys Town (Dowd & Tierney, 2005) model. Procedural fidelity checklists and directions for correct implementation of secondary intervention options were provided to teachers (Figure 7.4). Tina was available to teachers as a resource for any of these interventions. Procedural reliability data on these interventions was assessed indirectly and completed by the teacher at least one time in the school year for every intervention employed.

## Intensive or Tertiary-Level Systems of Support

*Tertiary Reading Interventions*

The BRIC adopted Reading Mastery Classic I (RM-I; Engelmann & Bruner, 1995a) as a tertiary intervention for kindergarten and first-grade students because it provides more intense and longer (i.e., 35–45 minutes) intervention, when compared to Practice Court, and the Reading Mastery programs were already in place as the school system adoption for special education in grades K–2. Reading Mastery Classic II0 (RM-II; Engelmann & Bruner, 1995b) was used as a secondary-level intervention for decoding in second grade because, unlike Practice Court, it addresses skills needed to bring students to a third-grade level in reading. Reading Mastery Classic I and II are designed to

**The BRIC Boys Town Individual Teaching Social Skill Treatment Fidelity Checklist**

In an effort to ensure that all instructors implement the intervention in a similar way, please use the following checklist to help ensure treatment fidelity. The checklist may be used indirectly (instructor self-report) or directly by an observer.

| When implementing **Individual Teaching Social Skill** instruction, the instructor should: | + Completed or observed<br>− Not completed or observed | Comments |
|---|---|---|
| Introduce skill | | |
| Provide examples of skill | | |
| Describe skill components | | |
| Demonstrate skill components | | |
| Provide rationale for the skill | | |
| Request acknowledgment | | |
| Provide practice cue | | |
| Provide practice feedback | | |
| Provide positive consequence | | |
| Prompt/praise future practice | | |

**FIGURE 7.4.** Sample social skill fidelity checklist.

teach phonemic awareness, word attack skills, and comprehension strategies. RM-I teaches many aspects of phonemic awareness necessary for a beginning reader. Phonics instruction in RM-I stresses letter–sound relationships, a blending technique, and acquisition of as many high-utility sight words as possible. RM-II expands on the decoding skills taught in RM I and teaches additional strategies for decoding difficult words. Reading Mastery Fast Cycle is an accelerated version that presents the same skills and concepts as RM-I and II. Our schools did not have the Fast Cycle edition, so instead they used the SRA chart for "fast cycling" through RM-I and II. These programs are based on Direct Instruction techniques, providing the kind of careful instruction that is needed to teach basic skills. It is a program that (1) emphasizes giving students strategies for decoding and comprehension, (2) provides careful instruction in all subskills that lead to mastery of those strategies, (3) provides for a carefully controlled sequence of skills through which those subskills are introduced and reinforced, (4) gives children adequate and realistic practice geared to the needs of children, and (5) provides individualizing provisions (i.e., placement, skipping). RM-I was also used during the IWT period.

### Tertiary Behavior Interventions

When a student attained six or more office referrals, or more than three class passes in a week for at least 2 weeks in the year, the PBS team reviewed the student for tertiary-level intervention, but often tertiary-level intervention was applied prior to those benchmarks given the student's clear need. Functional behavior assessments, individualized behavior support plans, and wraparound services were available as tertiary interventions for students requiring individualized behavior instruction and support. Social skill interventions discussed at the secondary level were also continued for many tertiary-level students. These evidence-based practices were implemented by teams of professionals within each school. The BRIC developed procedural fidelity checklists for each intervention with instruction for implementation. Leadership for community-based involvement in support of the child and family was assigned usually to the school psychologist, social worker, or family advocate. These plans were quite tailored to the individual student. Individual counseling sessions for tertiary-level students with one of these school professionals was a very common non-BRIC intervention employed at the school. In all tertiary cases, Tina played a supportive and consulting role. A summary flow chart for behavioral instructional decision-making and intervention selection is available in Figure 7.5.

## Screening, Scheduling, Progress Monitoring, and Instructional Decision Making in Reading

The BRIC reading model includes five key components which are integrated so that data from each component informs decisions that are part of the next component. Figure 7.6 illustrates the connections.

### Screening and Placement

Prior to the BRIC partnership with CMS and then during the first year of our implementation, the schools assessed students following each 9-week quarter, using a system-developed derivative of a North Carolina State literacy assessment for children in K–2. There were no clear guidelines as to how differentiation might occur for students who were not in special education but performed poorly on their system assessment.

The BRIC staff introduced DIBELS to our project schools in the first year of implementation and administered the benchmark assess-

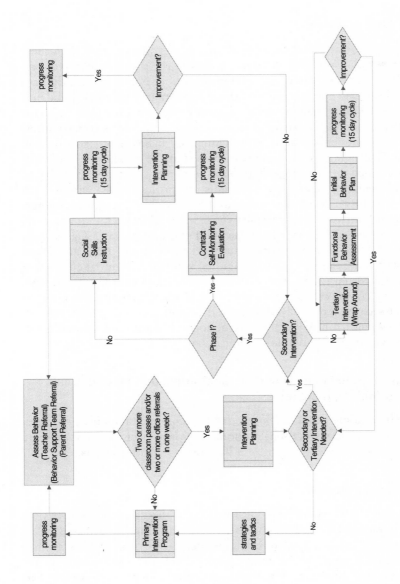

**FIGURE 7.5.** The BRIC behavior instructional decision-making model.

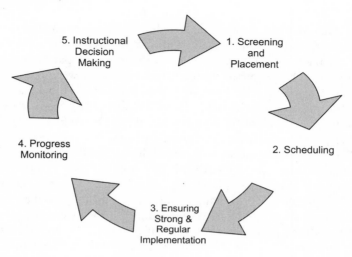

**FIGURE 7.6.** The BRIC comprehensive reading model.

ments to K–1 students at the beginning, middle, and end of our first year. During subsequent years, assessment teams and/or classroom teachers assumed responsibility for administering DIBELS benchmark assessments to students in K–2 as part of the CMS adoption of DIBELS.

We shared student-level outcomes with the CSC, principal, and teachers. We used the fall benchmark outcomes and teacher confirmation to place students, with DIBELS instructional support recommendations of strategic or intensive, into supplementary interventions. After the winter benchmark assessments, we reconsidered intervention placement for all first and second graders and for initial placement for kindergarteners. For those students already in intervention programs, the placement decisions were also considered at monthly meetings during the semester, when progress monitoring data suggested that a change in intervention was warranted. These placement decisions involved placement into the standard treatment protocols for each of the tiers. Decisions regarding change of tier were made at monthly meetings and following benchmark testing in winter.

### Scheduling Instruction

One of the greatest challenges each project school faced was the allocation of resources to support the interventions. We chose not to use the BRIC staff or university students to provide the interventions. Instead, each principal was given the challenge of identifying personnel in the school who could be trained and scheduled to provide the interventions as a regular instructional responsibility. Although some schools budgeted for reading tutors with some professional preparation, Eastside did not have this resource. Instead, paraeducators were given this instructional responsibility. Eastside scheduled literacy blocks at a common time for a particular grade level, but different times across grade levels. In this way, all of the K–2 teacher assistants could all be available for supplementary instruction during each grade level's literacy block. Supplemental instruction was scheduled during the IWT to avoid removing students from teacher-directed instruction in Open Court.

Students were given placement tests within the intervention program and then grouped so that all students in a group placed at the same point in instruction. Students were regrouped if they were not all able to keep up with the pace of the rest of their peers or following the DIBELS winter benchmark, when the needs of all students were reconsidered.

### Ensuring Strong and Regular Implementation of Interventions

To ensure that lessons in secondary and tertiary interventions were conducted regularly, we asked those conducting the sessions (i.e., tutors) to keep a record of each session taught, the students present for instruction, the reason why any lessons or students were not taught, and lesson outcome. The CSC collected these records each week and once a month summarized the session data. In addition, the CSC observed each tutor on a rotating basis so that each was seen approximately every 2 weeks during the first months of the school year and then at least once per month after that. The number of observations per tutor varied. For example, those tutors who experienced more difficulty were seen more often, whereas those who consistently demonstrated high-fidelity implementation were seen less often. We developed fidelity checklists for each secondary and tertiary program. When the CSCs observed, they completed the fidelity checklist, calculated the percentage of correctly presented elements, and indicated the follow-up that would be conducted (e.g., modeling, side-by-side coaching, giving guidelines or answering questions) for items on the checklist that were not at an acceptable level. Data from these observations also became part of a monthly report shared with principals and the classroom teachers.

### Progress Monitoring

All students receiving secondary or tertiary interventions were given DIBELS progress monitoring probes by the classroom teacher. Those students at the secondary level (i.e., identified by DIBELS as needing strategic support) were given probes every 2 weeks. Those students at the tertiary level (i.e., identified by DIBELS as needing intensive support) were given probes every week. The probes were from DIBELS progress monitoring materials and focused on the critical indicators of beginning reading, sequenced by difficulty in the following order: phoneme segmentation fluency, nonsense word fluency, and oral reading fluency. We prescribed the particular probe based on the entry lesson within the intervention program. For example, the students who placed in early lessons in Practice Court, were initially given probes from the DIBELS Phoneme Segmentation Progress Monitoring booklet, whereas students who placed in middle lessons in Practice Court started with the DIBELS Nonsense Word Fluency Progress Monitoring probes. The tutors established an aimline for students from the current performance to the next DIBELS benchmark level. Once students demonstrated that they were on or above the aimline for two or more probes, they switched to the next type of probe in the sequence. When students reached the Oral Reading Fluency probes, they were tested every week using the DIBELS grade-level passages. Students were required to meet benchmark level in Oral Reading Fluency for at least four probes before we released them from supplementary intervention. After supplemental intervention was removed we continued to monitor them until the next benchmark assessment. The individual student graphs showing data from these probes were printed from the DIBELS website and shared monthly with the principal and teachers.

## Instructional Decision Making

The principal and literacy team (e.g., CSC, literacy facilitator, and school psychologist) reviewed the progress monitoring graphs along with the monthly reports of students who were below the aimline. Instructional decisions were sometimes made by the Literacy Team or left to the teachers at the grade-level meeting. The CSC met with the grade-level teachers approximately once per month for the purpose of reviewing student data. First, the CSC handed each teacher the progress monitoring printouts for his or her class. Next, she presented the percentage of students in secondary or tertiary interventions that were on or above aimline. Then, the CSC and grade-level teachers considered changes for each student that might have a positive impact (e.g., ensuring more regular instruction, providing more professional development to the tutor, replacing the tutor, preteaching or reteaching lessons, adjusting tasks in the program to make them multisensory, or regrouping students). The decisions made at these meetings most frequently focused on modifications or elaborations of the instructional program; however, if a student had made little progress despite several modifications, the team could decide to move a student from the Tier 2 intervention (i.e., program) to Tier 3 intervention (i.e., program). Otherwise, changes from Tier 3 to Tier 2 or Tier 2 to Tier 1 were made at benchmark points when there were (1) data demonstrating benchmark performance in the highest level of the grade-level DIBELS subtests, and (2) benchmark performance had been sustained for a period of at least 8 weeks.

## Screening, Scheduling, Progress Monitoring, and Instructional Decision Making in Behavior

Screening, progress monitoring, intervention scheduling, and instructional decision-making functions were the responsibility of the school PBS team within the North Carolina behavior model. The team membership at Eastside included the principal, assistant principal, school social worker, school psychologist, family advocate, an exceptional children's teacher, and Tina, the CSC. The PBS team met at least monthly and often weekly to monitor student progress and once a semester also monitored teacher procedural fidelity data. Two major data sets were reviewed by the team each month. Office disciplinary referral outcomes were entered into the SWIS (May et al., 2000) database daily and outcomes monitored at least monthly by the team. Teachers were able to request SWIS data reports at any time. Tina developed a monthly profile for each meeting (Figure 7.7). The BRIC developed a SWIS compatible and CMS-aligned office referral form for all BRIC schools to facilitate data entry (Figure 7.8). As stated previously, infractions listed on the form required an immediate office referral except for disruption. The BRIC schoolteachers also collected data on every classroom rule violation that entailed disruption. The Eastside Record of Consequences (ROCs) data collection form recorded the type and number of disruptive events for every student in very class (Figure 7.9). Most team meeting time entailed screening SWIS and ROC outcomes for students who might need more intensive intervention, progress monitoring outcomes for students who were receiving more intensive intervention, and monitoring SWIS teacher-related variables to determine if additional support was needed. The team also discussed any problems with intervention scheduling and any school factors that might be undermining effectiveness of intervention implementation.

The BRIC Project maintained a database file of all students whose SWIS or ROC data indicated risk. In addition, the North Carolina Project in tandem with the other centers screened all students K–1 in year 2 of the project and K students in year 3 of the project using the Systematic Screening for Behavior Disorders (SSBD; Walker & Severson, 1992).

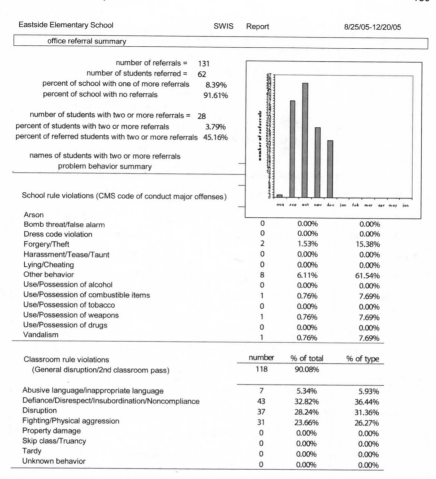

| office referral summary |
| --- |

| | |
| --- | --- |
| number of referrals = | 131 |
| number of students referred = | 62 |
| percent of school with one of more referrals | 8.39% |
| percent of school with no referrals | 91.61% |
| | |
| number of students with two or more referrals = | 28 |
| percent of students with two or more referrals | 3.79% |
| percent of referred students with two or more referrals | 45.16% |

names of students with two or more referrals
problem behavior summary

School rule violations (CMS code of conduct major offenses)

| | | |
| --- | --- | --- |
| Arson | | |
| Bomb threat/false alarm | 0 | 0.00% | 0.00% |
| Dress code violation | 0 | 0.00% | 0.00% |
| Forgery/Theft | 2 | 1.53% | 15.38% |
| Harassment/Tease/Taunt | 0 | 0.00% | 0.00% |
| Lying/Cheating | 0 | 0.00% | 0.00% |
| Other behavior | 8 | 6.11% | 61.54% |
| Use/Possession of alcohol | 0 | 0.00% | 0.00% |
| Use/Possession of combustible items | 1 | 0.76% | 7.69% |
| Use/Possession of tobacco | 0 | 0.00% | 0.00% |
| Use/Possession of weapons | 1 | 0.76% | 7.69% |
| Use/Possession of drugs | 0 | 0.00% | 0.00% |
| Vandalism | 1 | 0.76% | 7.69% |

| Classroom rule violations | number | % of total | % of type |
| --- | --- | --- | --- |
| (General disruption/2nd classroom pass) | 118 | 90.08% | |
| | | | |
| Abusive language/inappropriate language | 7 | 5.34% | 5.93% |
| Defiance/Disrespect/Insubordination/Noncompliance | 43 | 32.82% | 36.44% |
| Disruption | 37 | 28.24% | 31.36% |
| Fighting/Physical aggression | 31 | 23.66% | 26.27% |
| Property damage | 0 | 0.00% | 0.00% |
| Skip class/Truancy | 0 | 0.00% | 0.00% |
| Tardy | 0 | 0.00% | 0.00% |
| Unknown behavior | 0 | 0.00% | 0.00% |

**FIGURE 7.7.** SWIS monthly report sample.

The SSBD first requires teachers to identify students of most concern, and then teachers complete the Critical Events, Adaptive Behavior, and Maladaptive Behavior Scales on those students. Students who exceeded criteria for externalizing or internalizing conditions were reported to the Coordinating Center at Wisconsin and entered into the Project's behavior database. Project personnel would periodically discuss these students with each school's CSC, particularly if the student was not considered at risk using SWIS or ROC data, to be sure those students were not being inappropriately overlooked for intervention.

| Student's Name: | | Grade Level: |
|---|---|---|
| Referring Staff: | Date: | Time: |

**Location**

☐ Classroom   ☐ Playground   ☐ Commons   ☐ Hall   ☐ Cafeteria
☐ Bathroom   ☐ Gym   ☐ Library   ☐ Bus Loading   ☐ Parking Lot
☐ On Bus   ☐ Special Event   ☐ Office   ☐ Other   ☐ Unknown

**CMS Student Code of Conduct**

**Major Offenses**

On reverse side, describe specifically what the student did or said.

| ☐ Food/Beverages | ☐ Medication | ☐ Student Dress |
|---|---|---|
| ☐ Personal Property | ☐ Misrepresentation | ☐ Insubordination |
| ☐ Profanity/Obscenity | ☐ Trespassing | ☐ Unsafe Action |
| ☐ Vandalism | ☐ Use of Fire | ☐ Theft |
| ☐ Breaking/Entering | ☐ Burglary/Robbery | ☐ Extortion |
| ☐ Refusal to Allow Search | ☐ Misuse of Computer | ☐ Profane Material |
| ☐ Counterfeit Currency | ☐ Alarm/Bomb Threat | ☐ Physical Aggression |
| ☐ Sexual Offense | ☐ Illegal Substance | ☐ Dangerous Objects |

**Chronic Offenses**

☐ General disruption (2nd classroom pass Grade 2–6 plan)

Circle the rule violated most often.   1   2   3   4   5

**Possible Motivation**

☐ Peer Attention   ☐ Adult Attention   ☐ Obtain Items/Activities   ☐ Avoid Tasks
☐ Avoid Work   ☐ Avoid Peers   ☐ Avoid Adults
1 Unclear   ☐ Other   ☐ Unknown

**Others Involved**

☐ None   ☐ Peers   ☐ Staff Teacher   ☐ Substitute   ☐ Unknown   ☐ Other

**Administrative Action**

☐ Time in Office   ☐ Loss of Privileges   ☐ Conference with Student
☐ Parent Contact   ☐ Detention   ☐ Individualized Instruction
☐ In-School Suspension   ☐ Out-of-School Suspension
☐ Saturday School   ☐ Expulsion   ☐ Other   ☐ Unknown

**Comments**

Handled by: _____

**FIGURE 7.8.** Charlotte–Mecklenburg Schools BRIC Office Disciplinary Referral Form.

Behavior and Reading Improvement Center
Record of Consequences
ROC

Teacher: _____

Please list the students who had classroom passes/office referrals.
Week of: _____

Place your completed form in Tina's mailbox on Friday afternoons.

| Student's name | Number of classroom passes (tally) | Number of office referrals (tally) | Rule(s) # the student is having trouble with |
|---|---|---|---|
| EX. Little Jack Horner | III | I | 2, 3 |
| 1. | | | |
| 2. | | | |
| 3. | | | |
| 4. | | | |
| 5. | | | |
| 6. | | | |
| 7. | | | |
| 8. | | | |
| 9. | | | |
| 10. | | | |
| 11. | | | |
| 12. | | | |

**FIGURE 7.9.** Eastside record of consequences recording form.

## IMPLEMENTATION AND PROFESSIONAL DEVELOPMENT APPROACH COMMON TO READING AND BEHAVIOR

In addition to faculty serving as the Project Investigator and the two intervention directors, project staff included a full-time research associate for reading and a full-time research associate for behavior, and approximately six graduate students per year. Graduate assistants were hired to help with initial assessments and data collection and entry. As the schools assumed more of the data collection, fewer graduate students were needed because they only collected for data unrelated to school system requirements. Each year project personnel would develop an activity agenda that addressed perceived project needs and delineated responsibilities. Project personnel would meet monthly with CSCs and project graduate students on campus to discuss project progress, clarify tasks, and elicit concerns and ideas from the CSCs. Annual plans or components were then modified based on feedback received.

Project staff also met quarterly with all the BRIC treatment school principals to describe initiatives and discuss issues or problems. That quarterly meeting was directed by the assistant superintendent for exceptional children's services. The assistant superintendent was designated the lead liaison for the district with the BRIC project by the superintendent. At select meetings, other district personnel were invited. For example, at the superintendent's direction all regional elementary assistant superintendents (these assistant superintendents were responsible for all elementary schools in a geographical area of the countywide district) attended one meeting, and the superintendent also attended several. The principal at Eastside, along with other project principals, attended these meetings consistently and was an active participant. Each year the content of these meetings differed. In the early years, mutual problems concerning implementation were often discussed. In the final year, sustainability issues and scaling-up issues were predominant. Due to retirement of the Eastside principal following our 2nd year of implementation, we worked with two principals. The second principal assumed the same roles in our work as the first principal.

## Key Personnel

We established a system of communication and management at Eastside, similar to other schools in the project, which would allow for regular communication with the BRIC staff and across school staff. The key personnel included the school principal, the CSC who was responsible for ensuring that the BRIC's reading and behavior initiatives were implemented at the school, literacy facilitator (if not the CSC), the teachers, teacher assistants, and other supplementary staff when needed (e.g., school psychologist, assistant principal).

### Role of the Principal

The school principal had a key role in implementation of our reading and behavior models. As the instructional leader of the school, the principal was the first to learn of our plans and to provide feedback on how our model might work best within the context of the school. This feedback allowed us to make adjustments related to staff availability, numbers of students at risk, and the related scheduling challenges for interventions. The principal was key to promoting the acceptance of our model. We introduced our model to the school staff with the principal communicating that she embraced the BRIC model as holding promise for increasing the reading and behavior achievement of the children at Eastside. She spoke about the benefits and how she and other staff would be a part of ensuring the implementation. The principal assumed responsibility for allocating resources to allow for supplemental instruction of students in secondary and tertiary interventions.

### Role of the Center Support Coordinator

As the CSC at Eastside, Tina was responsible for attending monthly meetings where the BRIC staff introduced components of the BRIC model and provided professional development on implementation of the components as they were introduced. Tina and the other CSCs provided the BRIC staff with school information that helped us make changes or adjustments to our expectations. For example, we would learn how our assessment schedule aligned with other grade-level assessments required by CMS in reading. The CSCs informed us as to the number of intervention programs needed at each school, the dates that would work best for professional development, and described school initiatives, already in place, that might complement or conflict with our plans. Tina, along with other CSCs, gradually assumed responsibility for the professional development for their staff who were learning to implement the secondary and tertiary interventions. They were also responsible for collecting fidelity data on the implementation. Each observation was followed by an opportunity to provide modeling, coaching, or responses to questions regarding the programs, student responses or strategies for addressing challenges with implementation.

## Implementation Approach and Professional Development in Reading

Prior to the first year of implementation, there were several school system initiatives already in place which made the selection of the CMS advantageous. CMS required all schools to have at least one literacy facilitator in each elementary school. Due to the size of Eastside, there were two literacy facilitators, one designated for kindergarten through second grade and one for third through fifth grade. The basic role of the literacy facilitator is to share, train, and monitor CMS reading and writing initiatives within their school. The interpretation of that responsibility varied greatly across principals and literacy facilitators. However, support for the literacy facilitator position as a designated role within the school demonstrated system commitment to leadership in this area. One year prior to our work in the schools, Open Court had been adopted by CMS as the core reading program used in every elementary school. Additionally, CMS provided all elementary schools with evidence-based supplemental programs such as Reading Mastery and Corrective Reading to use with students identified for special education services in reading. Schools could also elect to use other programs meant to supplement Open Court (e.g., Accelerated Reader, Imagination Station, and Leap Frog) in the early grades. So, even though there was not an explicit model for placing students with interventions, K–2 classes had support materials available.

### Role of the Principal

As mentioned above, the principal had a number of functions that were common to reading and behavior. Specifically with reading, the principal reviewed monthly grade-level reports illustrating the reading progress of students receiving supplementary instruction and was key to celebrating growth and in making personnel changes when necessary. Professional development for the principal occurred in several ways. The BRIC staff visited the principal at the school to explain each new component of the model and to work with the principal and CSC on resolving particular issues at the school. At Eastside the principal was a former special educator and very familiar with the big ideas of early reading instruction.

### Role of the CSC in Reading

In addition to the responsibilities indicated above, the CSC was also expected to meet monthly with the principal and grade-level teams to discuss new reading information, go over DIBELS, explain the reports, and facilitate instructional decision making. Professional development for the CSCs occurred in the monthly staff meetings mentioned above and at the school site with our reading research associate. Until our last year of implementation, Tina served in the role of CSC for reading and behavior. During the final year of the grant, a teacher assumed the role of literacy facilitator for Kindergarten through fifth grades and served in the role of a CSC in reading. We provided approximately 2 hours each week of additional support from a graduate assistant funded by the BRIC grant.

### Role of the Teaching Staff

For the two supplementary programs designed for the primary level, BELS and FPPP, classroom teachers were invited to participate, engage in professional development, implement the programs, and collect data on student performance in these programs. The classroom teachers conducted progress monitoring probes for each of their students receiving secondary and tertiary interventions. They attended grade-level meetings to review lesson data and graphs of student progress to participate in instructional decisions for their students.

Supplementary staff, that is teacher assistants or reading tutors, were trained in grant-supported secondary and tertiary interventions. With the exception of a few teachers, these staff members had primary responsibility for the secondary and tertiary interventions. They kept session data on student progress through the intervention program, recording the number of lessons received, and student performance on program mastery checks. Their professional development was conducted by the BRIC staff until the last year of implementation when CSCs and literacy facilitators assumed this role.

## Implementation and Professional Development Approach in Behavior

The context for intervention was quite different in the area of behavior versus reading. Whereas reading intervention benefited from a system-wide evidenced-based reading adoption (Open Court, 2000), there was no district commitment to PBIS at the onset of the project. The system did have a district *Rules and Responsibilities Handbook* (Charlotte–Mecklenburg Schools, 2005) adopted by the Board of Education that explicitly defined offenses that could warrant suspension. However, schools responded to these guidelines quite differently. Therefore, the major implementation challenge facing the BRIC was the institution with fidelity of a schoolwide primary-level intervention grounded in the principles of PBIS and aligned with Board policy. Eastside has benefited from prior schoolwide workshops on classroom management that did support adoption of schoolwide rules, but the professional development was specific to the district. To foster adoption of PUBS, the BRIC model, project personnel met with the administrative teams of all intervention schools to describe the model, describe data collection requirements (SWIS), address any concerns, and plan for schoolwide in-service. The Eastside administrative team was supportive from the beginning. A total school in-service (K–5) was then delivered by the BRIC personnel for all staff in August on teacher work days prior to the beginning of the school year. By the time school had begun in the first year of intervention, schoolwide rules were adopted and teachers were prepared to implement. This procedure was followed at all treatment schools including Eastside. The major professional development, however, was the continuous, determined, and incessant coaching and modeling by Tina of PUBS instructional procedures throughout the project. The major "derivation" at

Eastside was that in the superiority of this CSC service at that school. Two follow-up, after-school, in-service workshops were conducted in the first project year to address any concerns and to assist staff in working through specific school problems related to the model. There were no schoolwide in-service workshops provided after that first year of intervention. All professional development needs in following years were identified by the PBS team, administrative team, or the CSC, and subsequent development was provided on a one-on-one basis by the CSC for any teacher in need, new teachers, or other new personnel. Two secondary and tertiary intervention in-services were provided by the BRIC personnel to related services personnel (school psychologists, social workers, parent advocates) and CSCs in the spring of the first year of intervention and the fall of the second. Once again, subsequent professional development was provided on a one-on-one basis by the CSC as needed, as identified by the PBS team or administrative team, and based on procedural fidelity and student outcomes.

## KEY OUTCOME DATA IN READING

### Eligibility

During the last year of the project, primary reading instruction was supported using BELS and FFFP. At Eastside, BELS was used in eight of the K–1 classrooms; FPPP was used in all five of the second-grade classrooms. In addition, all students identified as needing additional support, as indicated by DIBELS assessments, received supplemental instruction in reading. Practice Court served as a secondary-level intervention for kindergarten and first grade and as a tertiary intervention for second-grade students. Practice Court was used with 22 (16.7%) of the K–1 students and 8 (16.8%) of the second-grade students qualifying for tertiary support in the final year of the project. RM-I was used with 10 (7.6%) of the K–1 students and RM-II was used with 33 (28.2%) of the second-grade students in the final year of the project.

### Students at Benchmark

The percentage of students who were identified at "Benchmark" across years by grade level are presented in Figures 7.10–7.12. Each incoming class of kindergarteners over the last 3 years demonstrated greater challenge (i.e., a lower percentage were identified at benchmark). Also the results for kindergarten indicate that improvements occurred across all years, with more progress evident as the project progressed. First-grade results indicate modest changes across our years of implementation.

However, the entry points for first grade indicate improvements from the first year of implementation to the last.

Given the delayed treatment design we employed, second-grade data for the 2003–2004 school year are unavailable. Again, results indicate improvements in entry-level performance of second-grade students across the years of implementation. Improvements across the years were evident during the last 2 years of implementation. One possible reason for the modest gains and decrease between winter and spring is that the DIBELS Oral Reading Fluency measure is the only subtest that is used to determine the students' instructional recommendation. The goal increases from 68 correct words per minute (cwpm) in the winter to 90 cwpm by the spring.

## Changes in Instructional Recommendations

As explained earlier, DIBELS instructional recommendations (i.e., benchmark, strategic, and intensive) are used to identify students in need of supplemental support in reading. We calculated the instructional recommendations at the end of each year by grade level. The changes across grades are presented in Figures 7.13–7.15.

## Treatment Acceptability

We collected treatment acceptability data from all school personnel who delivered supplemental decoding instruction. An 11-item questionnaire

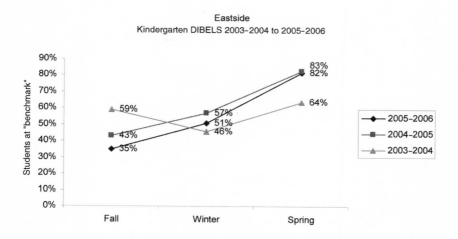

**FIGURE 7.10.** Percentage of kindergarten students at benchmark.

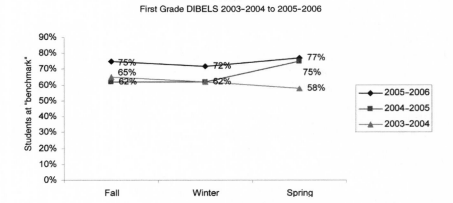

**FIGURE 7.11.** Percentage of first-grade students at benchmark.

was administered to each staff member who implemented Practice Court. A 4-point scale was used to determine tutors' perceptions of effectiveness and acceptability when delivering instruction using the program. Thirteen staff members provided instruction in Practice Court. Of the 13, 1 (7.7%) were reading tutors, 11 (84.6%) were instructional assistants, and 1 was a classroom teacher. Their experience implementing Practice Court averaged 18 months (ranging from 7 to 27 months).

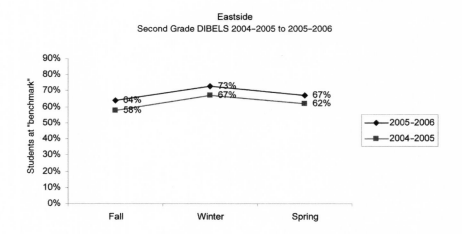

**FIGURE 7.12.** Percentage of second-grade students at benchmark.

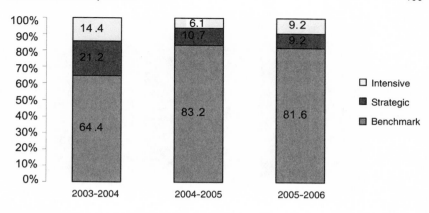

**FIGURE 7.13.** Kindergarten instructional recommendations across years of the project.

Overall, results indicated that staff had positive views of the program, found it easy to implement, and would recommend the program to others (Table 7.1).

An 11-item questionnaire was administered to each staff member who implemented RM-I or II. A 4-point scale was used to determine tutors' perceptions of effectiveness and acceptability when delivering instruction using the program. Ten staff members provided instruction in Reading Mastery overall. Of the 10, 2 (20%) were reading tutors, 6 (60%) were instructional assistants, and 2 (20%) were classroom teachers. Their experience implementing Reading Mastery averaged 12 months (ranging from 1 to 27 months). Similar to Practice Court, results indi-

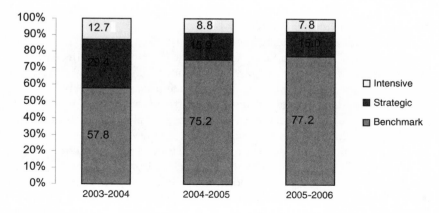

**FIGURE 7.14.** First-grade instructional recommendations across years of the project.

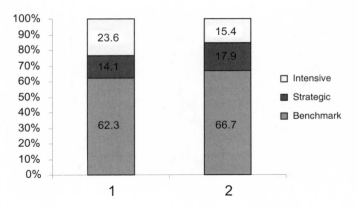

**FIGURE 7.15.** Second-grade instructional recommendations across years of the project.

cated that staff found the program easy to follow and effective in helping students gain basic skills and would recommend the use of the program to others (Table 7.2).

## KEY OUTCOME DATA IN BEHAVIOR

### School-Wide Evaluation Tool Outcomes

The School-Wide Evaluation Tool (SET; Sugai, Lewis-Palmer, Todd, & Horner, 2001) was employed to assess the critical features of schoolwide effective behavior support across each academic school year. The outcomes were used to determine features that are in place, determine annual goals for schoolwide effective behavior support, evaluate ongoing efforts toward schoolwide behavior support, design and revise procedures as needed, and compare efforts toward schoolwide effective behavior support from year to year. Information necessary for this assessment tool is gathered through multiple sources including review of permanent products, observations, and staff (minimum of 10) and student (minimum of 15) interviews or surveys. Levels implementation of positive behavior support, secondary and tertiary behavior interventions, and primary, secondary, and tertiary reading instruction were monitored with project-developed checklists and observations.

Evidence of key aspects of positive behavior support using the SET was gathered by trained observers annually, before schoolwide positive behavior support interventions began and 6 to 12 weeks after schoolwide positive behavior support interventions were implemented. SET

**TABLE 7.1. Treatment Acceptability Ratings for Practice Court**

| Item | | Eastside |
|------|---|------|
| 1. It is important for all students to acquire basic reading skills. | M | 4.0 |
| | SD | 0.00 |
| 2. It is important to have a supplemental program for students who are at risk for reading failure. | M | 3.89 |
| | SD | 0.33 |
| 3. The Practice Court lesson formats were clear. | M | 3.67 |
| | SD | 0.71 |
| 4. I was comfortable with the instructional procedures for Practice Court. | M | 3.44 |
| | SD | 0.73 |
| 5. The Practice Court lessons were easy to implement. | M | 3.44 |
| | SD | 0.73 |
| 6. The Practice Court script helped me implement the lesson. | M | 3.67 |
| | SD | 0.50 |
| 7. The paperwork for Practice Court was easy to manage. | M | 2.78 |
| | SD | 0.83 |
| 8. The Practice Court instructional materials (e.g., short books, passages) were easy to manage. | M | 3.44 |
| | SD | 0.53 |
| 9. Having students self-record their progress was useful. | M | 3.22 |
| | SD | 0.83 |
| 10. Practice Court is effective in improving basic reading skills of students who are at risk for reading failure. | M | 3.56 |
| | SD | 0.73 |
| 11. I would recommend the use of Practice Court to others. | M | 3.56 |
| | SD | 0.73 |

scores for control schools ($M = 36.67$, $SD = 35.56$) were significantly below ($t = -2,99$, $df = 5$, $p < .05$) those for treatment schools ($M = 90.00$, $SD = 8.26$). After implementation, SET scores for the original control school improved significantly to levels comparable to those of treatment schools implementing positive behavior support for 2 years (see Table 7.3). SET scores were consistently 90% or above for schools implementing positive behavior support over 2 consecutive years. During the most recent school year, SET scores were above the recommended benchmark for all schools implementing schoolwide behavior interventions (Figure 7.16) and Eastside met benchmark every year of treatment.

## Positive Behavior Support Procedural Fidelity Outcomes

When key elements of positive behavior support were compared in treatment and control schools, spring observations revealed differences in teacher reinforcement, teacher correction, reinforcement-to-correction

**TABLE 7.2. Treatment Acceptability Ratings for Reading Mastery I or II**

| Item | | Eastside |
|---|---|---|
| 1. It is important for all students to acquire basic reading skills. | M | 4.0 |
| | SD | 0.00 |
| 2. It is important to have a supplemental program for students who are at risk for reading failure. | M | 4.0 |
| | SD | 0.00 |
| 3. The Reading Mastery lesson formats were clear. | M | 3.62 |
| | SD | 0.51 |
| 4. I was comfortable with the instructional procedures for Reading Mastery. | M | 3.46 |
| | SD | 0.52 |
| 5. The Reading Mastery lessons were easy to implement. | M | 3.54 |
| | SD | 0.52 |
| 6. The Reading Mastery script helped me implement the lesson. | M | 3.69 |
| | SD | 0.63 |
| 7. The paperwork for Reading Mastery was easy to manage. | M | 3.31 |
| | SD | 0.63 |
| 8. The Reading Mastery instructional materials (e.g., storybooks, take-home worksheets/books) were easy to manage. | M | 3.31 |
| | SD | 0.75 |
| 9. Mastery tests were useful in monitoring student progress. | M | 3 |
| | SD | 1 |
| 10. Reading Mastery is effective in improving basic reading skills of students who are at risk for reading failure. | M | 3.85 |
| | SD | 0.38 |
| 11. I would recommend the use of Reading Mastery to others. | M | 3.85 |
| | SD | 0.38 |

ratio, total rule violations, teacher monitoring of rule violations, and teacher use of appropriate voice tone. The positive elements of behavior instruction were more evident in treatment classrooms, and effect sizes reflecting practical significance of these outcomes were large (Table 7.4). Again Eastside Elementary was a high-fidelity treatment school on these PUBS measures.

## Secondary and Tertiary Intervention Fidelity Outcomes

The secondary and tertiary levels of intervention involved implementing small-group and individualized interventions for children requiring more intensive attention to behavior improvement. Secondary interventions included teacher and student behavior monitoring, contracts, teacher and student evaluation models, and group and individual social skills instruction. Functional behavior assessment and individualized behavior

**TABLE 7.3. Schoolwide Evaluation Tool Scores before and after Implementing Positive Unified Behavior Support**

| School | 2003–2004 | 2004–2005 | Independent t-statistic | Dependent t-statistic |
|---|---|---|---|---|
| Control | 36.67 | 95.00 | −2.99* | −3.01* |
| | 35.56 | 4.00 | | |
| Treatment | 90.00 | 93.50 | 0.39 | −1.12 |
| | 8.29 | 5.69 | | |
| Eastside | 81.00 | 91.00 | | |

*p < .05.

plans were used for students needing tertiary intervention. Treatment fidelity observations were completed for a random sample of children participating in secondary and tertiary interventions (Table 7.5) and across participating schools (Table 7.6). Levels of treatment fidelity ranged from 0.78 to 1.0 for secondary and tertiary interventions and were similar in schools participating in the project for 1 (0.84) or 2 years (0.91).

## Student Behavioral Outcomes

### Office Referral Outcomes

The Eastside Elementary rate of office disciplinary referral was below the mean for the BRIC schools and the BRIC mean was below the na-

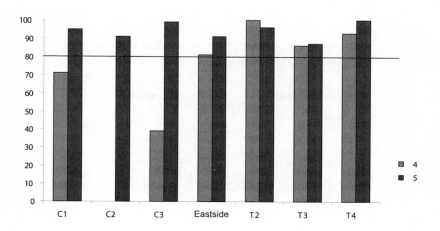

**FIGURE 7.16.** School-wide evaluation tool benchmark comparison.

**TABLE 7.4. Positive Unified Behavior Support Procedural Fidelity Comparison**

| Measure | | Control | Treatment | Obtained $t$ | Effect size | Eastside |
|---|---|---|---|---|---|---|
| | | | All schools | | | |
| Time for observation | M | 35 | 30 | 2.85* | | 26 |
| | SD | 8 | 4 | | | |
| Teacher reinforcement | M | 11.23 | 16.74 | −1.75 | 0.84 | 15.00 |
| | SD | 6.59 | 14.06 | | | |
| Teacher correction | M | 6.27 | 1.72 | 6.84* | 1.12 | 5.00 |
| | SD | 4.05 | 1.63 | | | |
| Reinforcement/correction | M | 3.59 | 11.24 | −2.50* | 1.55 | 5.68 |
| | SD | 4.92 | 13.96 | | | |
| Total rule violations | M | 6.87 | 1.80 | 7.48* | 1.28 | 5.06 |
| | SD | 3.80 | 1.64 | | | |
| Teacher monitors rule violations | M | 82.67 | 98.17 | −3.83* | 0.77 | 89.71 |
| | SD | 20.17 | 8.17 | | | |
| Teacher uses appropriate voice tone | M | 88.27 | 97.86 | −2.85* | 0.68 | 100.00 |
| | SD | 14.01 | 9.34 | | | |

*$p < 0.05$

tional mean and goal. Only 2.9% of students experienced 6+ referrals (tertiary level) and only 8.6% of students experienced 2 to 5 (secondary) referrals. The average daily referral rate for Eastside was a very low 0.26/100 students per day (Table 7.7). The type of offense that resulted in office disciplinary referral was very similar across the BRIC schools with chronic disruption as the major referral problem (Figure 7.17).

Eastside also performed well regarding frequency of preoffice referral corrections in comparison to the highest performing BRIC school. Only 17% of students received a class pass (a nonexclusionary time-out in another teacher's classroom for no more than 15–20 minutes) (Table 7.8).

**TABLE 7.5. Secondary and Tertiary Level Intervention Fidelity**

| Intervention | Overall fidelity |
|---|---|
| Secondary | |
| Teacher monitoring | 0.84 |
| Student contract | 0.78 |
| Teacher evaluation | 1.00 |
| Boys Town Individual | 1.00 |
| Boys Town Group | 0.93 |
| Books 'R Us | 1.00 |
| Games 'R Us | 1.00 |
| Tertiary | 1.00 |

**TABLE 7.6. Secondary and Tertiary Level Intervention Fidelity across Schools**

| School | Fidelity |
|---|---|
| A | 0.92 |
| B | 0.67 |
| C | 0.73 |
| D | 0.95 |
| E | 1.00 |
| F | 0.98 |
| Eastside | 0.95 |

## Secondary–Tertiary Intervention Outcomes

A prevalence of 14.9% of the students at Eastside was identified for possible secondary or tertiary intervention. This prevalence includes the students identified through SWIS benchmarks, and other students identified through class passes, and screening measures used to establish the tracking sample for the Coordination Center at Wisconsin (Table 7.9). Teachers at Eastside rated the effectiveness of the secondary–tertiary interventions lower than the mean across the BRIC schools. Only 5% were deemed effective but 66% were deemed partially effective. The not-effective rate (29%) was slightly above the mean rate. These low rates are reported in spite of success at the primary level and better than mean rates on procedural fidelity measures (Table 7.10). The school principal has suggested that the data reflected a desire among faculty for more intensive secondary options in particular, and this issue is discussed in the Summary.

**TABLE 7.7. Office Disciplinary Referral Outcomes**

| ODRs | Eastside | School A | School B | School C | School D | School E | School F | All project schools | USA |
|---|---|---|---|---|---|---|---|---|---|
| 6+ referrals | 2.91 | 1.97 | 2.78 | 4.31 | 3.98 | 5.24 | 3.26 | 3.42 | 5.00 |
| 2–5 referrals | 8.61 | 4.82 | 7.03 | 11.81 | 14.75 | 13.81 | 16.98 | 10.98 | 10.00 |
| 0–1 referrals | 88.48 | 93.21 | 90.19 | 83.88 | 81.27 | 80.95 | 79.76 | 85.60 | 80.00 |
| Referrals/100 students | 45.56 | 40.57 | 61.71 | 95.69 | 92.04 | 99.79 | N/A | | |
| Referrals/100 students/day | 0.26 | 0.23 | 0.34 | 0.53 | 0.51 | 0.55 | N/A | | 0.39 |

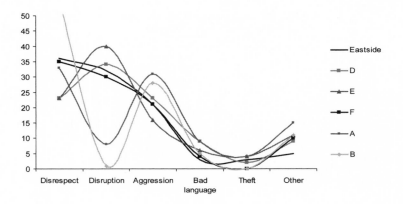

**FIGURE 7.17.** Percentage of referrals across categories.

**TABLE 7.8. Summary of Selected Intervention Outcomes across Participating Schools**

|  | School | |
|---|---|---|
|  | Eastside<br>($n = 685$) | Highest<br>performing<br>school<br>($n = 445$) |
| *Screening outcomes*<br>*(continuous monitoring/record of consequences)* | | |
| Fewer than two passes or office referrals | 83% | 85% |
| Two or more classroom passes or office referrals | 17% | 15% |
| *Intervention outcomes for students*<br>*with two or more classroom passes*<br>*or office referrals* | | |
| Primary intervention support | 40% | 46% |
| Secondary intervention | 44% | 48% |
| Waiting list | 16% | 6% |
| *Treatment fidelity*<br>*for secondary intervention* | | |
| Treatment fidelity 80% or more | 61% | 88% |
| Treatment fidelity less than 80% | 39% | 12% |
| *Treatment outcomes for secondary*<br>*interventions with different fidelity* | | |
| Treatment fidelity 80% or more | | |
| Fewer than two passes or referrals | 63% | 61% |
| Two or more passes or referrals | 37% | 39% |
| Treatment fidelity less than 80% | | |
| Fewer than two passes or referrals | 18% | 50% |
| Two or more passes or referrals | 82% | 50% |

**TABLE 7.9. Prevalence of Secondary and Tertiary-Level Students**

| Schools | Eastside | School A | School B | School C | School D | School E | Total |
|---|---|---|---|---|---|---|---|
| Total enrollment | 685 | 712 | 413 | 467 | 712 | 409 | 3398 |
| Total secondary | 83 | 126 | 132 | 73 | 75 | 77 | 566 |
| | 12% | 17.7% | 32% | 15.6% | 10.5% | 18.8% | 16.7% |
| Total tertiary | 20 | 25 | 15 | 4 | 16 | 8 | 88 |
| | 2.9% | 3.5% | 3.6% | 0.8% | 2.2% | 2% | 2.6% |

*Note.* Data for one BRIC school not submitted.

## Other Key Behavior Outcome Data

CMS regularly administers attitude surveys to parents, staff, and students in all elementary schools. The items address opinions about discipline and school climate, communication and parent involvement, effective instruction and administration, and overall "grade" for the school. Results from these surveys were regularly reviewed by project personnel and school partners in efforts to evaluate overall progress as well as to identify areas in need of change. Opinions in the BRIC treatment schools were consistently higher than those of respondents in control schools and CMS elementary schools in general regarding parents' attitudes toward "discipline and school climate" (Figure 7.18) and teachers attitudes toward "safe and orderly environment"(Figure 7.19).

## SUMMARY AND CONCLUSION

## Unique Benefits and Challenges Represented in This Three-Tiered Model in Reading

When we began the project, we did not have a clear picture of our model. Rather it evolved through our work in the schools. We began with the use of DIBELS assessments and established clear guidelines for our schools to use to identify students who were in need of additional

**TABLE 7.10. Rated Success of Secondary/Tertiary Interventions**

| | Eastside | School A | School B | School C | School D | School E | Total |
|---|---|---|---|---|---|---|---|
| Yes | 5% | 31% | 32% | 43% | 36% | 34% | 31% |
| Partial | 66% | 42% | 41% | 50% | 48% | 38% | 44% |
| No | 29% | 27% | 27% | 7% | 15% | 28% | 24% |

*Note.* Data for one BRIC school not submitted.

support in reading. We also identified specific decoding programs for each tier of instruction. As the project moved forward, we developed specific guidelines to use for progress monitoring, instructional materials to strengthen the core program (i.e., BELS and FFFP), guidelines for student movement between tiers, training materials and support systems for CSCs to provide professional development to school staff, procedures to make data collection more efficient, and a process for monitoring student progress regularly. By the middle of the 3rd year we had a clearly articulated model in place but did not have consistent implementation until the 4th year. One of the most important lessons we learned was that to ensure the success of the model it was critical to have a literacy leader in place. This leader is a key player in implementing each component of the model; she or he participates in assessment, assists with scheduling decisions, collects treatment fidelity and provides support to staff, examines progress monitoring data, presents data to the principal and grade-level teams, and assists teachers in making appropriate instructional decisions for students. Our schools' literacy leader was the CSC; however, we realized this position would be eliminated at the conclusion of our grant. We recognized that the only way to maintain the model would be to transfer the responsibilities of the CSC and bring about the schools' ownership of the model.

## Sustainability

During the 2005–2006 school year, we withdrew our direct involvement in the schools and focused specifically on sustainability. We found that

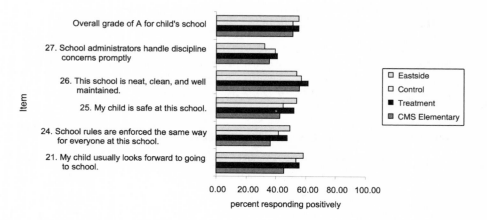

**FIGURE 7.18.** Parent attitudes regarding school climate.

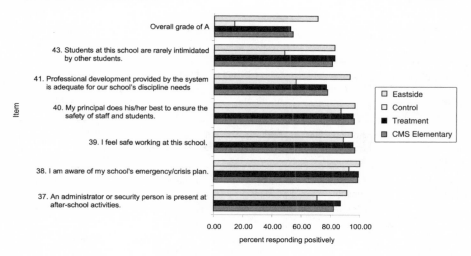

**FIGURE 7.19.** Teacher attitudes regarding school climate.

although the literacy facilitator and school staff were familiar with specific components of our model (e.g., assessment, specific interventions) they didn't necessarily recognize the relationships among the components or view the model as a school initiative. We wanted the schools' literacy facilitators to begin to take ownership over the model and present/incorporate it as a school initiative, not as a BRIC activity.

In the summer prior to our 4th year, we invited each of our schools' CSC and literacy facilitator to attend a full-day training session led by project staff. The purpose of the training was to provide professional development support and materials to prepare the CSCs to transfer their responsibilities to the school's literacy facilitators. We also emphasized that the BRIC model was to be presented as their school's reading model. Before school started the literacy facilitators at our project schools, with assistance from the CSC, presented the schoolwide model to the K–2 staff at her respective school. Again, the purpose was to create the school's ownership of the model. In addition, we created a planning sheet (Figure 7.20) to determine how the model could be sustained by the school. Project staff met with each school's CSC, literacy facilitator, and principal to determine the specifics of what was required to implement the model and how it would be done within the school.

As the 2005–2006 school year progressed, we were interested in determining how well the literacy facilitators at our seven schools understood our model as well as how comparison schools understood the school system's comprehensive reading model. An individual with no af-

| Components of reading model | Who? | How? | When? | Professional development provided by |
|---|---|---|---|---|
| Conducting screening (and benchmark assessments) | Assessment team | Using DIBELS assessment materials | Fall, winter, spring | School system, Literacy facilitator |
| Planning and scheduling of students | Administration, Literacy facilitator | Meet to discuss school schedule | Fall (Review after winter benchmark assessment) | N/A |
| Ensuring strong and regular implementation | Literacy facilitator/ Lead teachers | Training, using fidelity checklists | Ongoing** | School system and Literacy facilitator/Lead teachers |
| Progress monitoring | Assessment team and/or Classroom teachers | Using DIBELS assessment materials | For students identified "Strategic": every 2 weeks. For students identified "Intensive": every week | Literacy facilitator |
| Instructional Decision making | Classroom teachers and Intervention team | Review student progress, frequency of implementation, fidelity of implementation | During grade level meetings, monthly meetings with principal, and intervention team meetings | Literacy facilitator |

**FIGURE 7.20.** School-wide Reading Model Planning Sheet

filiation to our project conducted telephone interviews with the literacy facilitators at our seven project schools as well as with literacy coordinators at seven comparison schools. The purpose of the interview was to gather descriptions of how they interpreted their school's comprehensive reading model. For five of the seven comparison schools, we spoke with the schools' K–2 literacy facilitator. The remaining two comparison schools had literacy facilitators recently appointed and unfamiliar with specific practices in place, so instead we spoke with the schools' kindergarten lead teacher. The lead teacher was selected by the grade-level team to lead meetings and initiatives of the grade level.

The literacy facilitators at our project schools were able to correctly identify and explain the five components of the comprehensive reading model. However, across comparison schools the comprehensive reading model was regarded as including the identification of schoolwide reading programs and assessment. All seven literacy coordinators from comparison schools indicated that the major component of the comprehensive model included the primary reading program that had been adopted across the school system. Three of the seven literacy coordinators mentioned the use of DIBELS assessment; however, none referred to the ongoing progress monitoring essential to the comprehensive model. In addition, only one literacy coordinator mentioned the importance of team planning and shared decision making. Perhaps the key difference between our project schools' and the comparison schools' understanding of the comprehensive reading model is the level of school involvement. Because our BRIC schools had an articulated comprehensive reading model and were more actively involved in making the model fit the context of their schools, they were able to be more systematic in the ways they supported the needs of their students.

## The BRIC Influence on School System Comprehensive Reading Model

Prior to implementation, the school system had adopted a model for providing reading instruction. A set of literacy assessments were administered at the end of each quarter; however, there were no specific guidelines used to identify students in need of additional support in reading. And although different levels of support were identified in the school system's model, there were no specific guidelines as to which programs or materials to use. Rather, a variety of suggestions were provided. Schools identified their own system for identifying students in need of support and then selected or created their own method and materials to meet the needs of the students.

Over the years of implementation, the school system elected to incorporate some of initiatives set forth by our project. For example, during year 2 of implementation the school system piloted DIBELS across 17 schools, in addition to the six BRIC schools; then the following year, DIBELS was adopted systemwide with over 100 elementary schools. During the fall semester of our fourth and final year of implementation, we shared data from our interviews with the BRIC and non-BRIC literacy facilitators regarding their understanding of their Comprehensive Reading Model. The comparison data were presented in a report that was a contributing factor to redefining the system's Comprehensive Reading Model and role of the literacy facilitator. Additionally, when Practice Court was published as *Early Reading Tutor*, it was purchased for all elementary schools as a secondary intervention.

## Unique Benefits and Challenges Represented in This Three-Tiered Model in Behavior

The BRIC project defined a PUBS-like model for the primary level of intervention as part of the original proposal. The engagement with the BRIC schools, however, has led to some very important refinements, particularly concerning the instruction, cueing, and prompting of appropriate behavior. We believe the replicable and operationally defined PUBS model is one way of implanting PBIS that is worthy of replication and further inquiry. It has been received across schools with a high level of treatment acceptability. However, the BRIC posited a less well defined model for secondary and tertiary intervention. We anticipated that there might be common interventions at those levels required across centers, but this did not happen. So, the BRIC secondary–tertiary behavior model evolved over time. The secondary-level interventions that evolved entailed a less obtrusive series of evidence-based teacher or self-mediated interventions that could easily be implemented in classrooms. However, it was difficult for the schools to implement fully the more obtrusive secondary social-skill pull-out instructional interventions. The CMS had adopted the Boys Town model as the preferred social skills model, and the BRIC aligned with that decision. However, even with that district-level support, it was difficult for schools to identify available instructors and to schedule and maintain consistently group social-skill instruction. In hindsight, we have discussed a more intensive and functional-based intervention at the secondary level, the Behavior Education Program (Crone, Horner, & Hawken, 2004) as a possible substitution for a pull-out social-skill intervention. That program does not require the difficult pull-out scheduling and personnel reallocations. At the tertiary level, idiosyncrasies among related services personnel (school psychologists, social workers, family advocates) had a major influence on use of the BRIC tertiary model. Some favored functional assessment, others did not. Some embraced wraparound planning, others did not. Eastside Elementary has hired this academic year from another BRIC school a new school psychologist who was an active supporter of the BRIC model, and so the future is brighter at Eastside but perhaps dimmer at the other BRIC school.

## Lessons Illustrated by This School Exemplar in Reading

As mentioned earlier, during the final year of implementation, the CSC at Eastside became a full-time support for behavior initiatives. Without the direct support from a CSC in the school, we had less control over implementation. The K–2 literacy facilitator assumed responsibility for

Eastside's reading model, and she perceived that her job responsibilities were to the school system, rather than our project. Therefore, there were deviations in how the reading model was used in the last year. For example, although the literacy facilitator met regularly with the principal and grade-level teams, the meetings were not focused around the monthly report. Instead, she generated her own ideas for discussion. As more schools in our system begin to use literacy facilitators to carry out the Comprehensive Reading Model, it will be important for us to determine to what extent deviations will affect student progress.

## Lessons Illustrated by This School Exemplar in Behavior

Eastside Elementary demonstrated the effectiveness of the BRIC behavior model when that model is supported by the school principal and the principal delegates PBS oversight to a committed, dogged, and insistent teacher of positive behavior interventions and supports. The PBS team took its responsibilities (professional supports, fidelity monitoring, student progress monitoring) very seriously. The team and Tina consistently reinforced teachers implementing the BRIC interventions with high fidelity and coached assiduously teachers who were implementing with less fidelity. Students were also monitored closely, and there was widespread support for positive intervention versus exclusionary and punitive practice. Eastside also demonstrated the cumulative effect of school-level behavioral momentum. The school improved each year, and success begat success to the point that there is strong consensus among staff in favor of PBIS.

## Future Outlook for This School

As discussed previously, CMS has already "scaled up" to the system level DIBELS K–3 assessment, progress monitoring, and data-based decision making, and the district has also set 2008 as the timeline for districtwide scale-up of positive behavior support. However, CMS like many large urban school system is consistently in transition. Of the seven BRIC schools, five experienced a principal change during the project. The project was able to sustain and in some cases improve effort in spite of this significant leadership change given strong support by the CMS interim superintendent. This year, however, the system hired a new superintendent. The previous interim superintendent was a staunch supporter of evidence-based reading programs and PBIS and strongly supported the BRIC effort. The elements of the BRIC model have been maintained at Eastside with continued support from Tina and the school principal, this first academic year post the BRIC project. We anticipate a continued strong implementation of the BRIC model at Eastside assuming that the leadership of the school remains constant and assuming that there are no major changes at the district level regarding support for evidence-based reading programs and PBIS.

## REFERENCES

Adams, M. J., Bereiter, C., McKeough, A., Case, R., Roit, M., Hirschberg, J., et al. (2000). *Open Court reading*. Columbus, OH: SRA/McGraw-Hill.

Algozzine, B., Marr, M. B., McClanahan, T., & Barnes, E. (2006). *Basic early literacy skill activities*. Charlotte, NC: Behavior and Reading Improvement Center.

Carnine, D., Silbert, J., Kame'enui, E. J., & Tarver, S. (2004). *Direct instruction reading* (4th ed.). Upper Saddle River, NJ: Prentice Hall.

Charlotte–Mecklenburg Schools. (2005). *Rules and responsibilities handbook*. Charlotte, NC: Author

Crone, D. A., Horner, R. H., & Hawken, L. S. (2004). *Responding to problem behavior in schools: The behavior education program*. New York: Guilford Press.

Dowd, T., & Tierney, J. (2005). *Teaching social skills to youth*. Boys Town, NE: Boys Town Press.

Engelmann, S., & Bruner, E. C. (1995a). *Reading Mastery Classic I*. Columbus, OH: SRA/McGraw-Hill.

Engelmann, S., & Bruner, E. C. (1995b). *Reading Mastery Classic II*. Columbus, OH: SRA/McGraw-Hill.

Gibbs, S., Campbell, M., Helf, S., & Cooke, N. (2007). *Early reading tutor*. Columbus, OH: SRA/McGraw-Hill.

Gibbs, S., Campbell, M., Helf, S., Cooke, N., & Algozzine, B. (2004). *Practice court*. Charlotte, NC: UNC Charlotte Behavior and Reading Improvement Center.

May, S., Ard, W., Todd, A., Horner, R., Glasgow, A., Sugai, G. et al. (2000). *School Wide Information System* (SWIS). Eugene: University of Oregon, Educational and Community Supports.

National Institute of Child Health and Human Development. (2000). *Teaching children to read: An evidence-based assessment of the scientific research literature on reading and its implications for reading instruction* (NIH Publication No. 00-4769). Washington, DC: U.S. Government Printing Office.

Simmons, D. C., & Kame'enui, E. J. (Eds.). (1998). *What reading research tells us about children with diverse learning needs: Bases and basics*. Mahwah, NJ: Erlbaum.

Sugai, G., Lewis-Palmer, T., Todd, A., & Horner, R. (2001). *School-wide Evaluation Tool (SET)*. Eugene: University of Oregon, Educational and Community Supports.

Walker, H. M., & Severson, H. H. (1992). *Technical manual, systematic screening for behavior disorders*. Longmont, CO: Sopris West.

study, the school served 45 ELL students. The increased ELL population, for the most part, was Hispanic.

The faculty demographics at Oak School were typical of most of the school district's schools. Districtwide, 50% of teachers have 12 or more years of experience in the classroom and more than 70% of teachers have master's degrees or higher. At Oak School, there are 20 female classroom teachers, K–6. One teacher is Hispanic. The remaining teachers are European American.

Oak School is a district center for students with multiple disabilities. As many of these students required one-to-one paraprofessional help and remained in self-contained classrooms, they were not part of the current study. K–3 students with a classification of learning disabilities were part of the regular education classroom structure and received services from one special education teacher and two paraprofessionals. IEPs specified the intensity and duration of those services. Most students who received special education services also participated in interventions introduced through this project.

Prior to the Kansas prevention model, a full-time reading specialist provided remedial reading intervention services for students not identified for special education. Students who received remedial reading services were identified through use of an informal reading inventory that was required by the district. However, this measure was not tightly linked to individual student instructional decision making. Throughout the length of the project, the reading specialist in the building was also responsible for providing ELL services. Although general education teachers worked to provide additional academic and behavioral support, at the classroom level, this help was informal. There was no specific schoolwide discipline system in place. Beyond sending students "to the office" and suspensions, few procedures were in place to provide behavioral support for students with challenging behavior.

From initial meetings with the principal and staff, it was clear that Oak School was struggling to meet the changing instructional and behavioral needs of their students. The opportunity to enter into a university/school collaboration focusing on implementing a systematic tiered prevention model that improved student outcomes for reading and behavior and its sustainability was welcomed, and instructional and behavioral changes were desired.

## SCHOOL READING AND BEHAVIOR RISK ASSESSMENT

The initial risk assessment of Oak School students in the first year (see details below and Tables 8.1 and 8.2 for reading and behavior assessments) produced the following schoolwide profile based on measures and benchmarks described later in the chapter. More than half of students (54.5%) were identified with some form of risk. This included 36.4% at risk for reading problems, 10.3% with reading and behavior risk, and 7.9% with behavior risk (see Table 8.3). Compared to the average risk profile of all Kansas experimental and comparison schools in the study, it can be seen that Oak School was representative in terms of population factors and risk (Figure 8.1).

**TABLE 8.1. Oak School Reading Assessment Schedule**

| Participants | Assessment | Schedule |
|---|---|---|
| | School | |
| K–3 staff and administrators | Schoolwide Evaluation Tool for Reading (SWETR; Abbott, Kamps, & Arreaga-Mayer, 2003) | Yearly |
| Reading team | Reading team meeting fidelity of implementation | Twice yearly |
| | Teacher: fidelity of implementation | |
| Primary instruction | General education *Open Court* Teacher fidelity | Yearly |
| Secondary and tertiary instruction | Small-group intervention fidelities: Kindergarten Peer-Assisted Learning Strategies (K-PALS) Early Interventions in Reading (EIR) Read Naturally (RN) Language Arts Multisensory Program (LAMP) | Twice yearly |
| | Student | |
| All K–3 | Dynamic Indicators of Basic Early Literacy Skills Battery (DIBELS; Good, Gruba, & Kaminski, 2002) | Fall, winter, spring |
| Targeted below-benchmark students with parental consent | DIBELS: Progress monitoring | Monthly |
| Below-benchmark students with parental consent | Woodcock Reading Mastery Test (WRMT) Reading Battery (Woodcock, 1988) | Baseline and spring of each year |

**TABLE 8.2. Oak School Behavior Assessment Schedule**

| Participants | Assessment | Schedule |
|---|---|---|
| | **School** | |
| Principal interviews a random selection of staff and students | Schoolwide Evaluation Tool (SET) | Yearly |
| All staff | Positive Behavior Support (PBS) Survey | Yearly |
| SWPBS team | Schoolwide PBS team meeting fidelity of implementation | Quarterly |
| | *Office disciplinary referral data from the School-Wide Information System (SWIS) | Monthly review |
| | **Teacher: fidelity of implementation** | |
| All staff | Sections of survey | Yearly |
| Secondary/targeted intervention providers | Interventions: Class-Wide Function Based Intervention Teams (CW-FIT) Social Skills Club | Twice yearly |
| | Check-in/check-out *Office referral data (SWIS) | Weekly review |
| | **Student** | |
| All teachers screen all students | Systematic Screening for Behavior Disorders (SSBD) | Fall |
| Targeted students meeting SSBD criteria with parental consent | Social Skills Rating System (SSRS) *Office disciplinary referral data (SWIS) Direct observation/FBA | Fall/Spring Weekly review As needed |

## CORE PROCEDURES: COMMON AND CRITICAL THREE-TIERED FEATURES

### Early, Frequent Screening, and Progress Monitoring with Decision Making

Center staff conducted universal screening on reading and behavior measures to identify student risk. *Student risk* is defined as those students who fall within the Tier 2 strategic (secondary) or the Tier 3 intensive (tertiary) ranges on an academic and behavior continuum. After screening, strategic and intensive students were assigned to receive intervention. For this core screening, schoolwide, central data systems were established.

**TABLE 8.3. School Characteristics**

| | | Experimental | | | | | Control | | | |
|---|---|---|---|---|---|---|---|---|---|---|
| Variable | n | M | SD | Min | Max | n | M | SD | Min | Max |
| Schools | 10 | | | | | 7 | | | | |
| Enrollment | | 349 | 85.6 | 245 | | | 507 | 341 | 133 | 193 |
| % minority | | 56.0 | 36.5 | 8.0 | 99.0 | | 39.4 | 33.7 | 10.0 | 91.0 |
| % free lunch | | 54.4 | 34.0 | 5.0 | 90.0 | | 43.1 | 35.2 | 13.0 | 97.0 |
| IEPs | | 9.1 | 3.1 | 5.0 | 14.0 | | 11.6 | 4.7 | 5.0 | 19.0 |
| ELLs | | 10.4 | 16.5 | 0.0 | 49.0 | | 8.7 | 13.2 | 0.0 | 37.0 |
| No risk | | 51.6 | 11.1 | 38.1 | 72.1 | | 52.9 | 10.7 | 377 | 685 |
| Reading risk% | | 33.5 | 7.6 | 18.6 | 45.4 | | 36.0 | 149 | 13.0 | 53.8 |
| Behavior risk% | | 6.6 | 4.9 | 1.5 | 17.2 | | 4.5 | 3.9 | 1.1 | 11.1 |
| Both risk% | | 8.4 | 3.8 | 3.0 | 143 | | 6.5 | 3.0 | 2.8 | 11.8 |

*Reading*

Dynamic Indicators of Basic Early Literacy Skills (DIBELS) was used for the reading screening (Good, Gruba, & Kaminski, 2002). DIBELS subtests are 1-minute fluency checks in the skills of letter knowledge, phonological awareness, and oral text reading. Kansas Center staff collected this data and shared it with faculty. Teams of approximately 12 to 15 research assistants trained and monitored by Center staff spent 1 to 2 days at Oak School assessing K–3 students with DIBELS and other reading measures used as part of the larger evaluation of the model. Before the end of the project, Oak School and other district schools became trained in DIBELS administration and began collecting DIBELS data that was continued to be entered by Center staff. Data collected was entered into the schools' password-protected site on the national DIBELS website (*dibels.uoregon.edu*).

Based on DIBELS benchmarks for each grade level, individual students were classified as benchmark or on target, strategic (some risk), or intensive (high risk) (Good, Simmons, Kame'enui, Kaminski, & Wallin, 2002). Depending on individual performance, students at risk were assigned to receive or continue receiving strategic or intensive reading interventions in addition to the universal general education reading instruction.

*Behavior*

Students qualified for behavioral risk in one of two ways. Either a teacher identified students or the students received office disciplinary referrals for behavior problems. In the fall of each year, all teachers com-

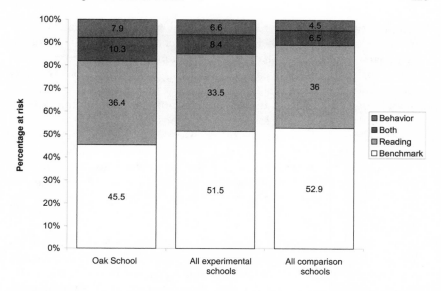

**FIGURE 8.1.** Oak School schoolwide risk profile compared to the mean of all experimental and comparison schools.

pleted the Systematic Screening for Behavior Disorders (SSBD; Walker, Severson, & Feil, 1992). The SSBD is a multiple-gating measure consisting of a ranking to identify students of most concern, followed by a rating scale to describe their behavior, followed by a direct observation. For the current purpose, only the ranking and rating components were completed. Teachers ranked their students from high to low relative to the occurrence of behavior problems. For those highest ranked, teachers completed the SSBD teacher rating consisting of three scales: (1) Critical Events, (2) Adaptive Behavior, and (3) Maladaptive Behavior. In its entirety, this screening took 45 minutes for teachers to complete for their class. The technical manual for the SSBD (Walker et al., 1992) provides normative criteria used to determine the risk status of students. Students exceeding normative criteria were eligible for secondary- or tertiary-level interventions.

A second measure was the School-wide Information System (SWIS) developed by the Oregon Behavior Center (Irvin et al., 2006). It is a computerized system for tracking all office disciplinary referrals and reporting trends in referrals over time (May et al., 2000). These data and reports generated from the national website (*www.swis.org*) were used by the school behavior team to evaluate and plan individual and schoolwide progress reducing behavior problems serious enough to prompt office disciplinary referral. Students at any time could qualify for strategic or intensive behavioral intervention because of (1) office disciplinary referral data—having two or more major behavioral events or three or more minor events, (2) suspension event records—students that may not have met other criteria yet became eligible as a result of a major incident, and (3) teacher nomination throughout the year to the team. At Oak School, students were considered for strategic interventions if they had two to five office disciplinary referrals and for tertiary interventions if they had six or more office disciplinary referrals. A suspension from school resulted in the automatic consideration for a tertiary intervention. Teacher nominations of students throughout the year led to data gathering (office disciplinary referral, screening records, and interviews) to determine the level of intervention most appropriate.

In addition to monitoring student's progress with SWIS office disciplinary referral data, teachers completed a pre- and post rating (beginning and end of year) of student's problem behaviors and social skills. The rating tool was the Social Skills Rating System (SSRS; Gresham & Elliott, 1990). Teachers completed this rating (approximately 5 minutes per student) for students screened at risk for reading, behavior, or both. The data provided information to inform interventions, measure outcomes, and guide SWPBS team decision making for such things as the need for more or different interventions.

These centralized data systems for reading (DIBELS) and behavior (SWIS) enabled reading and behavior teams at Oak School to access rich sources of information at the level of individual students, classrooms, and the entire school as a basis for decision making about changes in intervention and for monitoring progress over time.

## Schoolwide and Classwide Universal Systems of Support

The Kansas model of schoolwide prevention followed the three-tiered framework based on a risk-level approach to intervention (e.g., Fuchs & Fuchs, 2006). The goal was to provide an appropriately intensive experience to all students based on early-risk status and short-term progress over time. Instruction was intensified for students who were not measurably responsive to the universal intervention supports for reading and behavior.

At the outset, the Kansas Center staff had compiled a menu of secondary- and tertiary-level evidence-based reading and behavior programs/interventions/curricula (see Table 8.4). To be selected as "evidence-based" the following minimal levels of evidence supporting the effectiveness of the curriculum/intervention was required: (1) the

**TABLE 8.4. Kansas Center Prevention/Interventions at Oak School by Focus and Tier**

| Tier | Features | Intervention focus | |
| --- | --- | --- | --- |
| | | Reading and supporting evidence | Behavior and supporting evidence |
| 1 | All students; school- and classwide; all grades | Open Court Reading Curriculum (Foorman et al., 1998) Kindergarten Peer-Assisted Learning Strategies (K-PALS[a]; Mathes et al., 2003) | Schoolwide positive behavior support (SWPBS; Marquis et al., 2000) (Expectations, skill instruction, rewards and consequences) |
| 2 | Small groups (3 to 6) | Early Interventions in Reading (EIR[a]; Mathes et al., 2005), first and second grades Read Naturally[a] (Buck & Torgesen, 2003) second and third grades | Social Skills Club (Lewis, Dugai, & Colvin, 1998) Mentoring (Dubois et al., 2002) Check-in/Check-out (Crone, Horner, & Hawken, 2003) |
| 3 | Individual, one-on-one | EIR[a] in Reading (Mathes et al., 2005), double dose first and second grades Language Arts Multisensory Program (LAMP; Moats & Farrell, 2003; Torgesen et al., 2001), first through third grades | Social Skills Club (Lewis et al., 1998) Check-in/Check-out (Crone et al., 2004) |

*Note.* All interventions were evidence-based. Tier 1 interventions were received by all students. Tiers 2 or 3 were in addition to Tier 1.

[a]This practice was subsequently favorably reviewed in the What Works Clearinghouse website.

curriculum was applicable to small-group instruction as a secondary- or tertiary-level intervention within the three-tiered model, (2) published research showed effectiveness of the curriculum or curriculum components, and (3) the curriculum lessons provided structured content and lessons in the alphabetic principle (phonemic awareness, phonics, decodable text, fluency). Similar criteria were required for selection of behavioral prevention/intervention strategies: (1) the intervention fit within the context of the (SWPBS) three-tiered model for teaching appropriate behaviors as required in the original RFP, (2) published research showed effectiveness of the intervention or specified components of the intervention (e.g., differential reinforcement, token economy), and (3) the intervention provided instruction in targeted behavioral or

social skills for students. Schools in the Kansas study were able to ex-
plore the options in this list and chose among the curricula and interventions that they felt were a good fit to school's student population,
the staff, and most closely aligned to the district's curriculum philosophy and policies.

### Universal Reading

The Open Court Reading Series (McGraw Hill, 2005) was used for universal reading instruction at Oak School. Open Court is an evidence-based
curriculum with a focus on systematic, explicit, code-based instruction
(*www.mheducation.com/programs/files/Results_with_Open_ Court.pdf*)
(Foorman, Francis, Fletcher, Schatschneider, & Mehta, 1998). The curriculum included a scope and sequence, teacher manuals, student workbooks,
and ancillary materials. The general education daily literacy block of instruction was 90 minutes a day for first through third grade and 30 minutes a day for the half-day kindergarten. Because Open Court was already
in place, Kansas Center staff only observed universal classroom instruction to assess classroom teacher fidelity of implementation of the curriculum, but provided no training, coaching, or mentoring regarding its use.

### Universal Behavior

SWPBS (*www.pbis.org*) was selected for universal behavior prevention
(National Technical Assistance Center on Positive Behavioral Interventions and Supports, 2006; Marquis et al., 2000). At Tier 1, procedures
focused on teaching behavioral expectations and supports (i.e., proactive
discipline) to all students and staff, across all school settings that together served as the foundation for classroom and individual student behavior support. Universal PBS included teaching behavioral expectations
across settings (hallway, playground, cafeteria, and classroom) and specific skill lessons. Three to 5 days of initial team training are recommended prior to initial implementation of SWPBS.

## Strategic Level Systems of Support

### Reading

At the strategic Tier 2, Kansas Center project staff worked with the reading team and individual teachers to implement selected evidence-based
curricula in the context of small groups. These experiences were provided to students in addition to universal instruction increasing the total
time of each student's daily total reading experience. The evidence-based
interventions selected for this purpose were those with a focus on spe-

cific reading skills in which the skills were taught more explicitly than within the Open Court curriculum with additional academic reinforcement. Additional features were (1) small groups of six or fewer students, and (2) use of monthly DIBELS progress monitoring to inform short-term decision making (see Table 8.4).

*Kindergarten Peer-Assisted Literacy Strategies.* Kindergarten Peer-Assisted Literacy Strategies (K-PALS; Mathes, Clancy-Menchetti, & Torgesen, 2001) is a classwide peer-assisted 15- to 20-minute strategy that focuses on prereading skills. These skills include letter identification, rhyming, alliteration, first sounds, segmenting, and blending. By the end of the 60-lesson curriculum, students are sounding out real words. Each lesson includes a teacher-led minilesson with review of the material to be tutored from the two-page worksheet and peer-assisted tutoring between two students. At the end of the lesson, students regroup with the teacher and review the day's lesson. Materials for this curriculum include a teacher workbook and student worksheet pages. Half-day training is suggested for K-PALS implementation.

*Early Interventions in Reading.* The first- and second-grade teachers selected Early Interventions in Reading (EIR) as their targeted intervention (Mathes, Torgesen, Menchetti, Wahl, & Grek, 2004). EIR is a beginning reading intervention focusing on teaching four to six students in a group. It is teacher-led and scripted. It combines aspects of direct instruction and mastery learning methods. The suggested instructional lesson length is 40 minutes daily. The introduction and teaching of skills mirrors the Open Court series and uses many of the same readers and ancillary Open Court materials. EIR Level One has 100 lessons and is expected to be completed in one school year. Materials include a teacher manual, student workbook, and ancillary reading materials. The program has a strong phonological awareness, alphabet knowledge, and word recognition focus combined with fluency building. Specific activities found in the EIR program include (1) phonemic awareness tasks of oral blending, stretching, and sound discrimination; (2) letter sounds (new and review) using "see, hear, say, write" practice; (3) alphabetic decoding using sounding out, reading fast, and chunking tasks; (4) reading of tricky words, connected text, step-by-step stories (from the Open Court series), and phonics minibooks to build fluency; (5) comprehension activities including sequencing, retelling, story grammar; and (6) writing of sounds, words, and sentences. Three days of training are suggested for Level One implementation.

*Read Naturally.* Third-grade teachers worked with text fluency (speed and accuracy) and word recognition with students who needed secondary-level intervention using Read Naturally (Ihnot, 1992). Students listen to text and then practice reading the text. Worksheets are provided that include comprehension questions. Students are assessed on the pre- and postreading of each passage. Although this is considered a small-group intervention, the teacher/student ratio can comfortably range from one to seven. Materials include story CDs and student worksheets. Two days of training are recommended for Read Naturally.

*Strategic-Level Behavioral Interventions*

At the strategic tier, Kansas Center project staff worked with the SWPBS team to implement interventions that were provided to students in addition to universal instruction. These interventions were established as efficient and effective supports in which students at risk could be placed within 72 hours (as a goal) of being identified or referred. Additional features were (1) small groups of six or fewer students for groups that met outside of class (social skills club), and (2) use of monthly SWIS office disciplinary referral data and intervention records to monitor progress and to inform short-term decision making. As fidelity of primary-level implementation was established, the team began implementing various secondary-level supports. Those interventions included social skills club, check-in/check-out, and mentoring.

*Social Skills Club.* The social skills club (Lewis & Powers, 2002) is an intervention designed for students with deficits in social skills that appeared to lead them to problems sometime during the school day. The SWPBS team considered fall screening data, teacher nominations, and reviewed office disciplinary referral data to identify students for this program. Sixteen weekly 30-minute social skills sessions were held for five to nine students in a group (a maximum of six students with social skills deficits). Each group also included peer models. A typical lesson involved a review of the behavior expectations for the session, introduction of a skill, role-play, feedback, a review of prior homework, and a plan to practice new and old skills throughout the week. Materials were also given to the students' primary teachers to practice skills in their classroom. The social club curriculum addressed major topics such body language, following directions, using self-control, dealing with teasing, playing cooperatively, accepting "no," and using adults as resources. The schools' PBS coach attended a full-day training session on the intervention and then led several groups in the first year. By the second year of implementation five teachers volunteered, were trained, and led groups.

*Check-In/Check-Out.* The check-in/check-out program (Crone, Horner, & Hawken, 2004) involves a morning check-in during which students receive a behavior monitoring sheet for the day. Sheets list the expectations and provide a grid for student's behavior to be rated during each major setting and subject of the day (e.g., playground, cafeteria, math, and reading) by the teacher or adult responsible for that time/activity. Ratings included 0 (Needs improvement), 1 (Okay) and 2 (Great job). If a student was working on a specific skill, it was listed under one of the expectations. Teachers used the sheets as instructional opportunities to remind the student, recognize appropriate behavior, and constructively provide feedback if corrections were necessary. At the end of the day, check-out, students reviewed their day based on the sheet with their "check-out" teacher. In this process, students based on merit were rewarded for meeting their individual goals. The student took the sheet home to be reviewed and signed by parent/guardian and returned to the teacher the next day. At Oak School, the music teacher, art teacher, and school nurse checked students in and out. The music teacher (who was also the PBS coach) entered daily percentages of total points possible for each student into a spreadsheet as a means of tracking progress over time. To get started, the PBS coach participated in a half-day training session on secondary interventions of which approximately an hour was devoted to check-in/check-out.

*Mentoring.* The mentoring program matched students to in-school staff mentors. Students identified as needing strategic supports that addressed a perceived function (SWIS office disciplinary referral data) of adult attention (needing positive adult attention and for some students a sense of stability). Mentoring programs such as this can improve student outcomes by helping to establish school relationships (Dubois, Holloway, Valentine, & Cooper, 2002). At Oak School, building staff volunteered to commit at least 10 minutes a week to meet with a student with whom they were paired. Mentors were taught to establish a positive relationship and advised not to counsel, nag, or reprimand. Mentors were expected to meet with students during the course of each school day and not to take the student on excursions outside of school. To monitor this program, the SWPBS team reviewed SWIS office referral data and received weekly updates from mentors that ensured that mentor commitments were upheld. Minimal training is needed for mentors or for team members to organize the mentoring program.

## Intensive Systems of Support

### Intensive Reading

Intensive intervention was typically defined by (1) very small teacher pupil ratios of no more than two students and (2) "double-dose" exposures to the same lessons a second time during the day, using (3) curriculum with a focus on specific reading skills that are introduced at a much slower pace over a longer period of time than the general education curriculum. Monthly performance monitoring occurs. For example, some students received a double dose of the EIR intervention, and a reduction in group size boosted instructional intensity. However, the Linguistic, Alphabetics, Multi-level comprehension, Phonetics, and Speed (LAMPS; Abbott, 2002) was provided to students with the greatest reading challenges.

LAMPS is a one-on-one, multisensory intervention. Compared to universal and strategic reading interventions that are not multisensory, the LAMPS provides extensive repetition of learned materials through audio, visual, tactile, and kinesthetic activities based on the evidence the most challenged students with significant delays benefit from skill building using multimodalities (Moats & Farrell, 2003).

Like other evidence-based reading practices, LAMPS instruction is teacher-led and uses direct instruction and mastery learning strategies. The evidence-based reading skills taught are highly focused on extensive phonemic awareness, phonics, sight-word recognition, and fluency work. Other reading, spelling, grammar, and writing skills are introduced at a slower pace than most interventions. Four days of group training with approximately 10 additional hours of individualized training are recommended for this intervention.

*Intensive Behavior*

Intensive and individualized behavior intervention plans were designed based on function-based behavior assessments with implementation for students who were unresponsive to schoolwide (primary) and targeted (secondary) interventions (see Table 8.4) or as previously stated, either were suspended or had more than six office disciplinary referrals. SWPBS team members received training in functional behavior assessments and function-based intervention planning and implemented the plans with students. The SWPBS team monitored the progress of students receiving intensive interventions on at least a monthly basis.

## IMPLEMENTATION APPROACH

The primary approach used by the Kansas Center was designed to foster local ownership of the three-tiered model reading and behavior model and use of data-based decision making and evidenced-based intervention practices from the beginning using faculty leadership teams.

three classroom teachers, the reading specialist, and one paraprofessional would provide the EIR intervention, and the other two paraprofessionals would divide up the benchmark students and oversee independent student work and a fluency reading time. A similar plan was created by the second-grade teachers.

Although no published intervention was slated for the third-grade students, third-grade teachers also specified a guarded time. During this time, teachers regrouped the lowest students based on screening score and teacher recommendation. Only one paraprofessional was required to make the third-grade proposed plan work. Classroom teachers kept the benchmark students in their respective classrooms and provided independent work. The small-group intervention time included high-frequency words and fluency training.

Successful initial implementation also involved problem solving. Initially, transitions for moving into and out of small groups took far too much time. It took several weeks of daily practice to shorten transition time so that 70+ children could move to and from their different classroom in only a minute or two at each end of the transition. Teachers also had initial challenges of having a rigid time schedule for "small-group time." For example, in the first and second grades, because small groups were organized by data outcomes and teacher judgment, most groups had students from at least two of the three different classrooms. Additionally, the benchmark students were divided up into two larger groups. This required many of those students to move to a different classroom.

**TABLE 8.6. Sample Small-Group Reading Schedule**

| Time | Days | Grade | Teacher | Intervention | No. of students |
|---|---|---|---|---|---|
| 8:40–9:00 | M, T, R | K | Mrs. V | K-PALS | Class |
| 1:00–1:20 | M, T, F | K | Mrs. V | K-PALS | Class |
| 10:20–10:50 | M–F | 1 | Mrs. A | EIR | 5 |
| 10:20–10:50 | M–F | 1 | Mrs. G | EIR | 5 |
| 10:20–10:50 | M–F | 1 | Mrs. J | EIR | 6 |
| 10:20–10:50 | M–F | 1 | Mrs. R | EIR | 5 |
| 10:20–10:50 | M–F | 1 | Mrs. F | EIR | 6 |
| 10:20–10:50 | M–F | 1 | Mrs. M | EIR | 6 |
| 9:30–10:10 | M, T, R, F | 2 | Mrs. K | RN | 6 |
| 9:30–10:10 | M, T, R, F | 2 | Mrs. S | EIR (high) | 4 |
| 9:30–10:10 | M, T, R, F | 2 | Mrs. L | EIR (middle) | 4 |
| 9:30–10:10 | M, T, R, F | 2 | Mrs. E | EIR (middle) | 5 |
| 9:30–10:10 | M, T, R, F | 2 | Mrs. R | EIR (low) | 4 |
| 12:15–1:00 | M, T, W, R | 3 | All grade 3 | RN | All grade 3 |

*Note.* EIR, Early Interventions in Reading; RN, Read Naturally; Class, all students in class participate; high, middle, low, level of current reading ability for students in group.

A system was eventually worked out in which the students lined up next to the small-group teacher and proceeded to the appropriate classroom. Teachers were encouraged to provide additional positive reinforcement for students who lined up quickly and orderly to expedite the process. Teachers learned that adhering to the beginning and ending times of small groups was critical to make the transition smooth and ensure that no children were left unattended at any time.

In successive years, it became clear that to reduce the number of students in the first through third grade who needed intervention, a specific kindergarten intervention was needed. The kindergarten teacher at Oak School focused on the social/emotional development of the students in her half-day kindergarten classes. At the end of year 1, only 8% of the students met literacy benchmark. At the beginning of year 2, the reading team encouraged the kindergarten teacher to more closely adhere to the Open Court curriculum and provide more literacy experiences within the classroom setting. It was strongly suggested by the team that the kindergarten teacher implement the class-wide K-PALS curriculum. Implementation of K-PALS nearly doubled the amount of instructional time spent on literacy instruction. Although the kindergarten teacher was resistant to the idea of additional literacy instruction, she agreed reluctantly to allow K-PALS implementation taught by paraprofessionals. At the end of year 2, 24% of students were at benchmark. At the end of year 3, 38% of the students met benchmark, and by the end of the fourth school year, 55% of kindergarteners met the end-of-the-year benchmark (see Figure 8.2).

In addition to the school reading team, intervention reading teams were formed to meet and discuss student progress within a specific intervention. Invention teams met at different intervals (weekly, monthly, or on an as-needed basis). For example, the third-grade Read Naturally intervention team met on a weekly basis to discuss student progress and make decisions about promoting students to the next academic level or increasing text fluency goals. For the LAMPS, our individualized intensive intervention, the interventionist and JGCP consultant met often (minimum of twice a month) at the beginning of the year and less often as the year progressed.

### Behavior Implementation

The behavior team began by developing effective operating procedures. They established regular meeting times, roles (e.g., leader, communications, secretary, task master, data manager) and an agenda format. The team created an action plan to facilitate implementation and referred back to their plan at each meeting. Kansas Center staff provided the

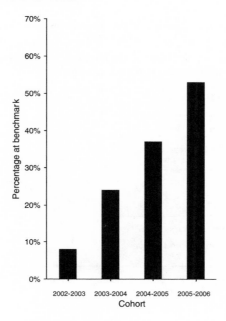

**FIGURE 8.2.** Percentage of kindergarten students at year-end benchmark across years.

team with an implementation start-up checklist (*www.pbis.org*; see Figure 8.3).

One of the first objectives the team accomplished was to develop school expectations and a definition matrix. The expectations the school staff chose were active listening, best effort, care for property, deepdown kindness, and extreme safety. Staff and students referred to these expectations as the Oak School "ABCs." The expectations and matrix were shared with the remaining staff. The SWPBS team then created the matrix by determining what the expectations would look like in the various settings of the school (see sample Oak School expectation matrix in Table 8.7).

Next, the SWPBS team planned an assembly to kick off the program. The assembly provided an opportunity to announce the initial changes to students (and again with staff) and to provide opportunities for practice. For example, teachers demonstrated the wrong way to line up, and then a group of students demonstrated the right way as they related to the expectations. The assembly was the first opportunity for students to learn about the rewards program that consisted of "loops" (nylon bands) that students earned for demonstrating the expectations. Students exchanged loops for privileges established by their classroom

School _____ Date of Report _____
District _____ County _____ State _____

INSTRUCTIONS: The SWPBS team should complete both checklists quarterly to monitor activities for implementation of PBS in the school.
EBS Team Members _____
Person(s) Completing Report _____

| Checklist #1: Start-Up Activity | | | | | |
|---|---|---|---|---|---|
| Complete and submit **Quarterly**. | Status: Achieved, In Progress, Not Started | | | | |
|  | Date: (MM/ DD/YY) | Oct. | Dec. | Mar. | May |
| Establish Commitment<br>1. Administrator's support and active involvement. | Status: | | | | |
| 2. Faculty/Staff support (One of top 3 goals, 80% of faculty document support, 3 year timeline). | Status: | | | | |
| Establish and Maintain Team<br>3. Team established (representative). | Status: | | | | |
| 4. Team has regular meeting schedule, effective operating procedures. | Status: | | | | |
| 5. Audit is completed for efficient integration of team with other teams/initiatives addressing behavior support. | Status: | | | | |
| Self-Assessment<br>6. Team/faculty completes EBS self-assessment survey. | Status: | | | | |
| 7. Team summarizes existing school discipline data. | Status: | | | | |
| 8. Strengths, areas of immediate focus and action plan are identified. | Status: | | | | |
| Establish School-wide Expectations<br>9. 3-5 school-wide behavior expectations are defined. | Status: | | | | |
| 10. School-wide teaching matrix developed. | Status: | | | | |
| 11. Teaching plans for school-wide expectations are developed. | Status: | | | | |

(continued)

| | | | | | |
|---|---|---|---|---|---|
| 12. School-wide behavioral expectations taught directly and formally. | Status: | | | | |
| 13. System in place to acknowledge/reward school-wide expectations. | Status: | | | | |
| 14. Clearly defined and consistent consequences and procedures for undesirable behaviors are developed. | Status: | | | | |
| **Establish Information System**<br>15. Discipline data are gathered, summarized, and reported. | Status: | | | | |
| **Build Capacity for Function-based Support**<br>16. Personnel with behavioral expertise are identified and involved. | Status: | | | | |
| 17. Plan developed to identify and establish systems for teacher support, functional assessment and support plan development and implementation. | Status: | | | | |

**FIGURE 8.3.** Effective behavior support team implementation checklist. From the Positive Behavioral Interventions and Supports website: *www.pbis.org* (U.S. Office of Special Education Programs). In the public domain.

teachers and for cumulative class participation in schoolwide celebrations.

Posters and bulletin boards detailing the school's "ABCs" (expectations) were placed prominently in the entry way to the school, every hall, the cafeteria, the library, and every classroom (see Figure 8.4). These posters provided an ongoing prompt for staff to use the expectation language in their praise and corrections. They also reminded students of what was expected.

After the assembly, it was clear that more practice was needed and that not all parts of the behavioral matrix could be implemented at once. The team decided to set some short-term goals and focus on cafeteria behavior first. Center staff guided the team through the following problem-solving process:

1. Define the problem and set goals.
2. Clearly define expected behaviors.
3. Identify strategies to teach appropriate behaviors.
4. Identify strategies to encourage appropriate behaviors.
5. Identify strategies to discourage inappropriate behaviors.

**TABLE 8.7. Sample School Expectation Matrix for Oak School**

|                    | Playground                                                                                                         | Cafeteria                                                                                                  | Hallway                                                                                                                            |
| ------------------ | ------------------------------------------------------------------------------------------------------------------ | ---------------------------------------------------------------------------------------------------------- | ---------------------------------------------------------------------------------------------------------------------------------- |
| Active listening   | Respond immediately after the whistle is blown (eyes on speaker, silent voices, ready to follow directions).       | Active listening within 2–3 seconds, eyes on the speaker, quiet chairs, and intent to cooperate.           | Silent voices, eyes look forward, ears ready to listen to any directions, follow the leader and directions.                        |
| Best effort        | Know the recess choices for your class and play games and use the equipment as taught.                             | Get everything you need before sitting down, and eat meal within time allowed.                             | Silent voices, space between people, body faces forward, avoid squeaking shoes.                                                    |
| Care for property  | Use equipment as it is intended to be used, keep balls inside the fence, and bring in all equipment.               | Keep all areas as clean and neat as possible and return dishes to washing in a neat and orderly way.       | Keep hands off walls and displays, wipe mud off of feet before entering the building, avoid making black marks.                    |
| Deep-down kindness | Use words of a good sport (good game, nice job, your turn, etc.) and include others in your play.                  | Use good manners as you eat, include others at the table in quiet and kind conversations, and thank others for serving and helping you. | Avoid racing to get ahead in line, allow others to step into their place in line, hold doors for others, use "excuse me" when moving in front of someone. |
| Extreme safety     | Appropriately dress for weather, use equipment as intended, and only throw and kick balls during a game.           | Walk at all times, avoid passing germs to others and their trays, and clean up spills.                     | Walk at all times, stay to the right side of the hall, keep arms at sides, look before rounding a corner.                          |

6. Identify system changes for adults to support practices.
7. Develop an action plan (including a follow-up meeting to review data).

## Full Implementation of the Three-Tiered Model (Years 2–4)

During full implementation, programs and curricula become fully operational in that teachers carry out the evidence-based practice with proficiency and skill. Implementation of the model has become "accepted practice." A measure of full implementation is found in teacher fidelity

**FIGURE 8.4.** Picture of expectations bulletin board

of implementation measures that are consistently above criterion levels. Programs and curricula at the new site produce similar effectiveness in student outcomes of the original evidence-based program. Additionally, schools are independent with their schedules, supervision, quality control, and data management.

### Reading

By the beginning of year 3, within a few days of DIBELS testing, the reading specialist at the school began downloading the data and providing it to the teachers prior to the reading team meetings, demonstrating an important level of independence in managing the three-tiered model. During the meeting, announcements were made, and then teacher teams broke into grade levels to discuss data. The scores of students who were already staffed into interventions were reviewed, and their interventionist gave a minute or less update on progress with recommendation about remaining in the current group or being moved to a different group within that same intervention or to a different intervention. For example, in year 4 at the beginning of second grade, five small groups of students below benchmark began in the EIR intervention. However, as the year progressed, more student groups (based on data and interventionist recommendation) were moved to the Read Naturally intervention. By the end of the school year, only one small group of students in EIR remained. The rest of the students had moved into the Read Naturally intervention.

For students who failed to meet benchmark for the first time, a discussion ensued about which intervention would best serve the student and then a decision was made about the best ability-group placement within that intervention. As soon as grade-level groupings were assigned, school personnel staffing assignments were made. For example, in the second grade, more classroom teachers moved from providing EIR interventions to providing the Read Naturally intervention. After every student was placed in an intervention, the grade-level team consulted with the Kansas Center reading coordinator and school reading specialist as to the intervention and grouping decisions that were made.

It took 2 to 3 years from the time a reading intervention was introduced for teachers to reach full implementation. One piece of evidence of full implementation was teacher fidelity of implementation. At the beginning of the implementation EIR teacher fidelity of implementation scores averaged 85%. At the end of the 3rd year of implementation their fidelity scores were consistently near 95%. For the LAMPS curriculum, beginning fidelity of implementation scores were 89%, and by the end of implementation year 3 fidelities were 100%.

## Behavior

With full implementation, the school had internalized responsibility for the programs/curricula and accepted the principle that fidelity of implementation is "best practice." Throughout years of the project, the SWPBS team continued to improve their universal or primary-level implementation. They kept good records and systematically created a system of schoolwide behavior expectations. As fidelity of primary-level implementation was established, the team began implementing various secondary-level supports. Those interventions included social skills club, check-in/check-out, and mentoring.

After 4 years of implementation, Oak School had established systems to internally assume responsibility for the SWPBS program. This independence, along with a general acceptance that the implementation is "best practice," is what Fixsen et al. (2005) considered full implementation. The team independently runs their meetings at high fidelity. They organize a first-quarter behavior screening and use data to determine which students need intervention. They maintain Schoolwide Evaluation Tool (SET; Horner et al., 2004) scores above 90% (see Figure 8.5) and continue to improve and evaluate based on SWPBS survey results (see Figure 8.6). The office disciplinary referrals for the 4th year indicate that primary- and secondary-level interventions are well in place and that the school can continue to improve support for tertiary-level students.

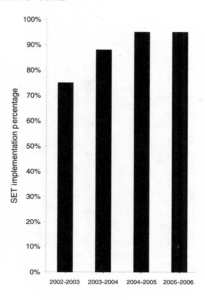

**FIGURE 8.5.** Oak School School-Wide Evaluation Tool (SET) implementation percentage by year.

## Innovation and Sustainability of the Three-Tiered Model (Year 5)

For purposes of this chapter, innovation and sustainability are briefly discussed. Fixsen et al. (2005) described innovation as refinement of programs and curricula. From the point of a research study, non-researched changes to programs and curricula are viewed as undesirable program drift and a threat to fidelity of implementation.

During sustainability, successive generations of teachers leave and come into the system (Fixsen et al., 2005). Funding for the model may change. The proof of how well the model was embedded into the school environment is tested. Although our schools had new staff and administrators throughout the project, Kansas Center staff was there to provide new staff with training and follow-up support. For 5 years Oak school had also benefited from two additional paraprofessionals for reading interventions that were employees of the school district but paid for by Kansas Center funds. These two individuals were excellent interventionists for all of the Kansas Center–sponsored interventions. After the end of the project, Kansas Center funds would no longer be available for these two interventionists. Although the school staff was quite competent in creating a structure of tiered instruction, lack of staff to support such interventions would be a challenge.

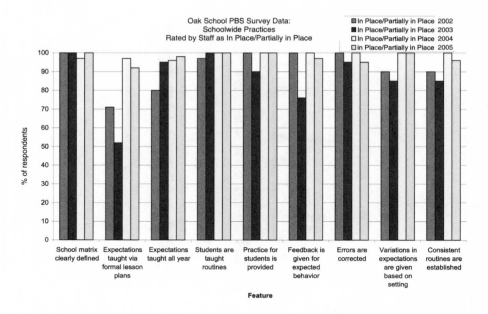

**FIGURE 8.6.** Positive behavior support (PBS) survey data with school staff as informants.

Sustainability for the reading model became strengthened by the school district–level systems and support for it. Over the course of implementation, the Kansas Center Staff met with school district leadership and experimental school principals, including Oak School. These meetings and the shared outcomes from the schools helped establish the districtwide initiative to implement DIBELS for K–2 in all of the district's elementary schools. The Kansas Center staff provided training to all 37 elementary principals on the use of the DIBELS web-based data management program (*DIBELS.uoregon.edu*) to the district. The Kansas Center then provided training for all K–2 staff, reading specialists, and administrators. This training included information about how to enter data and create reports and graphs, and make instructional decisions. In all, approximately 220 school staff were trained to use the DIBELS management system. Additionally, by the end of the collaboration, the school district had decided to provide a full-time reading specialist and instructional aid to every elementary school. The focus of these instructional aids is to provide small-group intervention with evidence-based reading practices. The Kansas Center staff view this districtwide focus on small-group implementation as a positive sign and an indicator of sustainability.

## School and Teacher Implementation Fidelity

Even the best research-validated intervention when poorly implemented can produce poor student outcomes. Conversely, when teachers implement a research-based intervention with fidelity, optimum student outcomes should be produced. Therefore, when there is good teacher fidelity with a research-validated strategy and a student fails to make progress, it signifies that the academic problem is with the student's special needs, not the instructional intervention or the quality of instruction (Kamps & Greenwood, 2005).

To improve the chances for good student outcomes by monitoring teacher fidelity of implementation, Kansas Center staff created and conducted fidelities of implementation at the primary level of instruction as well as the secondary and tertiary levels. These were conducted over the course of the project. Table 8.8 provides sample fidelity items from various reading and behavior fidelities. The first 2 years teacher fidelity continued to improve and, for the most part, remained above the 90% level for reading and behavior implementation in subsequent years.

### Universal Schoolwide Fidelity

To assess the fidelity of Tier 1 intervention, Kansas Center staff used implementation checklists. The reading intervention checklist was the Schoolwide Evaluation Tool for Reading (SWETR; Abbott, Kamps, & Arreaga-Mayer, 2003; see Table 8.9) developed for this purpose by Center staff based on a similar tool for a schoolwide reading program implementation by Kame'enui and Simmons (2000). The behavior intervention checklist was the SET, developed by Horner et al. (2004). Both tools (*SWETR* and *SET*) were administered yearly by project staff and included an evaluation of existing curricula, use of the curricula during implementation, school data collection, use of the data collection, establishment of inclusive decision-making teams, team use of data in moving students in and out of intervention, and use of staff to provide intervention. The *Effective Behavior Support* (*EBS*) *Survey* (see *www.pbis.org*) was also used to evaluate the implementation of SWPBS. This annual assessment was completed by staff to evaluate (1) schoolwide discipline, (2) nonclassroom management systems, and (3) systems for individual students engaging in chronic behaviors.

In addition to these universal schoolwide fidelities, component checklists were used to assess the effectiveness of reading and behavior leadership team meetings. These were completed by project staff and focused on items such as (1) administrator was present at the meeting, (2)

**TABLE 8.8 Sample Reading and Behavior Fidelity Items**

Reading

Early Interventions in Reading

| | | | |
|---|---|---|---|
| Is pacing appropriate? | Yes | No | |
| Was the activity taught to mastery? | Yes | No | |

K-PALS

| | | | |
|---|---|---|---|
| Students take turns acting as the coach and reader with the work book materials | Does not do | Does on limited basis | Fully implements |

Read Naturally

| | | | |
|---|---|---|---|
| Teacher ensures that the daily record keeping workbook materials is performed by the students | Does not do | Does on limited basis | Fully implements |

Behavior

Check-in/Check-out

| | | | |
|---|---|---|---|
| Ratings are assigned for a range in performance | Yes | No | N/A |

Social Skills Club:

| | | | |
|---|---|---|---|
| Teacher presents the lesson as directed in script/manual | Yes | No | N/A |
| Students practice/role-play skill with teacher feedback | Yes | No | N/A |

data was used to guide decision making, and (3) meeting procedures included an agenda and recording the minutes.

### Universal Classroom Tier 1 and Tiers 2 and 3 Intervention Fidelity

For reading, an Open Court measure was created to assess fidelity at the classroom level. Unlike the *SWETR* checklist, the classroom checklist included the reading instruction components specified by the Open Court publishers and implementation standards adopted by the school district. A yearly primary-level fidelity was conducted on a representative sample of teachers at Oak School. Each year 50 to 70% of the first- through third-grade classroom teachers were observed on one or two different occasions.

Different fidelity measures were created for each of the small group interventions K-PALS, Read Naturally, and LAMPS by Center staff. The EIR fidelity was provided by the curriculum's principal author. Small-group intervention fidelity measurements were conducted by Kansas Center staff based on implementation procedures. Fidelity data collec-

**TABLE 8.9. Core School-Wide Evaluation Tool for Reading (SWETR) Items**

Core reading

A systematic core reading program with a documented research base has been adopted by the school and/or district.
0 = no documentation, more than 50% of students not at benchmark
1 = documentation that is correlational, meets need for 50% students
2 = causal documentation and curriculum adequately teaches 80% students

Core reading

Six classrooms across grade levels or more of the teaching staff have been observed conducting a reading lesson with average high fidelity.
0 = 0–50%,
1 = 51–89%,
2 = 90–100%
N/A if no observations

Secondary level

Additional instructional time (beyond primary instruction) is provided to 80% of at-risk students (i.e., students who fail to make adequate progress).
0 =  no additional time is allocated to students 80%+ of at-risk students
1 = 30 minutes 3–4 times a week in groups of 7–12 or less
2 =  30 minutes 3–4 times a week in groups of 6 or less

Secondary level

80% of teachers providing secondary-level group instruction across grade levels have been observed conducting a reading lesson with average high fidelity.
0 = 0–50% mean fidelity
1 = 51–89% mean fidelity
2 = 90–100% mean fidelity
N/A if limited observations

Instructional leadership, management of instruction, data-based decision making

A reading teacher or instructional leader uses DIBELS for data-based decisions and placement of students with risk in groups.
0 = no data-based decision making
1 = data reviewed, but instruction not modified
2 = data reviewed and instructional groupings modified

Instructional leadership, management of instruction, data-based decision making

A reading teacher/coach schedules reading intervention across grades, monitors to make sure groups are consistently in place and of high fidelity.
0 = no monitoring of schedules, or instruction
1 = coach monitors reading schedules, but feedback is inconsistent
2 = coach monitors reading schedules and observes 80% or more of classrooms and provides feedback

tion was closely tied to professional development and ongoing teacher mentoring. Kansas Center staff organized and offered the professional development training and then offered mentoring follow-up support. Within a month of initial professional development and intervention implementation, project staff conducted a fidelity of implementation assessment to determine the implementation quality. Teachers who failed to receive an 85% or greater received additional mentoring support and another fidelity of implementation was conducted after mentoring support. Intervention fidelities were collected twice yearly by Kansas Center project staff.

For the behavior interventions, the fidelities were used to evaluate school-level implementation and also provided information relevant to classroom and Tier 2 and 3 interventions (see tools at *www.pbis.org*), and followed the same process as the reading fidelities of implementation. The behavioral fidelities for check-in/check out, mentoring, and social skills club were created by the Kansas Center staff.

## Evaluation Relative to Need and Improvement on the Action Plan Goals

Throughout the project, data was used to improve intervention quality and student response to intervention. After each DIBELS occasion teams met to refine student placement in intervention. Behavior teams met monthly to discuss student placement in intervention. Over the years, as teachers became more familiar with interventions and the process of collaborative placement, Kansas Center staff observed refinements in (1) school efficiencies, (2) interventions and materials available and sustained use even with new staff, and (3) reading and behavior teams' independence. As an example, the Kansas Center rated teams' reading and behavior independence at the end of each year. Components such as teams' consistent implementation of secondary and tertiary interventions, and data management were rated as total independence, partial independence, and dependence. The reading team improved from a score of 61% in the 3rd year to 83% in the 4th year. The SWPBS team improved from 72% to 94%.

From year to year it was evident that Oak School staff was finding new ways to increase efficiencies in running interventions. For example, a good indicator of efficiency is their check-in/check-out program (see previous program description). For example, the art teacher, music teacher, and school nurse devised a check-out system so that students could check out in one location with any of the three available staff. When checking out students, each adult would determine the percent of goal obtained, and the students recorded it on a roster. The art teacher

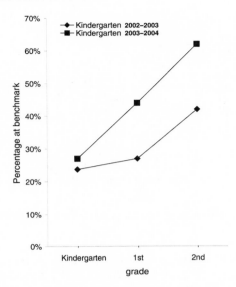

**FIGURE 8.9.** Percentage at benchmark of two cohorts over 3 years.

the same grade level of students and the same teachers providing the same intervention. For both graphs, the bottom line is the 1st year of implementation. The middle line is the 2nd year of implementation and the top line are student scores the 3rd year of implementation. Each cohort of students began at approximately the same level of achievement. However, as teacher fidelity of implementation improved (noted above), so did the slope of student achievement each year.

The top graph illustrates nonsense word fluency (NWF) outcomes for kindergarten and first-grade students. The benchmark for NWF is 50 sounds per minute by the middle of first grade. Notice that with the cohort that began the first year of implementation, it was the fall of second grade before those students reached the NWF benchmark. For the cohort who began the 2nd year of implementation, the NWF benchmark was met the spring of first grade, and for the cohort who began the 3rd year of implementation, the benchmark was met right on target in the winter of first grade.

The results are mirrored in the bottom oral reading fluency (ORF) graph that begins at winter first grade and ends spring of second grade. The 3rd-year intervention cohort of students come the closest to reaching the ORF goal of 90 correct words per minute by the end of their second-grade year.

Figure 8.12 reports results for the LAMPS, a tertiary-level interven-

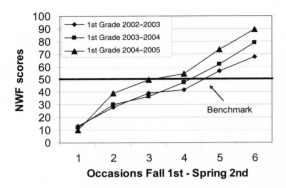

**FIGURE 8.10.** Early Interventions in Reading (EIR) student nonsense word scores.

tion for students across several experimental elementary schools with 12 matched-paired sets of students (experimental/comparison) over the course of 1–2 years on DIBELS ORF. Four of the experimental students were from Oak School. Using a two-way analysis of variance for repeated measures with factors of between group (experimental vs. control) and time within groups (fall pretest vs. spring posttest), a significant group by time interaction was detected. Both groups improved, but the LAMPS students improved at a significantly faster rate (the Cohen's $d$ effect size was 1.11, where effect sizes of 0.8 are considered large). These data suggested that with the LAMPS intervention, students not only im-

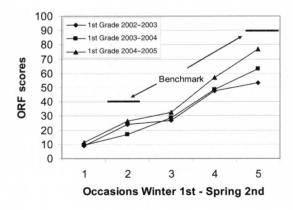

**FIGURE 8.11.** Early Interventions in Reading (EIR) student oral reading fluency (ORF) scores.

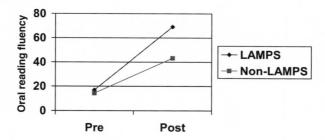

**FIGURE 8.12.** Linguistic, Alphabetics, Multilevel comprehension, Phonetics, Speed (LAMPS) data on 12 matched-pair sets of second- to fourth-grade students.

proved decoding skills but also improved their text fluency in contrast to matched peers.

## Student Outcomes for Behavior

As measured by the SSRS, students at risk for reading, behavior, or both, made improvements in behavior. Table 8.12 depicts pre- and post-standard scores for social skills and problem behaviors based on teacher ratings. Prescores were the initial ratings completed by the teachers when students were designated to be at risk. Postscores were the final teacher rating of the student. A total of 51 students at Oak School had SSRS ratings, 10 with a one-year pre–post rating, 16 with ratings over 2 years, and 25 with ratings spanning 3 years. A change of 10 points in the standard deviation is considered an indicator of important change in behaviors. As depicted in Figure 8.3, the percent of students who increased 10 or more points for social skills ratings was 41%, 73%, and 47%, respectively, for reading, behavior, and reading and behavior risk groups. Desirable changes on the Problem Behavior subscale are indicated by decreasing ratings and raw scores, thus higher standard scores are indicative of an above-average level of problem behaviors. For problem behaviors the percent of students who decreased by 10 or more points were 31%, 64%, and 33%, respectively.

Effect sizes (ES) were moderate overall (ES = 0.53) for social skills ratings, and small for problem behavior changes (ES = –0.38). Large effects were noted, however, for the students with behavior only risks, ES = 1.82 and –1.41 for social skills and problem behaviors, respectively (see Table 8.13). ES for the students with reading-only risks were small; however, prescores were well within the normal range (98–105), thus a ceiling effect may have prevented any important changes for this group. For the students who were most at risk, having reading and behavior

**TABLE 8.12. Standard Score Means, Standard Deviations, and Effect Sizes for Social Skills Rating Scale by Risk Group**

| | Social skills | |
|---|---|---|
| Risk | Pre | Post |
| Behavior | | |
| M | 81.50 | 100.90 |
| SD | 9.360 | 11.836 |
| Reading | | |
| M | 98.21 | 104.86 |
| SD | 17.369 | 18.285 |
| Both Kansas | | |
| M | 82.33 | 89.92 |
| SD | 9.442 | 20.651 |
| Total | | |
| M | 91.20 | 100.57 |
| SD | 16.446 | 18.553 |

| | Problem behavior | |
|---|---|---|
| Risk | Pre | Post |
| Behavior | | |
| M | 124.20 | 108.00 |
| SD | 8.991 | 13.466 |
| Reading | | |
| M | 105.59 | 102.11 |
| SD | 15.401 | 16.408 |
| Both Kansas | | |
| M | 119.92 | 115.83 |
| SD | 8.639 | 14.352 |
| Total | | |
| M | 112.61 | 106.58 |
| SD | 15.234 | 16.146 |

risks, a moderate ES was noted for social skills ratings (ES = 0.47), with a small ES for problem behaviors (ES = −0.38).

Although improvements in the standard scores are the gold standard for indicating changes, analysis of raw scores of teacher ratings showed even higher percentages of students' social skills and behaviors improving. The mean gain in raw scores for social skills was 13.4 (range, 2–35), 17.3 (range, 5–35), and 16.3 (range, 6–30), respectively, across the three risk groups. These changes are indicative of the large numbers of students who improved with gains in social skills raw scores for 63%, 90%, and 67%, respectively, across reading, behavior, and reading and behavior risks. Similar patterns were noted for improvements in the Problem Behavior subscale. The mean decrease in raw score was 7.8

(range, 1–20), 11.3 (range, 5–17), and 8.0 (4–15), respectively, by risk. The percent of students whose raw scores decreased for problem behaviors were 58%, 80%, and 50%, respectively, across risk groups.

Additionally, throughout the years of implementation of SWIS data collection, the recommended average of office disciplinary referrals per day per month remained below recommended targets.

## PARTICIPANT SATISFACTION DATA

Table 8.13 provides teacher satisfaction survey data. Two questions are asked:

1. Are you likely to use this intervention with a student with similar problems?
2. Are you likely to recommend this intervention to another colleague?

With one exception, teachers rated their satisfaction at somewhat likely, likely, or very likely to use and recommend. One LAMPS teacher stated that she would not recommend the intervention to a colleague.

**TABLE 8.13. Percentage Rating of Teacher Satisfaction on Secondary and Tertiary Interventions**

| No. of teachers | Intervention | Unlikely | Somewhat likely | Likely | Very likely |
|---|---|---|---|---|---|
| | Likelihood of using this intervention with a student with similar problems | | | | |
| 2 | CW-FIT | | 37% | | 63% |
| 9 | Social skills club | | 22.5% | 22.5% | 55% |
| 4 | Mentoring | | | 25% | 75% |
| 9 | EIR | | | | 100% |
| 6 | Read Naturally | | | | 100% |
| 2 | LAMP | | 50% | | 50% |
| | Likelihood of recommending this intervention to a colleague | | | | |
| 2 | CW-FIT | | | | 100% |
| 9 | Social skills club | | 12% | 44% | 44% |
| 4 | Mentoring | | | 25% | 75% |
| 9 | EIR | | | | 100% |
| 6 | Read Naturally | | | | 100% |
| 2 | LAMP | 50% | | | 50% |

## SUMMARY AND CONCLUSIONS

We found our Oak School and Juniper Gardens Children's Project collaborative effort to implement a three-tiered model successful. We were able to assist the school in infusing the five evidence-based practices of implementation defined within the Fixsen implementation framework (Abbott, Greenwood, Buzhardtr, & Tapar, 2006; Elmore, 2004; Fixsen et al., 2005). First, we were able to obtain buy-in from a majority of administrators and teachers to implementation of the model. Second, through completing installation and initial implementation steps, most Oak School staff recognized the benefits of using the three-tiered reading and behavior model, and improved results became the driving force in continuation of its implementation. For example, a teacher (the SWPBS coach) made the following comments about their adoption of SWPBS and how it has been helpful to their school.

> "One of the most helpful things has been the use of the same expectation language across the entire school. At first it was by name only. The expectations posted were not yet really part of the everyday language. It took time and much effort to get teachers to use the language on a daily basis. The focus on the positive has changed how some have taught."

This SWPBS teacher/coach went on to describe how much more academic content is now covered in her own classroom compared to before the Kansas model. She wasn't sure if it was due to her own improvements in classroom management skills learned in the project or the cumulative effect of SWPBS on students coming into her class. Either way, she knew that she was spending more time teaching instead of reactively dealing with behavior problems.

Second, we were able to help the school establish reading and behavior teams that made "data-driven decisions," and this created an intentional process for reinforcing change in teacher behavior to monitor student outcomes and make instructional intervention decisions. Watching the reading and behavior teams develop over the course of the project was a powerful experience. For example, prior to the Kansas Center model, the reading team had worked with the teaching staff at each grade level for state-mandated school-improvement reporting. The teachers had received input from specialists about how to best provide for struggling students. And the reading specialists had previously collected district-mandated assessments. However, whole grade levels of teachers, building specialists, and administrators had not consistently convened to look at primary (K–3) data, discuss every child that needed intervention, and then created a comprehensive K–3 plan for providing intervention for all of the school's struggling readers. Over the years, as the reading team continued to meet, teachers and interventionists at each grade level became the motivating force to engage in ongoing conversations about what interventions were working for which students and to make modifications in the instructional placement.

Third, throughout the project, Kansas Center staff provided professional development, ongoing instructional support, and mentoring with an external system of evaluation of good teaching practice with teacher fidelity of implementation. Every year Kansas Center staff provided the recommended professional development for each of the interventions. However, there was evidence that individual teams of teachers in different experimental schools extended those professional development activities by having other teachers observe intervention instruction and/or organize activities that recreated professional development experiences. This was especially true at Oak School for reading and behavioral interventions.

Finally, all of the above parts of the Kansas Center model culminated in the creation of an infrastructure to support and sustain new roles and procedures. We view the school district's districtwide adoption of the "evidence-based practices" we recommended at each experimental school as confirmation that, at least in this school district, many of the constructs of three-tiered instruction are likely to continue. In addition to the districtwide implementation of DIBELS screening, the last year of implementation, the district placed a minimum of one full-time reading specialist and paraprofessional interventionist at every elementary school regardless of school risk. Elementary schools in the district with greater risk received additional personnel. In exchange for additional staff, the school was required to provide to the district the specific evidence-based interventions that new staff would use for intervention.

## Unique Benefits and Challenges Represented in This Three-Tiered Model

One of the unique benefits of this project was the involvement of staff at every level of the decision making. The teaching staff had input on the interventions they used and were involved at every level of intervention from placement to providing the interventions. Classroom teachers were, at first, not accustomed to delivering small-group instruction and were resistant. However, by this year (year 5), classroom teachers providing small-group intervention had become a seamless operation of testing, grouping, and providing intervention.

Another unique benefit and also a challenge were in simultaneously implementing reading and behavioral interventions. Schools can only absorb so much change over time. The behavior team quickly figured out that secondar- and tertiary-level interventions would need to be delayed until the schoolwide universals were in place.

A final unique feature to the model was the level of ongoing professional development, mentoring, and fidelity of implementation. Our budget provided the financial means for school districts to send teachers to training. As our training continued over the years, teachers who had become skilled interventionists naturally took on mentoring responsibilities at each school and became the school "expert." Teachers used fidelity of implementation checklists to monitor their own implementation. As a result, at the end of the project we had a sizable number of empowered teachers who thoroughly knew the Kansas Center three-tiered model of implementation and would be able to use the model in future years.

## Lessons Learned and Challenges to Implementation

The greatest lesson we learned is that it is quite effortful to change the way we educate children, and this effort directly addresses the barriers to implementation. The greatest identified barriers involved the flexibility to create a schedule with sufficient teacher and support staff to provide a strong enough mix of intervention strength and duration. Within the 1st year, teachers became skilled at rearranging the instructional day to create small-group time. The difficulty was in staffing the large numbers of intervention groups throughout the day. To address this issue, Oak School reorganized nonclassroom teacher staff and paraprofessional assignments. For example, prior to implementation of the Kansas Center model, the art and music teachers were hall monitors at the beginning and end of the school day. The behavior team made the determination that a more beneficial use of their time would be to implement the check-in/check-out behavioral intervention. For reading interventions, two paraprofessionals whose prior main responsibilities entailed copying, lunch room monitoring, and filling-in to provide secretarial breaks took responsibility for monitoring independent reading activities with benchmark students during small-group reading interventions. Additionally, Kansas Center provided the school district with funds to employ two reading intervention paraprofessionals. These personnel were critical to the success of the implementation and provided reading interventions throughout the day. Kansas Center staff was encouraged that, by the end of the project, the school district decided to unilaterally increase the number of reading interventionists in every elementary school by at least one and a half staff positions.

A related barrier to sufficient staff is that school systems are not easily set up to provide a substitute or replacement personnel to run interventions if someone is absent. In most cases the intervention is cancelled just for the length of time of the absence. In response, the Oak School reading team decided that small-group intervention was the most important part of the instructional day. The team created back-up plans to ensure that reading interventions happened every instructional day. Sometimes this meant dividing students into larger temporary groupings during teacher absences or shortening the intervention time when there was an assembly or field trip. On the behavior team, the music and art teachers took major roles in creating and staffing schoolwide and small-group intervention. We learned that flexible scheduling of small groups and creative use of staff resources were critical to reading and behavioral interventions.

A second important lesson was that early screening and data-based instructional decisions are critical to intervention design, implementation, and progress monitoring. For reading screenings, Kansas Center staff provided the reading screening assessors. Therefore, the screening process was not a major responsibility or barrier for schools. Additionally, from the beginning of the project, classroom and related instructional staff were trained in DIBELS and the behavioral screening procedures. This allowed school staff to become comfortable with the process before they became completely responsible for screening by the end of the project.

A related lesson we learned was that it was essential to plan in the spring for intervention implementation the next fall. The years that we failed to do spring planning, intervention groups got a later fall start-up date. This evoked a new way of thinking for the school. Teachers were at first quite hesitant to begin intervention groups in the first several weeks of the beginning of school based on spring scores. Traditionally, the reading specialist tested most children before intervention began. That process often took 4 to 6 weeks. Through team discussions, we helped teachers to create reading and behavior plans that began almost immediately. These small groups were revised after the fall screenings. What teachers found out was that spring data and their professional judgments resulted in very few children needing to move to different instructional groups. New students to the school, who teachers thought might need intervention, were given a quick screening prior to the whole-school screening to assess the need for intervention. Intervention began earlier in the school year and continued through the end of the school year. Most years, this planning added 4 to 7 weeks of actual intervention implementation during the school year.

A third lesson learned was the importance of advancing through the intervention curriculum in a timely fashion or lesson pacing. For example the EIR Level 1 intervention is meant to be completed during the first-grade year. Because the program is based on mastery this was not possible for all groups to complete Level 1 in one academic year. However, we did find that, in successive years, as the teachers became familiar with the curriculum, they were able to cover more material within a given year. The completion of the curriculum sequence that focused on explicit phonics instruction then allowed the teachers to change the intervention focus to fluency and comprehension building that is critical to the second-grade year.

A fourth barrier/lesson learned was how to create a system for classroom teachers to provide mentoring and implementation support to other teachers while working with students. This process was not difficult when the Kansas Center staff consultants provided instructional support because we did not have teaching responsibility at the school. However, when teachers at the school began to assume more responsibility for mentoring, we found that the team mentor and the classroom teacher who needed mentoring lost instructional time. Although no one wanted to give up planning time; that, however, is what was often required. We also found that instructional observations initially made teachers feel uncomfortable. Eventually, most teachers accepted these observations as opportunities to improve instruction. As always, issues of mentoring with teachers for reading and behavior initiatives required extensive administrative support in allocation of time. We found that when there was strong administrative support, the staff was more accepting of outside forces helping to implement change.

A final barrier/lesson learned revolved around the understanding of a fused reading and behavior approach to improve student outcomes. With national and state initiates, the district and school had given considerable thought to improving reading scores. And the school had become quite aware that as their demographic of children had changed so had the academic and behavioral needs of their student body. However, a specific link between the two that resulted in an effortful plan had not yet formed. With extensive professional development and team mentoring, the staff learned that the schoolwide rules with rewards built consistent discipline across the school, and that this culture of positive supports reduced inappropriate behavior. Reduced aberrant behavior led to more appropriate focused behavior during intervention, which improved reading outcomes for students. Oak School also learned from multiple years of reading data that systematic phonemic awareness,

# PART III

# IMPLICATIONS
# AND CONCLUSIONS

# CHAPTER 9

# Multi-tiered Prevention Models
## *Implications and Future Perspectives*

MELISSA CLEMENTS *and* THOMAS R. KRATOCHWILL

T he purpose of this book is to present illustrative findings from each of the six centers, through the eyes of one of their participating schools, and to report integrated lessons learned overall about implementation across the centers. The book reflects a pioneering effort to reform schooling based on research evidence. Although each effort sought to affect sustainability as well as the quality of model implementation, it was not possible to report on the actual sustainability of each model beyond the involvement of the research partners.

The prevention models described throughout this book were implemented as part of each center's local research agenda and as a component within a cross-center study of multi-tiered models designed to address the needs of schools and their students in the areas of reading and behavior. The Office of Special Education Programs (OSEP) funded six Research Centers (referred to in this chapter as the Kansas Center, Nebraska Center, North Carolina Center, Oregon Reading Center, Oregon Behavior Center, and Texas Center) and a Coordination Center. The role of the Coordination Center was to plan for common research questions and measures in a separate effort to assess the implementation and impacts of coordinated systems of prevention within approximately 50 schools across five states (Kansas, Nebraska, North Carolina, Oregon, and Texas). This multisite study became known as the K–3 Reading and

Behavior Intervention Models Project (OSEP K–3 Project), and reports of this effort are currently in preparation. Each Research Center participated in this common evaluation of the effects of their efforts to implement reading, behavior, or reading and behavior models that incorporated tiers of intervention at primary, secondary, and tertiary levels. For more information on the common project, the reader is referred to the Coordination Center (Coordination Consultation, and Evaluation Center) website at *www.wcer.wisc.edu/cce/*.

To demonstrate the implementation of the six Research Centers' prevention models in real school settings, this book includes a compilation of case studies describing exemplary school-based efforts within which these models were implemented. A diverse sample of seven schools participated in the case studies representing four regions of the country including the Southeast (North Carolina), Southwest (Texas), Midwest (Kansas and Nebraska), and the Pacific Northwest (Oregon). Staff at each center selected a school(s) that was representative of schools in that local program as well as was an example of excellent implementation of the model. There was a range of income levels across the schools spanning from about 20% of students being eligible for free/reduced lunch to about 75% being eligible. The racial makeup of the schools also varied. Two of the case studies included schools with a large population of minority students ranging from 80% to 90% of students being of minority status. The other case studies included schools with rates of minority students ranging from approximately 12% to 30% of students. School student bodies ranged from 300 to nearly 700 students across all case study schools.

## CAVEATS OF IMPLEMENTATION

From the outset, it is important to emphasize that the multi-tiered models were implemented within the context of a research study. Given the newness of the policies, practices, and the limited knowledge base currently existing to support multi-tiered models in schools, the case studies provide the reader with highly important new information. The extent to which components of the program were implemented and/or supported by research staff versus school and district staff varied across models and across the duration of the study. Some of the models required more school independent implementation by school staff whereas in others research staff played a larger role. For example, in Oregon, the schools took on more responsibility for the reading and behavior programs because they already had exposure to and were implementing some aspects of the model through participation in prior research studies. Similarly, school staffs in North Carolina and Kansas were largely responsible for the implementation of the primary reading program because the schools had already adopted the core program prior to the current study. Typically, more responsibility was transferred onto school staff as the study progressed and as schools became more proficient with the implementation of each model. This continuum of researcher versus school ownership over implementation highlights the delicate balance between ensuring the model was accurately implemented with a high degree of integrity and ensuring that schools could likely sustain the models without researcher support. We elaborate more on issues of integrity and sustainability later in this chapter.

Perhaps most important, all of the Research Centers worked closely with school leadership and personnel to collaboratively implement the intervention models and to cultivate sustainable systems of prevention and intervention within the schools. Thus, the multi-tiered models described in this book provide unique insights into how to effectively implement evidence-based models, the influence of such models on real schools, and how these models may be integrated into school systems in the absence of the additional support, guidance, and funding that accompanies a research study.

Another caveat is that the case studies presented here were not necessarily entirely representative of the complete multi-tiered model implemented by a Research Center or implementation across all schools. For example, the Texas Center chose to focus their case study on their primary intervention level given the foundational nature of the primary tier. However, their model also included secondary and tertiary interventions. In addition, as previously mentioned, the case study schools were selected partly because of their exemplary status to showcase best practices for implementation of each of the models. The remainder of this chapter provides a synthesis of what the case studies have taught us about the multi-tiered model and its implementation, how to sustain such models in real-world school settings, and finally, what questions remain regarding the implementation and sustainability of multi-tiered models.

## WHAT WE KNOW ABOUT THE MULTI-TIERED MODEL

Although it was common for the schools participating in the case studies to already have a core reading or behavior management program in place and be providing supplemental intervention to struggling students, what was unique about the multi-tiered models was that the levels of intervention were implemented in a coordinated and systematic fashion to meet the differentiated needs of students through interventions and professional development grounded in evidence-based research. The multi-tiered models exemplified in this book brought to the schools an aligned system of support for which student data were used to make instructional decisions. A rich array of practices was used across centers to implement their models but common to all centers was the use of a response-to-intervention (RTI) methodology (see Jimerson, Burns, & VanDerHeyden, 2007; National Association of State Directors of Special Education [NASDSE], 2005). Multi-tiered models can be thought of as fitting within the larger framework of RTI models.

The OSEP K–3 Project that began in 2001 predated the 2004 reauthorization of the Individuals with Disabilities Education Act (IDEA) for which two primary shifts occurred relevant to this work. As mentioned in earlier chapters, one such shift is that states may now use some of the funds allocated for special education services toward early intervening services: the primary, secondary, and tertiary services described in this book. A second is that states are no longer required to use an IQ–achievement discrepancy method of identifying students for special education services and may now use a student's response to scientifically based instruction. Much of the same research and expert recommendations that drove these revisions to IDEA also influenced the design of this larger investigation including research demonstrating that prevention and early intervention are more effective and less costly than remediation or special education at later stages of development (Kamps, Kravits, Rauch, Kamps, & Chung, 2000; Kratochwill, Clements, & Kalymon, 2007; Walker & Shinn, 1999; Vaughn & Fuchs, 2003) and the criticisms leveled against selecting students for services based on the discrepancy between intellectual ability and achievement (e.g., represents a wait-to-fail model) (D. Fuchs et al., 2003; Gresham, 2006). RTI models are thought to be powerful tools for identifying and selecting students for services and one way of improving the accuracy with which students are placed in special education services (Fuchs, Mock, Morgan, & Young, 2003; Vaughn & Fuchs, 2003). RTI has its roots in the academic model of Deno and colleagues (Deno, 1985; Deno & Mirkin, 1977) and the behavioral consultation model of Bergan and colleagues (Bergan, 1977; Bergan & Kratochwill, 1990). From these origins, RTI models are conceptualized as including the following key components (NASDSE, 2005):

- High-quality, evidence-based instruction/intervention,
- Schoolwide screening,
- Continuous progress monitoring,
- Instructional decision making,

- Tiered service delivery,
- High-quality professional development, and
- High fidelity of implementation.

Although the specific methods used to implement these practices vary from case study to case study, these above features can be found in each of the models discussed in this book. It is also important to note that the K–3 Research Centers were directed to develop a multi-tiered model as part of the research agenda. However, other models of prevention services exist and may be considered for implementation in schools. For example, prevention models can include resilience approaches and positive youth development where there is not just a focus on risk variables such as in the RTI approach (Small & Memmo, 2004). Nevertheless, the Research Centers in these research projects used a risk model with screening and multi-tiered intervention options in academic and/or behavioral domains.

## Evidence-Based Instruction/Intervention

*High-quality evidence-based instruction* has been defined as "instruction or intervention, matched to student need, that has been demonstrated through scientific research and practice to produce high learning rates for most students" (NASDSE, 2005, p. 5). The evidence-based instruction movement has helped conceptualize evidence-based practices in the academic and mental health fields and promote the use of evidence-based practices (Kratochwill, Albers, & Shernoff, 2004; Kratochwill & Shernoff, 2004; Kratochwill, 2004). As we noted in Chapter 1, research has shown that prevention and intervention programs that are evidence-based and implemented with fidelity can have positive effects on reading and behavior outcomes. Furthermore, policies such as IDEA and the No Child Left Behind Act of 2001 (NCLB) mandate the use of evidence-based programs.

The multi-tiered models described within this book began with an evidence-based core program. Open Court (McGraw Hill, 2005) and schoolwide positive behavior support (SWPBS; Horner & Sugai, 2000) were commonly used primary reading and behavior programs implemented across case studies, though not the only primary interventions used. Table 2.1 (see Chapter 2) shows the variety of primary interventions used across centers. However, the true commonality and the more important take-home message was that the primary programs used had prior research supporting their effectiveness and could be aligned with the other tiers within the model. Many of the Research Centers also chose prevention systems that would fit the school's existing philosophies or chose schools that were already implementing certain core programs. For example, Open Court was already being implemented in most of the schools for which reading models were put into place. The primary intervention summarized in Chapter 5 was unique in comparison to the other primary-level interventions assessed in this study in that the primary tier examined was the center's professional development program.

## Schoolwide Screening

Universal screening of all students allows school staff to assess the effectiveness of classroom instruction, determine the ability level of each student, and identify specific students that need further monitoring for academic or behavioral difficulties (NASDSE, 2005). If the majority of the students in a classroom score above the cut-off criterion for satisfactory performance on the screening measure, the core program is likely effective. Changes to the instructional environment may be necessary for any students scoring below the cut-off. Screening holds a very critical role in the implementation of prevention models because it is the first gateway for students to be identified for services (Albers, Glover, & Kratochwill, 2007). One challenge in the screening process is that over- and under-identification of student need can and does occur in practice (L. S. Fuchs & Fuchs, 2006; L. S. Fuchs, 2003; Speece, 2005). Some estimates have been as low as 50% accuracy for identifying students based on initial screening measures of their response to the core instruction (Compton, Fuchs, Fuchs, & Bryant, 2006). Although casting a wide net will ensure all needy students get services, overidentification can result in the diluting the available resources for those students most in need.

Some have conceptualized screening as including level and growth or the student's initial status and rate of learning over some period of time (L. S. Fuchs, 2003; Speece, 2005). L. S. Fuchs and Fuchs (2006) recommend coupling assessment at the beginning of the year with multiple assessments over a short period of time (5 weeks) to identify students needing instructional modifications. They have found that this practice considerably improves accuracy of identification.

Surprisingly few reliable and valid screening measures exist which creates another challenge for accurately identifying students (Albers et al., 2007). Common screening measures used to identify at-risk students within the case study schools were empirically based and included the Dynamic Indicators of Basic Early Literacy Skills (DIBELS; Good & Kaminski, 2002) for identifying students with reading difficulties and the Early Screening Project (ESP; Walker, Severson, & Feil, 1995) or Systematic Screening for Behavior Disorders (SSBD; Walker & Severson,

1992) for identifying students with behavioral difficulties. In addition, behavioral screening measures also included frequency of office discipline referrals obtained from the School-Wide Information System (SWIS; May et al., 2000) and teacher professional judgment. Identifying students for behavioral intervention is more likely to be influenced by subjective factors such as school and teacher tolerance for certain behaviors. Nevertheless, improvement in these measures in the future will assist schools in reliable and valid identification of students in a program of screening.

## Progress Monitoring and Instructional Decision Making

A cornerstone of the models implemented by the Research Centers was the reliance on data to make instructional decisions. To be most effective and useful, progress monitoring tools need to be quick and easy to use, reliable and valid, sensitive to change, and representative of what the student is being taught (Ardoin, 2006; Coyne & Harn, 2006; Ardoin, 2006). Ideally, progress monitoring data should be collected multiple times during the year for all students and especially for students identified as having elevated risk due to poor performance on screening measures (L. S. Fuchs & Fuchs, 2006; NASDSE, 2005). The emphasis on data-based decision making for assessing programs and their effects on student outcomes has grown in recent years (Stone, 2001).

In addition to screening at the beginning of the school year, each of the centers in the OSEP K–3 Project also monitored student progress regularly, particularly those students identified as needing supplemental instruction. Collecting benchmark and progress monitoring data allowed for making informed instructional decisions about which level of intervention was needed and when to move students to higher or lower levels of intervention or out of supplemental intervention altogether (receiving primary-only). Each Research Center had its own entrance and exit criteria for determining when to move students across levels of intervention or exit students out of secondary or tertiary intervention. Table 2.1 in Chapter 2 shows the screening and progress monitoring schedule used by each center.

## Tiered Services

The multi-tiered model is typically conceptualized as including three progressively more intense levels of intervention: primary, secondary, and tertiary levels. At the primary level, all students are exposed to a core curriculum or set of practices. At the secondary level, students that are nonresponsive to the core program are provided more intense and usually small-group interventions. At the tertiary level, individualized interventions are provided to students with more serious and chronic difficulties. Traditionally, approximately 80% of students can be expected to respond to primary intervention, approximately 15% of students will need secondary intervention, and approximately 5% of students will need tertiary intervention. However, these numbers are not necessarily based on empirical data and may vary considerably from school to school (Kratochwill, Clements, & Kalymon, 2007).

Interventions used within the schools exemplified in this book had to meet several criteria including the following: (1) more intensive than the core program but aligned with the core program and the other levels of intervention, (2) supported by prior research (evidence-based), (3) address the necessary instructional needs, and (4) in some cases, aligned with the school or district's educational mission or other options offered by the school. Aligning new programs with existing policies can facilitate acceptance by stakeholders (Fixen, Naoom, Blase, Friedman, & Wallace, 2005) and is strongly recommended for adoption and sustainability.

The actual secondary and tertiary programs selected varied more across case studies than did the primary interventions (see Table 2.1). A common theme across some of the models was to provide a menu of evidence-based interventions from which schools and teachers could choose the intervention that worked best for their school or classroom. Typically, the secondary interventions were implemented in small-group settings, and the tertiary intervention was more intensive and implemented with individual students or very small groups of students. Often interventions were grade specific such as using Early Interventions in Reading (Taylor, Short, Frye, & Shearer, 1992) for first- and second-grade students and Read Naturally (Ihnot, 1992) for third-grade students at the secondary level. The reading interventions focused on bringing students up to grade level on their reading skills by increasing vocabulary, word study skills, reading comprehension, text reading, and oral reading fluency skills. Behavior interventions focused on social skills building, friendship development, problem solving, and confidence building. In the case of more severe behavioral difficulties, interventions such as functional behavioral assessment were used to target specific behavioral changes. Nearly all of the interventions were primarily school-based. Many reading and behavioral interventions involved families by fostering family–school communication and providing a feedback loop to the parents regarding their child's progress. The interventions implemented within the Nebraska Center model actually included home-based components involving parents in the provision of the intervention to the child and offering therapeutic services to the entire family.

## High-Quality Professional Development

Providing high-quality professional development is foundational to effectively implementing the multi-tiered models described in this book. The trainings offered by centers in the OSEP K–3 Project covered areas such as understanding and implementing evidence-based primary, secondary and tertiary interventions; screening, progress monitoring, and data-based decision making; and monitoring and evaluating the implementation process. Those providing the training were sometimes research staff or other staff funded by Research Centers and sometimes existing school staff such as expert teachers who monitor and provide feedback to other teachers.

The actual professional development practices used by the Research Centers for this study were aligned with recommendations from the professional development literature in general and the emerging literature on professional development for RTI models more specifically (Gusky, 2003; Kratochwill, Volpianski, Clements, & Ball, 2007). Professional development practices should be embedded in the typical school environment, sensitive to the needs of the learner, aligned with other goals and policies of the school, collaboratively oriented, and ongoing with regular follow-ups (Guskey, 2003).

Professional development strategies implemented in the case study schools ranged from in-services to job-embedded training such as participating in grade-level team meetings and being mentored by a reading or behavior coach. Continuous professional development training was offered with refreshers and follow-ups as needed. Instruction was monitored, and teachers received constructive feedback to help build their knowledge and skills related to implementing the prevention models. Another key aspect of high-quality professional development included creating collaborative environments that encouraged active engagement in the learning process and allowed teachers to be a real part of decision making at the schools. In the Texas case study school for instance, teachers had the chance to interact and share ideas with same-grade teachers from their school as well as other schools. We also found from the case studies that there was a focus on providing professional development that was timely (provided before or at the start of the school year), differentiated according to specific staff needs, and that covered content of high interest to teachers that could be applied in their own classrooms.

## High Fidelity of Implementation

How well the interventions were implemented was assessed through fidelity measures. It is not sufficient to choose a program that has been established in the research literature to be an effective program. Schools desiring to implement these evidence-based interventions and models will need to be prepared to assess whether the programs are being implemented as intended and provide feedback to the intervention agent(s) to continually improve the quality of implementation at their school. Research has demonstrated a link between integrity and intervention effects (McIntyre, Gresham, DiGennaro, & Reed, 2007). One of the key elements of integrity assessment in so far as it supports an RTI model is that it provides information on whether an identified problem is the result of the instruction provided or due to special needs of the student. If the quality of implementation is low that signifies that changes need to be made to the instruction before a true assessment can be made of the student's response to that instruction. In this way, integrity measures help to clarify the effects of programs by ruling out alternative explanations for the impacts of the program. If integrity data are not used and a student doesn't respond to the intervention, it will be unclear why the student did not respond. In some cases, lack of integrity data could result in the erroneous assumption that the student has a disability when in reality the intervention wasn't implemented appropriately (Cochrane & Laux, 2007). To address some of the barriers to assessing integrity, Power et al. (2005) proposed a researcher–interventionist partnership approach to examining integrity that facilitates the active involvement of the interventionist in the process.

Although the importance of collecting integrity data is clear, only a small percentage of studies in the educational and prevention sciences literature actually report these data (McIntyre, et al., 2007; Sanetti & Kratochwill, 2005; Smith, Duanic, & Taylor, 2007). Furthermore, in a survey of nationally certified school psychologists, all respondents indicated that assessing integrity was essential, but only about 4% to 11% said that they always collected integrity data and those data were usually based on indirect measures (Cochrane & Laux, 2007). Barriers cited to collecting integrity data included not understanding how to collect those data; teachers not understanding the importance of those data and therefore being less willing to provide the necessary information; and the additional time required to obtain those data.

Research Centers in the OSEP K–3 study used a variety of direct and indirect methods to assess fidelity including checklists, observations, and staff self-assessment surveys. The fidelity measures were used to target changes needed to the system and guide professional development efforts. Intervention coordinators typically collected the fidelity data and provided feedback to staff on improvements needed to reach an established fidelity criterion. The integrity with which the instruction or intervention was implemented was examined as were other activities that supported the implementation of the model such as activities that took place during the meetings. For example, at the Kansas Center, the effectiveness of leadership team meetings was assessed to determine whether the administrator was present during the meeting, data-based decision making was occurring, and there was compliance with the meeting procedures.

It sometimes took several years for schools to reach desired levels of integrity. It is not expected that new models and programs will be implemented with the highest degree of integrity in the first year of implementation. However, schools should set integrity goals and timelines, have clear measures for determining if and how those goals are being met, and have a feedback system for continual improvement toward meeting their integrity goals. The reader is referred to the summary provided in Chapter 8 by the Kansas Center on the steps of implementation outlined by Fixen et al. (2005) beginning with Exploration and ending with Sustainability. In the next sections we elaborate on strategies and best practices for implementation.

## WHAT WE HAVE LEARNED ABOUT IMPLEMENTATION

So far we have outlined the conceptual model that a school might follow to implement a multi-tiered system of intervention at their school, but we have said little about what it actually takes to put such a model in place. There is more to the process than knowing what ingredients to include. Schools also need to know how to staff and schedule the programs, provide training, and get school personnel to accept the new model that will inevitably require motivation and collaboration across staff, an additional time commitment, and creative use of resources. Fortunately, the case studies in this book provide very useful examples of what is involved in implementing multi-tiered models in schools. The authors of the case study chapters have also been forthcoming in sharing their challenges in implementing these models. From the case studies we gleaned several "lessons learned" regarding implementing schoolwide prevention models grounded in multi-tiered frameworks that were common across the case studies: establish buy-in, incorporate strong leadership and coordination, use teams of professionals who communicate regularly, and address challenges flexibly and proactively. A summary of these lessons follows.

### Establish "Buy-In"

As indicated in the case studies, prior to implementing multi-tiered models, administration and other school personnel need to fully commit to the model. This commitment is facilitated when staff understands the potential benefits of the model. Principals and those in leadership play a key role in establishing "buy-in" at a school. This finding was demonstrated, for example, by the actions of the Texas school principal who was very supportive of the model and highly involved in all aspects of the implementation. The authors of the case study for the Reading Center in Oregon referred to the importance of having a shared vision focused on student success. This shared vision exemplifies the type of commitment that can promote positive outcomes. The authors reported that it is most beneficial if principals and district leadership share this vision. However, they note that when those in leadership are "distracted by other business" the model can still be successfully implemented through the shared vision of other school personnel responsible for implementing the model.

### Strong Leadership and Coordination

As indicated above, the role of administration was very important to successful implementation. Principals set the tone for the implementation of the models by communicating the expectations, helping staff to see the positive impacts of the program, and providing support and coaching. In addition, each of the multi-tiered models included a lead coordinator that was referred to by different names (e.g., primary intervention coordinator, Center Support Coordinator, PBS coordinator) and had somewhat different roles across the models but whose primary role was to oversee and facilitate implementation activities. A good example of this lead coordinator was the center support coordinator (CSC) included within the North Carolina Center's model. The CSC at Eastside assisted with assessment, data-based decision making, and scheduling. She also provided coaching and training, held staff meetings, collected integrity data, and provided feedback for continual improvement of the model implementation. The CSC was credited with playing one of the most important roles in the success of the model.

### Teams of Professionals and Regular Communications

Across case studies, teams of professionals (e.g., teacher assistance team, behavior support team, literacy team, leadership team) met regularly to discuss student progress and make instructional decisions. During these meetings, teachers, administrators, research staff, and other specialists reviewed student data and discussed the types of interventions to provide struggling students. These meetings allowed for a collaborative and supportive environment to problem-solve and make decisions about the

when to move students across tiers. In addition, we know that even with evidence-based intervention practices there will be variation in how students respond and some modifications to those interventions will be necessary to meet the needs of diverse learners. Schools will need further guidance on how to make these types of decisions.

Another question is how to deal with staff turnover. Probably the best defense is having an atmosphere of acceptance of the model at the school as a whole so that a shift in personnel, even key personnel like the principal, won't have as debilitating of an effect. This harkens back to the "shared focus" mentioned in the Oregon Reading Center's case study. A related question is how to fit everything into a school day, especially without neglecting other instructional topics. For instance, if students need a great deal of instruction in reading, they may not be able to spend as much time on other academic subjects.

The multi-tiered models focused on kindergarten through third grade, but some have asked what can be done to extend these models into higher grades. At higher grades there are different standards and expectations including a greater emphasis on high-stakes testing. It is clear that intervention needs to occur early in a child's development, but perhaps the multi-tiered models can be formally extended into higher grades so as to have coordinated systems of support in higher grades and continuity of support across the educational trajectory. Such models would need to consider the learning needs and greater demands placed on students in higher grades (Mastropieri & Scruggs, 2005).

Finally, there is still a need for randomized controlled trials to experimentally examine the effects of multi-tiered models. Although initial evidence of the effects of these models is positive and they are conceptually appealing, more rigorous tests of their effectiveness will be important going forward (Kratochwill, 2007).

## HOW TO STRENGTHEN AND SUSTAIN
## IMPLEMENTATION AT SCALE

Schools participating in the case studies had the benefit of Research Center support and funding to implement the multi-tiered models. After the research projects and support ended schools would have to find other ways to sustain the models. As Sugai and Horner (2006) indicated, "an organization is defined by the extent to which collective behaviors of an organization's membership move the organization toward a common goal" (p. 248). Sustaining these models in practice will require the collaboration, resilience, flexibility, and adaptability of all involved.

During the course of the study, there were examples of activities put into place to help sustain the models beyond the life of the study. These efforts began with the selection of interventions. The Behavior Center in Oregon emphasized the practicality of the PBS intervention due to the efficiency with which it can be implemented. In addition, their school's district promoted sustainability of the PBS model through establishing a district-level PBS leadership team and a PBS district coordinator to provide support and training for the model. The county and state also offered PBS support and conferences. At Eastside in North Carolina, the literacy facilitator at the school was recruited to take over the role of the all-important CSC for the reading model. Research Center staff met with school staff to discuss how the CSC's responsibilities could be transferred to the literacy facilitator, and a planning sheet was developed outlining how this transfer could occur.

Paramount in sustaining these models are the best practices reviewed in this book that have been cultivated by the researchers and schools participating in the case studies. Much effort was expended on the part of the researchers to build acceptance and buy-in of the models and provide necessary training. Participating schools also expended a great deal of effort and commitment to implementing the multi-tiered models. The efforts of the researchers, schools, and their districts appear to have paid off with high-quality implementation and improvements in the academic and behavioral adjustment of the schools and their students. Having the benefit of positive outcomes and being committed to the programs are probably the most important factors to sustaining these models into the future. Increases in social validity and perceived importance of interventions are more likely when teachers have the opportunity to see improvements in student skills from tangible, concrete data sources (Coyne & Harn, 2006). Although the multi-tiered models implemented in this study are comprehensive and require their share of time, resources, and funding, evidence suggests that they can be successful when best practices are followed.

## REFERENCES

Albers, C. A., Glover, T. A., & Kratochwill, T. R. (2007). Introduction to the special issue: How can universal screening enhance educational and mental health outcomes? *Journal of School Psychology, 45,* 113–116.

Ardoin, S. P. (2006). The response in response to intervention: Evaluating the utility of assessing maintenance of intervention effects. *Psychology in the Schools, 43,* 713–725.

Bergan, J. R. (1977). *Behavioral consultation.* Columbus, OH: Charles E. Merrill.

Bergan, J. R., & Kratochwill, T. R. (1990). *Behavioral consultation and therapy.* New York: Plenum Press.

Bradley, R., Danielson, L., & Doolittle, J. (2005). Response to intervention. *Journal of Learning Disabilities, 38,* 485–486.

Burns, M. K., Appleton, J. J., & Stehouwer, J. D. (2005). Meta-analytic review of responsiveness-to-intervention research: Examining field-based and research-implemented models, *Journal of Psychoeducational Assessment, 23,* 381–394.

Clements, M., Bolt, D., Hoyt, W., & Kratochwill, T. (2007). Using multilevel modeling to examine the effects of multitiered interventions. *Psychology in the Schools, 44,* 503–513.

Clements, M. A., Reynolds, A. R., & Hickey, E. (2004). Site-level predictors of children's school and social competence in the Chicago Child Parent Centers. *Early Childhood Research Quarterly, 19,* 273–296.

Cochrane, W. S., & Laux, J. M. (2007). Investigating school psychologists' perceptions of treatment integrity in school-based interventions for children with academic and behavior concerns. *Preventing School Failure, 51,* 29–34.

Compton, D. L., Fuchs, D., Fuchs, L. S., & Bryant, J. D. (2006). Selecting at-risk readers in first grade for early intervention: A two-year longitudinal study of decision rules and procedures. *Journal of Educational Psychology, 98,* 394–409.

Coyne, M. D., & Harn, B. A. (2006). Promoting beginning reading success through meaningful assessment of early literacy skills. *Psychology in the Schools, 42,* 33–43.

Crone, D. A., Horner, R. H., & Hawken, L. S. (2004). *Responding to problem behavior in schools.* New York: Guilford Press.

Deno, S. (1985). Curriculum-based measurement: The emerging alternative. *Exceptional Children, 52,* 219–232.

Deno, S., & Mirkin, P. (1977). *Data-based program modification.* Minneapolis, MN: Leadership Training Institute for Special Education.

Ervin, R. A., Schaughency, E., Matthews, A., Goodman, S. D., & McGlinchey, M. T. (2007). Primary and secondary prevention of behavior difficulties: Developing a data-informed problem-solving model to guide decision making at a school-wide level. *Psychology in the Schools, 44,* 7–18.

Fixsen, D. L., Naoom, S. F., Blase, K. A., Friedman, R. M., & Wallace, F. (2005). *Implementation research: A synthesis of the literature* (FMHI Publication #231). Tampa: University of South Florida, Louis de la Parte Florida Mental Health Institute, The National Implementation Research Network.

Fuchs, L. S. (2003). Assessing intervention responsiveness: Conceptual and technical issues. *Learning Disabilities Research and Practice, 18,* 172–186.

Fuchs, L. S., & Fuchs, D. (2006). Implementing responsiveness-to-intervention to identify learning disabilities. *Perspectives on Dyslexia, 32,* 39–43.

Fuchs, D., Mock, D., Morgan, P. L., & Young, C. L. (2003). Responsiveness-to-intervention: Definitions, evidence, and implications for the learning disabilities construct. *Learning Disabilities Research and Practice, 18,* 157–171.

Good, R. H., & Kaminski, R. A. (Eds.). (2002). *Dynamic indicators of basic early literacy skills* (6th ed.). Eugene, OR: Institute for the Development of Educational Achievement. Available at *dibels.uoregon.edu.*

Gresham, F. M. (2006). Response to intervention. In G. G. Bear & K. M. Minke (Eds.), *Children's needs III: Development, prevention, and intervention* (pp. 525–540). Bethesda, MD: National Association of School Psychologists.

Guskey, T. (2003, April 21–25). *The characteristics of effective professional development: A synthesis of lists.* Paper presented at the annual meeting of the American Education Research Association, Chicago, IL.

Henggeler, S. W., Schoenwald, S. K., Borduin, C. M., Rowland, M. D., & Cunningham, P. B. (1998). *Multisystemic treatment of antisocial behavior in children and adolescents.* New York: Guilford Press.

Hester, P. P., Baltodano, H. M., Hendrickson, J. M., Tonelson, S. W., Conroy, M. A., & Gable, R. A. (2004). Lessons learned from research on early intervention: What teachers can do to prevent children's behavior problems. *Preventing School Failure, 49,* 5–10.

Horner, R. H., & Sugai, G. (2000). School-wide behavior support: An emerging initiative. *Journal of Positive Behavior Interventions, 2,* 231–232

Ihnot, C. (1992). *Read naturally.* St Paul, MN: Read Naturally.

Jimerson, S. R., Burns, M. K., & VanDerHeyden, A. M. (Eds.). (2007). *The handbook of response to intervention: The science and practice of assessment and intervention.* New York: Springer.

Kamps, D. M., & Greenwood, C. R. (2005). Formulating secondary-level reading interventions. *Journal of Learning Disabilities, 38,* 500–509.

Kamps, D., Kravits, T., Rauch, J., Kamps, J. L., & Chung, N. (2000). A prevention program for students with or at risk for ED: Moderating effects of variation in treatment and classroom structure. *Journal of Emotional and Behavioral Disorders, 8,* 141–154.

Kratochwill, T. R. (2004). Evidence-based practice: Promoting evidence-based interventions in school psychology. *School Psychology Review, 33,* 34–49.

Kratochwill, T. R. (2007). Preparing psychologists for evidence-based school practice: Lessons learned and challenges ahead. *American Psychologist, 62,* 826–843.

Kratochwill, T. R., Albers, C. A., & Shernoff, E. S. (2004). School-based interventions. *Child and Adolescent Psychiatric Clinics of North America, 13,* 885–903.

Kratochwill, T. R., Clements, M. A., & Kalymon, K. M. (2007). Response to intervention: Conceptual and methodological issues in implementation. In S. R. Jimerson, M. K. Burns, & A. M. VanDerHeyden (Eds.), *The handbook of response to intervention: The science and practice of assessment and intervention* (pp. 28–52). New York: Springer.

Kratochwill, T. R., & Shernoff, E. S. (2004). Evidence-based practice: Promoting evidence-based interventions in school psychology. *School Psychology Review, 33,* 34–48.

Kratochwill, T. R., Volpianski, P., Clements, M. A., & Ball, C. (2007). The role of professional development in implementing and sustaining multi-tier prevention and intervention models. *School Psychology Review, 36,* 618–631.

Lane, L., & Menzies, H. M. (2003). A school-wide intervention with primary and secondary levels of support for elementary students: Outcomes and considerations. *Education and Treatment of Children, 26,* 431–452.

Mastropieri, M. A., & Scruggs, T. E. (2005). Feasibility and consequences of response to intervention: Examination of the issues and scientific evidence as a model for the identification of individuals with learning disabilities. *Journal of Learning Disabilities, 38,* 525–531.

McGraw Hill Publishing. (2005). *Open Court Reading Series.* DeSoto, TX: Author.

May, S., Ard, W., Todd, A., Horner, R., Glasgow, A., et al. (2000). *School Wide Information System (SWIS).* Eugene, OR: University of Oregon, Educational and Community Supports.

McIntyre, L. L., Gresham, F. M., DiGennaro, F. D., & Reed, D. D. (2007) Treatment integrity of school-based interventions with children in the *Journal of Applied Behavior Analysis* 1991–2005. *Journal of Applied Behavior Analysis, 40,* 659–672.

Musti-Rao, S., & Cartledge, G. (2004). Making home an advantage in the prevention of reading failure: Strategies for collaborating with parents in urban schools. *Preventing School Failure, 48,* 15–21.

National Association of State Directors of Special Education. (2005). *Response to intervention: Policy considerations and implementation.* Alexandria, VA: Author.

O'Connor, R. E., Harty, K. R., & Fulmer, D. (2005). Tiers of intervention in kindergarten through third grade. *Journal of Learning Disabilities, 38,* 532–538.

Power, T. J., Blom-Hoffman, J., Clarke, A. T., Riley-Tillman, T. C., Kelleher, C., & Manz, P. H. (2005). Reconceptualize intervention integrity: A partnership-based framework for linking research with practice. *Psychology in the Schools, 42,* 495–507.

Reynolds, A. J., & Clements, M. (2005). Parent involvement and children's school success. In

E. N. Patrikakou, R. P. Weisberg, S. Redding, & H. J. Walberg. (Eds.), *School-family partnerships for children's success* (pp. 109–127). New York: Teachers College Press.

Sanetti, L. H., & Kratochwill, T. R. (2005). Treatment integrity assessment within a problem-solving model. In R. Brown-Chidsey (Ed.), *Assessment for intervention: A problem-solving approach* (pp. 304–325). New York: Guilford Press.

Sheridan, S. M., & Kratochwill, T. R. (2008). *Conjoint behavioral consultation: Promoting family school connections and interventions.* New York: Springer.

Small, S., & Memmo, M. (2004). Contemporary models of youth development and problem prevention: Toward an integration of terms, concepts, and models. *Family Relations, 53*(1), 3–11.

Speece, D. L. (2005). Hitting the moving target known as reading development: Some thoughts on screening for children for secondary interventions. *Journal of Learning Disabilities, 38*, 487–493.

Smith, S. W., Daunic, A. P., & Taylor, G. G. (2007). Treatment fidelity in applied educational research: Expanding the adoption and application of measures to ensure evidence-based practice. *Education and Treatment of Children, 30*, 121–134.

Stone, C. A. (2001). Issues in data-based decision making in special education: Introduction to the special series. *School Psychology Review, 30*, 463–465.

Sugai, G., & Horner, R. R. (2006). A promising approach for expanding and sustaining school-wide positive behavior support. *School Psychology Review, 35*, 245–259.

Taylor, B., Short, R., Frye, B., & Shearer, B. (1992). Classroom teachers prevent reading failure among low-achieving first-grade students. *Reading Teacher, 45*, 592–597.

Vaughn, S., & Fuchs, L. S. (2003). Redefining learning disabilities as inadequate response to instruction: The promise and potential problems. *Learning Disabilities Research and Practice, 18*, 137–146.

Walker, H. M., & Shinn, M. R. (1999). Structuring school-based interventions to achieve integrated primary, secondary, and tertiary prevention goals for safe and effective schools. In M. R. Shinn, H. M. Walker, & G. Stoner (Eds.), *Interventions for academic and behavior problems II: Preventive and remedial approaches* (pp. 1–25). Bethesda, MD: National Association of School Psychologists.

Walker, H. M., & Severson, H. (1992). *Systematic Screening for Behavior Disorders: Technical Manual.* Longmont, CO: Sopris West.

Walker, H. M., Severson, H. H., & Feil, E. G. (1995). *The early screening project: A proven child-find process.* Longmont, CO: Sopris West.

Walker, H. M., Stiller, B., Golly, A., Kavanagh, K., Severson, H. H., & Feil, E. G. (1997). *First steps to success.* Longmount, CO: Sopris West.

# Index

Figure numbers are indicated by *f*. Table numbers are indicated by *t*.